MAKING MOVIES

PHILLIP TURNER

Prospero Books
46 West Street
Chichester
West Sussex
PO19 1RP

A CIP catalogue record for this book is available from the British Library.

ISBN 1 84024 004 0

Printed in Great Britain by
Antony Rowe Ltd, Chippenham, Wiltshire

Preface

This is the true story of the three months that I and two university friends spent in America a few summers ago. We traveled on the British Universities North America Club (BUNAC) scheme. But this book is not a critique of the BUNAC scheme, it is simply the tale of our adventures in the States and the characters we met during our time there. Indeed, this book, I would hope, will encourage others to participate in the BUNAC scheme, which enables students to travel and legally work in the States for an extended period of time.

As soon as we had embarked on the trip so much began to happen and we had so many encounters, with so many amazing characters, that I thought it would be a crime not to keep a daily diary throughout our time there. As time progressed each page in the diary became more colourful and more involved, until the diary itself became more of a book.

My overwhelming feeling throughout the trip, especially the time spent in New York, was one of being an actor; we were not in a foreign country but rather on a film set. Everywhere we went we seemed to be stepping into a film set. Sometimes we moved from scene to scene in the same film, sometimes from film to film. Each situation we encountered seemed to have come straight out of the movies. Indeed I began to realise that the perfect backdrop to a film in America was America itself. We were making movies!

Phillip Turner
May 1997

Lights, camera, action...

Decisions

'I'm thinking of doing BUNAC next year!' exclaimed Mark.

'I wouldn't mind doing it either,' added Paul.

'The trouble with these is they go at the throat,' I said.

'Well, it will do if you keep on doing that to it,' Paul said, as he stood up and snatched the squash racket back from me and gave it close inspection.

We were all in our second year at university, reading Economics, sitting in Paul's room in a house that was under-lit and under-furnished, containing far too many people paying far too much rent; typical student accommodation. Paul returned to sit at his desk clutching his squash racket.

'Phil and I went to a BUNAC meeting last year in London,' Mark continued, 'but we didn't seem to get much further. I mean it would be worth doing while we're at university, we probably won't get the chance to do something like this again.'

'And what a classic meeting that was,' I added. 'The place was packed and it lasted for about three hours; all we did was get some stupid card signed, we didn't learn anything!'

'We did,' said Mark, 'We learnt not to go to another bloody BUNAC meeting.' I laughed.

'Ah, stop complaining. I can imagine you and Phil getting bored after the first minute,' said Paul . 'I think I would have found it very interesting.'

'You do come out with an amazing amount of rubbish, Paul, ' I said, while Mark jumped on Paul and proceeded to beat ten bells out of him for being sarcastic.

I stood up. 'Let's go, you two,' I said, as I tried to pull my squash bag from under Paul and Mark, who were now fighting on the floor.

We were on our way to play squash, an activity that, apart from shifting from student room to student room drinking coffee, took up most of our free time.

Our conversation about BUNAC continued in the beaten up student car in which we travelled. BUNAC stands for British Universities North America Club, and is an organisation that enables university students to work in America, legitimately. This means that students don't have to save up thousands of pounds by working every single day of their holidays in the town of Boring for 'Mr. Slime and Co.' in his warehouse, just to be able to afford a week in the States! In fact it offers the opportunity to spend literally months in the USA. By working as you travel it's possible to see all the tourist spots - even work at all the tourist spots - earning the money you need to live on as you move along; witnessing far more of the American way of life than 'Joe tourist'. While there you will also hopefully avoid 'Mr. Slime's' American subsidiary!

Our university gave us the opportunity to spend our third year on an industrial placement, which all three of us had decided to do and which we would begin within six months. The applications to BUNAC therefore, and all the organisation that was involved in planning a three month trip had to begin immediately. We were also taking up our placements in various places around the country making detailed communication difficult; none of us could write a coherent letter and we would probably only manage to call each other once every two months.

In reality Paul was the only one of the three of us who went to a 'various place' in England. Mark and I both landed industrial placements in 'The City' in London working for stockbrokers and would therefore be able to meet up and hopefully arrange details of the trip. But for a while the only thing we managed to arrange was who was to buy the next round of drinks, as most of our meetings took place in pubs with other friends that were working close by.

Mark and I rang Paul from time to time and whenever we did, good old Paul had a brand new piece of 'news'. 'You'll never guess what, I've lost my wallet, Mark, with all my cards in and everything,' or 'Hey Phil, sorry I haven't phoned but I've lost my address book.'

Paul was in fact a bit of a rascal. His middle name was 'organised'. He was late for almost every engagement and would often lose things. These were endearing qualities that Mark and I were by now used to, so we called Paul from time to time to check on his BUNAC activities. Discovering that he had done absolutely nothing, we proceeded to guide him toward eventual acceptance of the scheme.

The time soon came for Mark and I to attend a BUNAC meeting in London. We guessed it would probably be another marathon meeting, similar to the one we had been to the year before, but attendance was compulsory. Our expectations were not high. As it turned out the meeting was quite an event for Mark and myself.

When the day actually arrived we met after work and made our way to one of the colleges at the University of London where the meeting was to be held. By the time we arrived there was already a full lecture theatre and those that couldn't get in - about a hundred - including ourselves, sat in a grubby, smokey common room, just outside the lecture theatre.

'Let's just sit here,' I said, 'if you don't mind sitting on butt ends that is.'

'I think the place has character,' replied Mark. It was filled with padded plastic chairs, a few armchairs and a notice board along the side of the room that wasn't windowed, displaying notices about The University Parachute Club, A Junk Jewellry Sale, and a note about a missing cat.

Due to the massive turnout the BUNAC officials eventually decided to give two talks simultaneously, one in the lecture theatre and one in the common room.

Afterwards the presenters would swap rooms and give their lecture to those that hadn't heard it; in this way everybody would be lectured to without any time wasted.

After we had been in the room a short while listening to the BUNAC representative I started to receive strange glances from Mark. I soon discovered why. The chairs I had chosen for Mark and myself to sit on were in fact right at the front of the room, right next to the chap who was talking to the assembled group. We were actually facing the audience, resulting in everybody thinking that we were part of the presentation. The fact that we had both come directly from work in The City and were therefore in our suits and overcoats didn't help much either! There we were, dressed in suits, with those all around us in jeans and sneakers, sitting at the front of the room with about a hundred people continually staring at us, believing that we were incredibly important BUNAC representatives probably present to ensure that some sort of structured presentation took place and that it was half way decent. We tried to disguise our laughter by burying our faces in our hands, staring at the ground or having noisy coughing fits, all of which gave the game away to a ridiculous extent. The assembled students looked at us anxiously, curious as to what was going on. Why were two BUNAC officials in suits laughing at the presentation? And why was the chap giving the presentation ignoring them completely and looking embarrassed? Our position in the room, of course, meant that we couldn't move, and we simply prayed that the earth would swallow us up or that our BUNAC rep would finish in record time!

The talk didn't finish for some two hours, and by the end we couldn't wait to get out into the fresh air and get it all out of our system. We only had a short break though before the next lecturer was due to start. Having survived the first talk - just - the idea of sitting through another marathon lecture, in the same seats, listening to the same things we had heard at the BUNAC meeting a year earlier, didn't really appeal to us; anyway, we were in such high spirits we thought that it would be a shame to dampen the proceedings. We couldn't leave the area altogether though, as the whole point of attending the BUNAC meeting was to enroll onto the scheme by getting our BUNAC cards signed at the end of the meeting. This would enable us to continue onto the next stage in the proceedings. Neither Mark nor myself had had anything to eat that evening and it was by now eight o'clock. We decided to walk the dark London streets to find a fast food joint.

We left the college building and headed out into the London night. Apart from the usual street lights, the pavements were further lit by the lights from the University buildings and we walked slowly in search of food, in the knowledge that we had two hours to kill.

'What is the point in sitting in a series of talks for about four hours, which teach you nothing that you couldn't read in a small handout and which should only take half an hour to talk about?' Mark asked once we had sat down and ordered at a conveniently situated Pizza Hut. 'Most of it is only common sense anyway. It's ridiculous.'

'Listen,' I said, 'we must be the smartest kids there; nip out, grab a pizza, stroll back and get our cards signed. Easy peessee, Japaneessee!'

Mark continued his praise of the meetings.'You've got to be on drugs to stay for the second part of that talk,' he said.

We returned after about an hour and a half to make sure we didn't miss the card signings. Those lucky enough to have stayed in the common room for the second half were now being lectured to again. We peered in through the window.

'God, look at them,' Mark said, 'almost four hours they've been in that room now, poor things.' We stood outside in the London cold for a while, our breath a bright white against the dark sky. We decided to wait in the hall!

After another ten minutes of chat Mark decided he needed to visit the Gents. He returned with a broad grin on his face.

'I've got a joke for you Phil, I read it in the Gents. What do you say to a former London University student with a job?' We started laughing before he'd even given the punchline: 'Large Mac and fries please!'

Regaining our senses, we noticed that people had started to filter through from the lecture theatre out of a side door, avoiding the common room. We quickly turned and from where we stood looked through the glass doors into the common room. Their talk had also finished and people were starting to approach the front to get their cards signed by a BUNAC rep. We approached the common room door with haste. I followed Mark and bumped into him as he stopped abruptly.

'Oh shit!' he exclaimed, 'There's somebody on the door stopping people getting in!' We looked at each other.

'Don't tell me that we've wasted all this time hanging around for no reason. What are we going to do?'

'We'll just have to hope that the guy leaves and then rush in.'

I was beginning to think that we hadn't been such 'smart kids' after all and after a few minutes things were getting serious. We looked at each other wide-eyed and laughed. Eventually though the chap on the door left his post, and we seized the opportunity, scrambling past those coming out, finally managing to get up to the front of the common room. BUNAC officials were signing everything stuck in front of their noses and we pushed our arms through the mass of students that had completely engulfed the tables, and our cards were signed.

'The business,' I said, as we sauntered out.

We then embarked on a course of intensive letter writing and form filling. We called Paul occasionally to see how he was doing. He too had attended a BUNAC meeting and things seemed to be going well. But all of a sudden there was a hitch. Paul had been asked if he would be best man at a wedding on July 23rd. This meant that he would have to wait until then before leaving for the States and cut his trip short by two weeks or so. Mark and I would have to leave earlier and arrange to meet Paul later on. We discussed the possibility of Paul returning for the wedding but decided that this would be impractical and would cost too much. The fact that we weren't all travelling out together did have a plus point though: Paul's notoriously bad time keeping. We had visions of waiting for him at the airport until just seconds before take-off, if he had ever turned up at all!

One of the conditions of the BUNAC scheme is that everybody has to have a 'Sponsor'; somebody who lives in the States and who could be contacted by the BUNACer, or by the authorities, should anything disastrous happen. Our Sponsor was Mark's elder brother, Richard, who was working in Highpoint in North Carolina for a reproduction antique furniture manufacturer. As it turned out Richard was not only our Sponsor but also turned out to be our saviour; without him we would have been destitute and would have probably returned early.

July came around quickly and we began to finalise plans for our leaving on July 13th, when we would be off across the Atlantic toward the 'land of opportunity'! All that was left to do was to swear and curse while trying to pack our rucksacks and phone Paul, to make sure that everything was all right for his arrival on the 24th, after his wedding duties.

The Outward Journey

As I lived in London, Mark and I decided that rather than meet at Heathrow it might be better if Mark came straight to my house to lessen the chance of any confusion on take-off day.

Mark arrived on the morning of the 13th July and we spent an hour in the kitchen checking that we had such essentials as 'shark-repellent spray'.

We were looking forward to the trip so much that we left for the airport far too early. When we arrived we witnessed the usual airport scenes: taxis, traffic, luggage and tears. It was a hot July day and passengers struggled through the electric doors with their baggage into Terminal 3. Mark and I were pleased to reach the air conditioning of the terminal building. Little did we know that this would be considered a cool day in New York at the height of summer! We walked over to the Pan-Am check in desk and handed in our rucksacks. We then searched for the BUNAC official. The airport was crowded with the world and his wife and it seemed as though today they had brought the kids along as well. When we found our BUNAC rep (he was wearing a green jacket and greeted us with a 'Hi') he set about checking our forms and tickets to make sure we were bonafide BUNACers. We were slightly apprehensive about this. We had filled in about twenty forms in the last few months and we might easily have forgotten to read certain small print or to bring documentation that was needed to legally work in the States.

'That all seems to be in order,' he said, handing back our forms and tickets. 'There's quite a time to wait before they call the flight so if you'd like to wait upstairs by passport control you'll be sure of getting through first without having to queue too much.' He smiled.

'Thanks,' Mark and I said in unison.

We wandered up the carpeted stairway and found the usual mix of nationalities sitting on the moulded blue plastic chairs that grace each terminal building, all chatting loudly and waiting for their respective flights. We found a couple of free chairs, dumped our stuff and immediately headed for the Skyshop.

'I'm starving,' announced Mark. I agreed. We probably were starving but never actually made it to the Skyshop on our first attempt; the flashing lights on a line of video game machines against the wall had caught our attention. We were feeling rich and tried our hand at every game. We ended up throwing a disgraceful amount of money into Deathrace. None of the other video games came close to this fantastic game of skill, adventure and outright destruction. Although rusty to begin with, it didn't take long for us to master Deathrace. Mark was soon in the middle of an extremely fortuitous run.

'Ah, incredible!' he exclaimed, screwing up his face, putting his foot further down on the accelerator and grasping the steering wheel ever tighter. 'A mixture of intense concentration and skill,' he continued. I started laughing as his entire score was due to luck.

On our second attempt we actually made it to the Skyshop. On the way, while Mark was still idly boasting about his incredible talents on Deathrace and wondering whether he should turn professional, we passed two airport policemen. They were both dressed in black and wore the uniform of normal police officers, but were carrying machine-guns. This was a sight that many travellers - including ourselves - had not yet become accustomed to and we consequently gave them fearful looks. Although the guns were tightly held against their bullet-proof vests, the gun barrels weren't pointing in any particular direction. As Mark and I passed by, the guns seemed to be aimed directly at our heads. Although we continued walking passed them, the incident stopped our conversation in its tracks.

'That's bloody dangerous,' Mark exclaimed.

I simply opened my eyes widely and looked back at the two policemen, aghast.

'They've probably got hair triggers on those machine guns,' Mark continued. We looked at each other.

'Even Britain's being run by heavily armed bully-boys,' I said. 'What's gun crazy America going to be like?'

The Skyshop was more or less empty, and once we had seen the prices and the small but perfectly shaped British Airways 'teddy' mascots that were available, we understood why. We browsed for a while, though, and then Mark approached me.

'Going to buy something to read?' he asked.

'Probably. Are you?'

He shoved a magazine under my nose.

'Golf Monthly?'

'Yeah; just reading up on the finer points of my game. With a bit of luck we'll be able to play a fair bit in the States and I can sort out that slight swing deviation I've got.' I smiled.

'Seriously though, I might buy a set of clubs while we're out there; they're really cheap,' Mark said.

'How cheap?'

'Half price, maybe less.'

'I might buy some myself, then,' I said. 'Although I've only ever played once I couldn't really miss that sort of opportunity. Even if I never use them its still a chance to make some money. The entrepreneurial flame shines bright, as Arthur Daley would say.' Mark laughed.

'When we're out there I bet you use them. Once you buy a set of clubs you get hooked on the game. I love it, it's a great game; just wish we had better courses in England.'

Mark bought Golf Monthly, and I bought nothing.

We made our way back to our seats, avoiding machine gun fire, and sat and waited for a while before going through passport control. After a couple of quick camera snaps of

'Us At The Airport', the time came for us to move through to the departure lounge. It wasn't long before we were airborne on a Pan-Am jumbo.

We found we had been given seats bang in the middle of the aircraft - the noisiest place to be situated as it's just behind the engines. We couldn't have wished for worse seats and I hoped that this wasn't a bad omen for the whole trip. Our seats on the plane turned out to be more important than we could have ever guessed.

There were quite a few BUNACers on the flight, three were sat directly in front of us and another at the end of our bright red three seater row. Having taken a few snaps of the bright blue sky and the cumulus cloud formations below out of the small quadruply glazed window , we struck up conversation with the fellow BUNACers.

We soon realised that the row in front of us and the chap on the end of our row were all from the same university. Two of them had been 'BUNACing' before. (You are allowed to participate in the BUNAC scheme only once; but the opportunity to 'BUNAC' more than once is given to those that offer to become BUNAC reps for their particular university. This is a clever idea, because those that have had a good time on their first trip are likely to give an impressive talk to other students about life in the States.)

'So you've graduated then, have you?' I asked.

'Yes,' came the reply from one of them - a small blond-haired chap with a fat face who had just stood up to adjust his Walkman. Initially he didn't seem too keen to talk, but once he had swung the topic of conversation around to his favourite subject - himself - he was quite willing to chat forever. By the time he finally stopped talking, he had managed to leave us with the impression that we had been incredibly lucky to have ever met this chap and that our lives had now been fulfilled. Mark and I looked at each other after he had finished his speech and smiled: yes, the trip was not going to be 'stupid git' free.

On the plane there was a choice of food; you either had the pasta or you didn't eat. The other item on the menu was supposed to be chicken, but it really didn't look like it.

Although the flight took some seven hours, hiding our blond-haired 'friend's' Walkman and taking plenty of trips up and down the plane made the time pass quickly. We were soon able to view 'The Big Apple' from the air. The view into the John F. Kennedy (JFK) airport was quite spectacular, especially because we approached at night: a mass of orange and white lights.

Once on American soil the usual announcements were made by the cabin staff,

'...and we would appreciate it if passengers would remain in their seats until the aircraft has come to a complete standstill', upon which everybody scrambled for their luggage and headed for the exits.

The walk from the plane took us through various corridors and eventually into the Arrivals Hall. The heat was tremendous. It was 10pm and 90 degrees outside. The hall itself was quite large but it was filled by the long queue snaking through it. Immigration control was tight and we were in the hall for over an hour.

After immigration, we collected our rucksacks from a small carousel in the luggage hall. This is the time that everybody dreads; wondering whether their luggage is going to appear or whether it's going round and round on a carousel at a small airport in Austria. Fortunately our rucksacks arrived with the plane. By the carousel there stood four black janitors, all leaning on their brooms on the tiled floor, waiting for the passengers of the last flight in to claim their luggage, so that they could get home.

'Right, 1,2,3,4...' A BUNAC rep dressed in shorts, a T-shirt and a ten gallon hat was counting people out for the coach. Everybody was tired, sweating in the humid heat of a New York night and looking for a quick way out of the airport. BUNACers and their badly-packed luggage were crammed solid into the small hallway leading out to the bus.

'Great,' I said as Mark and I were chosen almost immediately. We walked out into the dark muggy night and were instantly face to face with an enormous coach. It was quite awesome: much taller, wider and longer than any British coach, with shiny steel bumpers protruding like tusks from the front.As we walked down the length of the coach to stow our luggage the terminal lights made the coach's burnished steel sides glow orange. The thick black tyres were shoulder height. It surely belonged in a science-fiction film. The scene was set for our first role in the movies!

New York, New York

Once full, the coach set off and emerged from the airport
tunnel into a sea of road and car lights. This was our first
glimpse of New York and it looked like absolute chaos.

'We're here, I can't believe it, the States!' I exclaimed
studying the scene. Cars whizzed by us as we approached
the main highway route into the centre of New York, the
Van Wyck Express Way. It was midnight and the roads
were packed with everybody driving like crazy; there
seemed to be no lane laws and the 55 m.p.h. signs seem to
have been a waste of tax payer's money.

'Yeah, come on then you wanna play with mama?' the
coach driver suddenly shouted as he dared a small
hatchback to pull in front of his massive beast. Our driver,
a small grey haired man, continued to insult and curse
everyone that passed us, or any driver that threatened to
pull in front of us. This shocked a few of the BUNACers
on the coach and when he continued with such phrases as

'Come on baby, let's play ball,' and 'Oh yeah, sleaze
bag?' many hurriedly opened their insurance paperwork
to see if any exemption clauses mentioned New York
coaches.

For most of the ride the coach was quiet with everybody
too tired to talk and too busy watching the chaos. We
passed signs to Flushing Meadows - the famous tennis venue
- and were soon crossing onto Manhattan Island through
the Mid-Town Tunnel. A few minutes later we had arrived
outside the YMCA, the building that would give us our
first night's rest in the US - or so we thought!

We disembarked in front of the massive YMCA buiding,
and looked skywards.

'Is this it?' Mark asked. 'It's quite small really isn't it?'

The YMCA building looked old and somewhat tatty,
and even a bit eerie, lit only by fluorescent yellow street
lights.

Our gaze was brought right down to street level by a BUNAC rep who had suddenly appeared under the long blue canopy that covered the building's main doorway. He was wearing long fawn shorts and a white T-shirt but still seemed uncomfortable in the humid night.

'Can you all come this way please?' he shouted from the doorway, anxious - as we all were - to move to somewhere cooler. We moved inside, with those last off the coach still struggling with their over-filled rucksacks that the small driver was systematically pulling from the luggage holds. We all trailed crocodile fashion in and out of halls and rooms and eventually arrived in a small, barren room, full of chairs laid out in rows. This is where we were to be briefed about our first night in the US. The room was very hot. In the US, as in most industrialised countries that experience high temperatures and humidity, almost everywhere has air conditioning; thus you move from air conditioned car to air conditioned offices, to an air conditioned home. But the YMCA was not equipped with such a modern luxury. With over fifty people per sitting in the room and with the humidity at 90 percent, the heat was stifling.

'Right, if you could just dump your stuff at the back and grab a chair.' There were two more reps at the front of the room. One was perched on a table and the other was standing, arms folded, studying the new intake.

'Quickly, please.' The rep on the table began to talk while most people were still struggling with their rucksacks at the back of the room. The briefing about life in the YMCA lasted about ten minutes. It seemed strange to have so many people in one place at two o'clock in the morning dressed only in T-shirts and shorts.

In the dimly lit room we were told to keep ourselves to ourselves, keep all our belongings locked away in our rooms and any valuables on our person. We were all given a small box to lock away our not-so-important valuables, and the key to our rooms. All doors would lock once closed and therefore we had to keep our keys with us at all times even if we were just popping along the hall to see a friend, 'or visit the khazi' - as the rep put it.

Mark and I had rooms on the eighth floor and when the briefing had finished we dashed off to grab some rest. When my door closed behind me I dropped my rucksack. I didn't bother with the light as the room seemed to be well lit by the orange street lights. I struggled with the window and eventually managed to get it open. My view was of a flat roof and office windows beyond. To my left was the street below.

'So this is New York,' I said quietly to myself. Looking out into the night my thoughts were constantly interrupted by the sound of wailing police sirens.

'Just like the movies!'

There was a knock on my door. It was Mark, of course. He was occupying the room opposite.

'Shall we go and get a can of something, Phil, I'm thirsty?'

'Yeh, good idea. Where will we be able to get one from at this time of night, though?'

'Are you kidding?' said Mark. 'we're in the city that never sleeps, the Big Apple, everywhere's open; and besides I think there's a little shop directly over the road that's open twenty-four hours.'

'You seem to know New York quite well, Mark'.

'Well I did some extensive research on the area in which we would be staying before we arrived,' he commented from the doorway and we both laughed. Mark was right. This was it, The Big Apple: there was not a moment to waste. We left our rooms, took our keys and ventured out to spend some 'greenbacks'.

On our way to the lift we met two other BUNACers, two girls, who were also in search of a drink and had had the same idea as us. In fact we discovered on our 'refreshment trip' that there were quite a lot of other people, just like us, wondering around, excited, and frightened they might miss something if they went to sleep.

Either that or we had missed out on a cocaine-snorting session! We accompanied the girls to the store.

Laughing and joking we walked out into the New York night and onto the New York sidewalk. It was now almost three in the morning and still 80 degrees. In the distance was the gentle hum of traffic and every so often the wail of a police siren. The small isolated store was directly opposite and the bright white light emanating from its large glass frontage made it stand out in the dark night, as if it were glowing. Outside the store was a black and white police patrol car: a classic movie shot. We could see two policeman inside buying a couple of cans of Coke each.

We entered the store and immediately noticed the policemen's guns. Mark and I looked at each other with a frightened smile and decided to give them a wide birth. The store looked like a classic shop set from Magnum Force. We all took a can each from the 'cool cupboard' and approached the counter. The policemen were still waiting and we queued up behind them. It looked like every American TV cop show I had ever seen. Suddenly I dropped my can. It landed side-on on the linoed floor with a loud 'bang'. Both policemen instantly turned around quickly placing their hands on their holstered guns and had their gazed fixed upon me within a split second. Stories I'd heard of New York cops accidentally shooting innocent people suddenly raced through my mind and I was rooted to the spot. There was a split second when I thought that my 'movie' would come to an abrupt end. Fortunately for me, neither of them was of a nervous disposition.

'Ooops,' I said, still staring into their tense faces. They both smiled and turned back to the counter. I picked up my can trying to ignore a smirking Mark.

'Could have been killed,' I whispered to him.

'They both have 45 Magnums, the most powerful hand gun in the world and it could of blown your head cleeeeeeeean off.'

The girls meanwhile were making sure that they didn't have to walk all of the fifty yards back to the YMCA alone and wanted us to wait for them after we had paid.

Neither Mark nor myself got much sleep that night and unfortunately it had nothing to do with the girls we had just met. The rooms were extremely hot and opened windows only seemed to increase the room temperature. So once I had returned to my room I gazed into the night. It began to rain, but that didn't make it less humid, just put a shine to the flat roof that I looked out upon. I stayed at my window for the precious little that was left of the night and as dawn broke the gentle hum of traffic turned into a roar.

Eventually, I collected my thoughts, stood up and made for Mark's room. I knocked at his door at 7.00am and discovered that he had had much the same night as me. We both showered in the supremely unhygienic shower room and attended breakfast in the cafeteria. It was self-service, fully plastic and designed to make as little use of the available space as possible. The food was quite awful and the conversation was almost on a par: we were joined at our table by the same motley crew that we had met on the plane the previous day. We didn't really get a word in edgeways as 'Superman' spent the entire time talking about himself again. His only saving grace was that because of his previous BUNAC experience we could now take the opportunity to pick his brains for tips. We asked various questions of 'Superman' hoping to make the most of our trip and to avoid any wrong turnings that would cost us time and money. Ironically it was the tips he gave us, and the information that he supplied, that led us to take a major wrong turning, that would cost us both time and money!

One of this little chap's 'handy hints' was that being an English waiter in a restaurant was the way to earn big money. The salary itself wasn't very good, but you could double your salary in tips.

'Myrtle Beach, that's the place to go,' our big-mouthed friend informed us. 'I was there last year and earned about two thousand dollars.'

'Quite a lot,' I said.

'Yeah, it meant I could travel a fair bit and didn't really have any great financial constraints about where I went. I would really recommend it.'

We took note of his suggestion. When he eventually left the table with his two sidekicks Mark and I both looked at each other.

'Did he love himself or what?' Mark said distastefully.

'Just a bit.'

'Suppose we'd better take a look at this Myrtle Beach place then. If we can earn as much money as that chap did we'll be laughing.'

We finished eating and went to gather our stuff together.

We were all to attend a briefing session that morning but had to vacate our rooms first. Being one of the last to arrive we didn't have much of a choice as regards seating and had to sit at the front. Before us was a small American chap, slightly built with blond hair.

The meeting was entitled 'Orientation'. It was intended to give us a brief guide to the 'Do's and Don'ts' in New York and to help us in our initial searches for employment. We learnt a lot of important information and it was useful. But we were keen to get on; we knew where we were headed.

After about an hour and a half of sitting in the un-airconditioned room in the heat of a New York summer, Mark and I began to feel restless and our presenter's jokes began to wear a bit thin. Consequently, we started to take the mickey out of almost everybody that was in view. Soon we were having problems disguising our laughter. Our presenter had noticed our 'silent chatter' and gave us a stare or two. We calmed down for a while and listened to him talk about his favourite topic, taxes. He spoke for well over half an hour on the subject, about all the minor tax laws, all the ways in which we might be subject to tax or in which we could claim it back. After having spent what seemed to be an age on the subject he paused.

'Are there any questions?' he asked. Mark turned around and whispered to me 'Yes, I've got a question. What do we do about taxes?' I nearly fell out of my chair. Our combined laughing now earned us severe looks from every section of the large, attentive room and glares from our host.

The meeting continued in the same vein for about another hour. 'Right are there any final questions?'

Mark turned to me and whispered, 'Yes, how do we get in touch with the A-team?' Our laughter was uncontrollable. It didn't seem to matter that we had drawn quite a large audience, we just laughed with our heads down in our hands, using the disguising techniques that we had perfected at our initial BUNAC meeting in London! Fortunately there was a reprieve from all the embarrassment we were causing. Somebody asked a question about car hire. The presenter began to talk about driving in the States, eligibility requirements etc. He suddenly mentioned, as an aside, that it wasn't advisable to drive in New York itself as driving habits in the city were pretty awful. At that point, from three large open windows situated along one side of the room, we heard a loud screech of tyres and waited for the bang. The bang didn't arrive but the whole room had erupted into laughter. It gave Mark and I an opportunity to release our pent up merriment without fear and the incident came as a massive relief.

The meeting had been wonderful entertainment and we had in fact learnt quite a bit about life in New York and about the pitfalls of obtaining a job in the States. After the meeting had finished we shuffled out with everybody else and collected our rucksacks from the mass pile of luggage that had accumulated just outside the room. We went down to the foyer where we attempted to find out about trains, planes and automobiles. The foyer was hot and densely populated with anxious students. The floor, by each of the variously coloured walls and large square pillars, soon turned into seating areas. This complicated matters and it was soon almost impossible to pass through the foyer.

As we entered the BUNAC office just off the foyer we met the two girls we had accompanied to the store early that morning. They were headed west, deciding to fork out about $100 each for a plane trip to Los Angeles. We ourselves were in search of car hire companies. Hiring a car, we had decided, was the best and most economical way down to Highpoint, in North Carolina, where Mark's brother was based. We were hoping to find a company that needed a car driven down to Highpoint and which would thus involve only a minimal charge. Travelling around the States by ferrying cars around for hire companies is a clever idea and is a classic BUNAC 'wheeze'; it's mentioned in almost every pamphlet. Still running on nervous energy, we made our way out of the YMCA. The next time we would stay here would be on our return journey and behind us would be a catalogue of stories and adventures, people and places.

The sidewalk seemed a world away from the dark and desolate night-time street of the early hours. People rushed this way and that and cars were nose to tail on the hot New York roads. We turned left and headed towards a telephone. We had collected some change and began calling various car hire companies from the kiosk. Carrying our Union Jack covered rucksacks, wearing shorts and looking as white as ghosts compared with everybody else, you wouldn't have needed a degree in geography to realise that we were British and probably carrying all our worldly possessions. Within minutes of us approaching the telephone kiosk I was aware of preying eyes. Our bags were tightly tucked together by our feet and I treated every passerby with caution while Mark rang around. I sensed eyes everywhere. Every street corner was literally crowed with young men - black, Hispanic and white - all pretending not to notice us through the traffic that moved along the roads, but at the same time making us aware of their presence!

Mark (who I was grateful to for being six foot three tall), seemed to take forever to phone around the various car hire agencies. When he finally hung up the phone for the last time his expression said it all.

'Nothing!' he said.

'Nothing?'

'The only thing to do is hire a car for the full going rate or go down by bus.'

'Well, how much will hiring a car cost us?'

'I'll just find out, Phil.' Mark once again had a broad smile on his face, and returned to the phone, possibly oblivious to the rising probability that someone would come running by and snatch a rucksack and, if he were lucky, manage to stab one of us to divert attention while he escaped!

Hiring a car turned out to be too expensive so we walked back down the street to the YMCA to find out about buses - a lot cheaper. On the walk down to the bus station, it seemed like New York was falling to pieces. This was the most we had yet seen of the city and the structural decay was quite a sight. It was sad to see that New York's infrastructure had been left to fall into such disrepair, when the city had so much life. Perhaps it was due to lack of public funds, or badly constructed buildings, or perhaps poor maintenance, but we were taken aback at the dirty streets, the unending graffiti and the large cars that spewed pollution. But what the heck, this was New York and we had seen it all before at the movies; now we were living it.

It's true to say that a perfect backdrop to a movie about life in New York is New York itself. There's no need for any artistic license on the part of the director; everything is catered for from the black and white police cars to the screaming taxi-cab drivers and harsh street-wise ways.

The main bus terminal in New York City is called the Port Authority and is situated on Eighth Avenue, a short walk from the YMCA. Stopping outside we were pushed and shoved by the passers-by.

Our rucksacks felt like lead weights on our shoulders; we were relieved that we had found the building so quickly. Upon entering we were greeted with a spacious tiled foyer. There were large pillars scattered around the vast interior and a few potted plants. I'm not sure whether the pillars were there to support the high ceiling, or simply for decoration. In any case the high ceiling made everybody look small, plants here and there suggested an attempt at 'going green' and there were kiosks dotted here and there selling freshly squeezed orange juice and snacks. There was a noticeable police presence. With our rucksacks becoming heavier by the minute we staggered up through the hall and joined one of six cues at the modern-looking ticket desks.

The whole place had quite a bad, although exciting, atmosphere. As we waited we noticed that there seemed to be twice as many people wandering around and generally doing nothing as there were honest-looking customers. P.C. Severe would have no problem in arresting a dozen people for 'Loitering with Intent'. It seemed to be a place for communal gatherings.

As both Mark and I were so obviously 'strangers in a strange town' we didn't have to wait long in the queue before we were accosted. A small black man wearing a tatty black leather jacket and a large black hat suddenly appeared and started talking continuously.

'Listen man you haven't got a dollar you could lend me have you man? Just a dollar? That's all I need, man. I have to get to see my Mam whose on the other side of the country, and all I need is one more dollar, man, for the bus ride.' Everybody in our queue turned to watch. Our 'Orientation' lecture came in useful. We were told that we would almost certainly be approached by someone and asked for some money. It would be a nominal sum and we might be tempted to give it to them. It wouldn't be the money that they would want, though. The aim was to see where we kept our cash or our wallets. Having discovered this, their accomplices would then later mug us, or we would be pick-pocketed: in both cases they would know exactly where to find our loot. Being wise to this classic piece of criminal maneuvering we consequently told the guy where to go - and it wasn't to see his Mam! He shuffled away slowly, looking at the floor.

'Just wanted to see where we kept our money,' I said.

'I know,' said Mark. 'I'll show him where I keep my fist if he appears again!'

We bought tickets to Greensborough (the nearest large town to Highpoint) and left our rucksacks - minus valuables - in the 'left luggage' department downstairs. Our bus didn't leave until 7.30 that evening so we headed for the tourist sights. What a relief it was not to have to walk about in the New York heat with 54lb packs on our backs.

Apart from the chap in the Port Authority asking us for some change, we had had no other confrontations with street life and we began to wonder whether all the hype about the tough New York streets was really true. We began to feel more at ease.

It was approaching lunchtime as we headed towards West 42nd Street and businessmen and women - wearing the usual out-of-office 'sneakers' - rushed by, heads down, looking incredibly stressed. Thank God we're on holiday over here, I thought, remembering the City stress Mark and I had left behind. The crowded streets now seemed less formidable and the New York buildings, all plastered with advertising, seemed to have character rather than simply looking decayed. When we reached the corner of Eighth Avenue and West 42nd Street our sense of direction failed us. Mark's 'extensive research' on New York City was revealed to have been limited to a one block radius around the YMCA.

All of a sudden there was a commotion and shouting from across the hot street.

'OK, man, easy!' came a loud, panicked shout.

'On the floor. Now!' shouted another man.

'OK! AGAINST-THE-FENCE!' Everybody turned to watch. These last words were unmistakably from a loudhailer. From absolutely nowhere what we took to be three unmarked police cars screeched to a halt. Out jumped eight men brandishing guns. They joined a further five plain clothed and five uniformed policemen who were already 'at the scene'. The shouting continued and fights broke out. The police soon over-powered those struggling. We were witnessing a drugs bust. Each of the men against the fence was being searched and packets taken from their jackets. They had probably been trading on the street corner and by the number of guys that had been handcuffed it looked like it had gotten a little out of hand. All the pushers were now either on the floor or against the fence of a building site.

'Aheeee!' exclaimed Mark, and we looked at each other in disbelief.

'A bust on a street corner. Just like the movies!', I said. 'This is what the States is all about, man!'

'It is! Where else would you see this sort of action? It's like The French Connection on high definition television!' We continued watching, though all the other spectators were now on their way. An everyday occurrence, I supposed, on the streets of New York, which didn't warrant a second look. The pushers were all either Hispanic or black and still making a lot of noise about the way they were being treated. But their screams of abuse soon died down and the everyday sounds of pedestrians and vehicles once again reigned supreme. The heavily armed police started pushing suspects into cars while simultaneously producing paperwork of some sort. It was all done pretty harshly but efficiently; even the drug pushers seemed to know the parts they had to play in this 'movie' and within minutes the street corner was completely cleared. Arriving just five minutes later you wouldn't know that anything had taken place at all - the set had been cleared.

'Well, that was bloody amazing!' I exclaimed.

'It was just unreal,' said Mark. 'And it all happened so quickly. What would we have done if we had been walking by and got mixed up in it? It happened so quickly we wouldn't even have had time to protest; and by now we'd be stuck in a police cell with loads of fat, sweating tattooed ex-cons, who hate the British.'

We pushed our way through the crowds up 42nd Street to Fifth Avenue and onto the first of the tourist sites, the Empire State Building.

Walking for any distance in any large city in the summer is very tiring, with the hard pavement beneath and the fume filled air above, but it's especially so in New York where your mind also has to cope with being bombarded by advertising everywhere you look. Your feet also have to cope with the sneakers that tread on everyone and everything. We were hot and sticky, and refreshment was long overdue. There was a McDonald's situated on the other side of the road to the Empire State Building and as we approached the Empire State we both gave the fast food joint a longing stare. Every tourist trip should be rounded off with a Big Mac or two!

As we entered the Empire State Building we squinted in an attempt to see anything in the dimly lit entrance hall. The floor was marble and we were greeted by an enormous sign listing all the companies that were resident in the building. There were a lot of people just milling about and a surprising number dressed formally, who looked as though they worked in the building. It was quite a surprise. You don't envisage people actually working there. In fact our tourist gear seemed incredibly out of place at one of the world's most famous tourist sites.

When the lift doors closed, Mark, myself and the other five tourists with us all waited in eager anticipation. As soon as the lift began to move we could feel our stomachs reach into our mouths and a small girl in the lift let out a small excited scream; everybody looked up at the numbers above the lift door to watch the floors pass by. In an instant we had reached floor 64, then sped up and up. The doors opened and we disembarked, paid a dollar or so at some booths, received a pink 'souvenir' ticket and then proceeded on, following the 'Visitors' signs. It became apparent that this wasn't the top of the building and with the others that had accompanied us in the first lift we took another, smaller lift to the very top. We stepped outside.

The view was really quite breathtaking, even though it was quite hazy. The whole of Manhattan Island lay below us: absolutely packed with buildings and infrastructure; there was not a spare foot of land to be had anywhere and buildings even seemed to have been built on top of other buildings, cramming as much onto the island as possible. It looked like thousands of giant people had jumped up onto a scrap of land to escape the water and were squeezed tightly together, clinging onto anything they could to keep themselves from toppling back.

Surrounding the top of the Empire State Building is a high wire fence, in place for obvious reasons. This obscured our cameras, and we had to poke our Pentax lenses through the fence to get a decent shot of all that was below. I had already taken one whole film in less than a day and I continued to snap away. Mark put forward a suggestion.

'I tell you what, Phil, why don't you grab my ankles and hang me over the edge. Then start to swing me so I can get some really spectacular shots?' In fact, we had taken photos from every conceivable angle: the only thing left to do was indeed to dangle Mark over the edge and swing him by his ankles!

From the top it was difficult to pick out the individual buildings that lay below us and even trickier to focus on the maze of streets, pathways and roads. Only the largest roads were really visible, crowded with literally hundreds of bright yellow taxis, weaving in and out of the other traffic like ants. Pedestrians were invisible from such a height, as we must have been to them. The only living thing big enough to be seen from street level would be King Kong!

McDonald's was our next stop. The meal tasted the same in New York as it had done in 'Old' London and the interior was similarly decorated. An English family sat next to us, the father with the latest Sony video camera tucked under his arm.

'Ah thank God, some air conditioning,' said the mother.

'Makes you wonder how people live in this heat all year round doesn't it?'

We spent the rest of the day walking around New York and later, having claimed our rucksacks, waited at the Port Authority Bus Terminal. We waited for almost an hour outside our allotted gate number - not because the bus was late, but because we were early and were now exhausted. We sat, not talking, on small, hard, green plastic chairs. The passengers that waited with us in the small low-ceilinged gate area were predominantly black; chatting and laughing to the policemen that seemed to be in abundance at the Port Authority.

Once again it seemed as though we had jumped forward in time, or were taking part in some futuristic movie in which everything was brightly coloured plastic or shiny steel and where daylight was a thing of the past, forcing us into a world of artificial light and conditioned atmosphere. The cramped area was hot and badly lit by a single strong spot light, which occasionally caught the sweating face of somebody swaying forward out of the shadows as they laughed with the policemen. Those that had missed out on the chairs were sitting in the dark on the floor, their features never revealed in the light. In my completely exhausted state everything had an artificial look about it. Or maybe Mark and I were in a psychological thriller, where at any moment all those present would stop laughing with the policemen and turn to us and begin to laugh loudly at us.

Midnight Express

Boarding the bus was quite a relief: at last we would be able to get some sleep. In fact, everybody that boarded the bus - including ourselves - looked as though they could have done with a bath and a decent night's sleep. The Greyhound, we had discovered, was the way that the more characterful individuals travelled around the States.

As the large silver beast left New York we settled down into our seats and tried to sleep; but we had been cast in another film, a comedy thriller. It didn't take us long to realise that we were travelling with a bus full of the most worrying individuals we were ever likely to meet.

Opposite us was a large black woman and her children. There was an outlandishly dressed girl of about sixteen, a boy of about twelve, who looked like he was high on drugs, and his younger brother, who had a glass eye and was aged about six. This younger kid was very energetic and began running up and down the bus as we started out of New York and headed for the wide roads of America. He stared at everybody with his one good eye, while his glass eye looked in completely the opposite direction. He tried to start up conversation with a few people but to no avail. As with all little kids he was greeted with a smile by everybody and then ignored; and like all little kids do he kept on going long after everybody was sick and tired of him. He began to smile at the fact that he was now the centre of attention and annoying almost everybody on the bus.

'If that little brat comes near me again I'll give him something to smile about!' said Mark. But the little chap eventually ran out of energy and fell asleep on his mother's lap.

We were also blessed, on this first trip on a Greyhound bus, with a mental patient, a black girl who looked to be in her late twenties. She appeared pleasant enough and was quite pretty with short unstyled hair. She sat two seats from the front and was accompanied by a white male psychiatric nurse, officially dressed and sporting a badge that revealed his occupation. We couldn't believe that a mental patient would be transported by Greyhound bus; what treats had she in store for us? Also on the bus were two chaps dressed like cowboys who looked as though they would have sold their grandmothers to make a fast buck, and a couple of hippies who sat at the back and smoked pot throughout the entire trip.

Our voyage to North Carolina took us all night and most of the following morning. We travelled down from Pennsylvania, through Virginia and into North Carolina. Mark and myself slept through most of the trip, careful to tuck our baggage under our feet during the night. At the first stop the drivers were changed. Our youngish driver left us and was replaced with a much older one. The psychiatric nurse was also changed and another male nurse accompanied the patient, who was being studied carefully by the others on the coach. The night passed slowly and as dawn broke we stopped for welcome breakfast. We all piled out and sat, looking worse than death, in a small road-side cafe. We stopped for only half an hour and hurriedly drank our coffee as the driver started up the bus again. There was a mad rush for the door; who wants to be left at a small road-side cafe in the middle of nowhere?

All seemed to be going well as we continued en route to Greensborough until people toward the front of the bus started talking loudly amongst themselves. The talking got louder and louder. I peered over the top of the seats to see what all the commotion was about. Our journey had continued from the breakfast stop with no minder for our psychiatric patient. Maybe the nurse had preferred to be stuck at a road-side cafe in the middle of nowhere!

'Looks like we've left the psychiatric nurse back at the cafe. But the patient's back on the coach.'

'You're joking?!' Mark started to laugh.

'Let's hope she's not in for mass murder' I said. The driver of course was unaware of the fact that the nurse had been left behind and probably even unaware that he had a patient on board. It wasn't long before the patient rose from her seat with a broad smile on her face. People cowered into each other's arms. Mark and I thought it was really neat. A bus, on the road to nowhere, completely controlled by a psychopath who would murder the passengers one by one with a rusty old carving knife in the most gruesome fashion possible! A classic 'B' movie script!

The patient's every move was watched by the now silent passengers. She walked slowly up to the front of the bus, right up behind the driver's chair. She waited a while. What was she going to do? Should somebody warn the driver that he was about to get a rusty carving knife jabbed between his shoulder blades? She stood and looked out the window for a minute or two then slowly and purposefully walked up to the front window, turned and sat on the large dash board area with her back to the road.

'Hey! What you doin' up here?' Asked the driver. 'Get back to your seat. You're not supposed to distract the driver; can't you read the signs?' He pointed to a small plaque instructing passengers not to communicate with the driver at all while he was driving. She ignored his remarks and the plaque. Then she smiled and spoke slowly.

'How long is it until we get to the next town?' Oh no. We were all to be massacred before we had a chance to reach help I thought. The road stretched out before us with no sign of life for miles in any direction. 'The Shining' re-worked for a female lead and incorporating a coach load of victims. The whole bus waited on her every word, trying to peer over the seats without being noticed.

'Well, about another hour to the next stop,' answered the driver. 'Now go and sit down and stop distracting me.'

'When you say about an hour does that mean fifty minutes or an hour and ten minutes?' the girl asked, frowning.

'Well, about an hour. I can't be exact.'

'Do you think it will be, say, one hour five minutes and thirty five seconds?'

'What you sayin'?' The driver was confused.

'And the town after that another two hours and twenty seven minutes six seconds.'

'Don't be stupid, nobody can be that accurate about times, woman; now take your seat.'

'Just take a guess,' she said. 'Do you think it will be that sort of time or perhaps a few seconds less?' The elderly black driver was by now pretty annoyed. He literally shouted at her to return to her seat. The rest of the bus cowered even futher back into their seats.

'Hope he knows what he's doin',' exclaimed one of the hippies at the back. He sounded frightened. The patient returned to her seat, perplexed. Was she taking her time before she pounced? A few minutes passed, then she again rose from her seat to repeat her questions to the driver. The driver by now had calmed down and realised that she wasn't all quite there. The rest of the bus became more sanguine about her, but continued to watch her every move. She approached the driver twice more with the same question before we reached the next town.

When we arrived in town she was waiting by the door to jump off. Although she had given the rest of us a frightened few miles on the bus, she had turned out to be harmless and the moment she walked off the bus was undoubtedly homeless. When she left the bus the driver looked around at an old lady at the front of the bus and said, 'She's mad that women, mad.' The old lady leant forward and said, with a straight solemn face, 'Yes, she is.'

As we continued on our route and approached Greensborough, the announcements over the bus' address system changed. We learnt that Highpoint, where Richard lived, was actually a town in which the bus would stop, although this wasn't made clear when we set out. We were naturally pleased about this as it would save us a further trip by bus, or save Mark's brother from trekking out to pick us up.

Greensborough arrived and we watched out of the windows as people disembarked.

'Hey, they're unloading our rucksacks' I yelled. Mark and I rushed off the coach.

'Wait, those don't come off here.' The driver stopped unloading the luggage and looked up at Mark and I.

'They've got Greensborough written on the luggage label,' he said.

'Yes, I know' I replied, 'but we now want to go on to Highpoint. We didn't know the bus went all the way to Highpoint when we booked the tickets, so our luggage was labelled up for Greensborough.' The drivers sweating face began to screw up.

'Shiiiiiiit, man; why didn't you say so in the first place? I've unpacked your luggage an' everything. Let me see your tickets.' We showed them to him.

'Well you can travel on if you want to, man,' The elderly black driver looked down at the heavy rucksacks and was almost in tears at the thought of rearranging his large luggage hold to make room for our rucksacks. He begrudgingly started to move things around. Mark and I looked at each other and felt guilty.

'It doesn't matter,' I said. 'It's all right, we'll stay here.'

The driver stood up from the luggage hold.

'Oh shiiiiiiit make your mind up, man.'

'Sorry, yes we will stay here, it's OK.' The driver continued to complain as he closed up the hold, adjusted his cap and got back into the bus. We watched the bus leave from the hot dusty ground where we stood, then headed inside the bus station building to call Mark's brother.

Richard duly arrived, picked us up and transported us on to his apartment in Highpoint. I had never met Richard before. He was tall, six foot two, with very light brown hair and was of a light build. He wore jeans and a T-shirt and had a big smile on his face when he turned up to meet us.

Local Hero

The trip to Highpoint gave us our first look at the typical US town during daylight and as we set off in Richard's black 16 valve Volkswagen Golf GTI, the first thing that struck us was the massive amount of advertising hoardings that completely engulfed the roadside. As in New York advertising was chucked down your throat.

The heat and humidity outside were as bad as they had been in New York, so the car's air-conditioning was very welcome. It didn't take long to reach the apartment and the thought of getting some decent sleep ensured that we unloaded the car with renewed strength. The apartment itself was quite smart and thankfully also air-conditioned. It was small but not cramped and was housed on a complex, which included a tennis court and swimming pool. There wouldn't be much room, but Mark and I would move on when Paul arrived from England in two week's time.

'Do you want to work this afternoon?' Richard asked as we wandered around the apartment, trying everything out. We were a bit taken aback with his question and stood in stunned silence for a while at the realisation that we were in the States to work. We had just spent two whole days travelling and didn't feel much like working. We reluctantly decided that we had to start some time and Richard took us into his work place after lunch.

Richard worked for a reproduction antique furniture makers and was in charge of the American outfit. He had been over in the States for about nine months before we arrived and had been doing well; although his social life was quiet due to his long hours at work.

The drive to Richard's warehouse and offices that afternoon only took about ten minutes and on the way he explained about the area and we saw Highpoint in full.

'Shopping mall in there,' he said, after we had only been travelling for about two minutes. The building in fact could be seen from the apartment, but we hadn't known its function.

'In America, everyone shops in these big air-conditioned shopping malls. They contain most stores and you can get practically anything in them; and there's the added attraction of 24 hour shopping in some supermarkets as well,' he said.

'They're just getting around to Sunday opening in Britain,' Mark observed and there followed a debate about the merits or otherwise of buying a tin of beans at 3.00am on a Sunday morning.

We were soon at the warehouse. It was a large single-floored building with an extensive tarmaced area at the front where just a few cars were parked. Richard stopped in front of the glassed office area of the building. Mark and I nervously followed Richard into the offices and we were immediately confronted by four secretaries. They seemed shocked by our arrival. We later discovered that this was because they had never seen anybody looking so white or so ill as Mark and I apparently did on that first day. It wasn't surprising really; we had come straight from jobs where we had been stuck inside for most of the daylight hours, with only a day's rest before embarking on a forty-eight hour non-stop trip of several thousand miles to North Carolina.

The secretaries all looked like classic American soap opera secretaries. There was Diane, Carol and Sarah. We wouldn't really have much to do with Carol and Sarah while we were there, but we would come to know Diane quite well as she lived on the same complex as Richard.

Beyond this first room, separated by a wall with a glass hatch, we could see Richard's office, which was furnished with reproduction antique furniture giving it a very English feel. There was a large map of the States on the wall from which we would plan future journeys.

Having joked with the secretaries for a while - I think the jokes were on us but we were too tired to care - Mark, his brother and I all walked on, through a small dark corridor into the warehouse. As we entered, the strong smell of furniture polish was almost overpowering. We glanced around. There were freshly polished large wooden table tops and chairs lying on various pieces of soft materials; and other furniture leaning up against the walls. Vats of polish stood in a small semi-enclosed area. The enclosure was supposed to stop the polish fumes from spreading around the warehouse; sack the guy who had constructed it.

Richard introduced Mark and myself to Cheryl (a male with a female name), who was a short, lean chap with blonde hair, and Daniel, a little black chap who was also quite lean. They were both wearing jeans, sneakers and sweatshirts. Cheryl was also wearing a leather apron to protect him from the chemicals and polishes that were used. Neither Cheryl or Daniel said much, they were quite shy and as we didn't really know what to say either, introductions were short.

We walked on through the warehouse, past a blond-haired woman, Donna, wearing a T-shirt and jeans, and who looked to be in her early thirties. She was quite pretty and was kneeling on a table, using an industrial staple gun to fire large staples into a chair. She looked up and smiled as we passed. She was, we discovered, in charge of upholstery. I looked at Mark as we passed and he smiled. I knew he had had the same thought as me; apart from the obvious thought about Donna, we both had the idea that the large industrial staple gun she was using would be quite a cool weapon. Games such as 'Get To The Emergency Exit Door Without Me Sticking Twenty Industrial Staples Into Your Body From Ten Yards' came to mind.

'She does the upholstery,' Richard called to us.

'That would explain the staple gun,' I shouted back with a smile.

'Yeh, it does make a bit of a noise doesn't it?'

To our right were stacks of shelves full of reproduction furniture. Chairs, tables, cabinets and the like. They stretched all the way back to the wall on the other side of the building, with larger pieces of furniture that were too big for the shelves filling the floor space. To our left were smaller shelves with smaller items of furniture on them. As we turned a corner we saw the packing area and more furniture out to the right. Here we were introduced to Mike, Cheryl's brother. He had a thin moustache and nodded and smiled when we were introduced. We would get to know Mike very well over the coming weeks. We also met Steve who was a large - well, fat - black chap. He wore a scruffy T-shirt and scruffy jeans, with a pair of sneakers that looked about three sizes too big. Both Mike and Steve seemed shy and greeted us in much the same way as Cheryl and Daniel had done, with an air of caution.

'Well, I'm on my way back to the office,' Richard said. 'I'll leave you to sort them out, Mike. Can you give them some packing or something to do?'

'Yeh,' Mike said with a smile. Richard departed and we were left standing with a couple of complete strangers at the end of a reproduction furniture warehouse in the middle of North Carolina! We were soon given our first task of the afternoon. We had to wrap up walnut coffee tables and dining chairs with a sort of green spongy wrapping material. The fact that each object was probably worth more than we would be paid for our entire time in the warehouse ensured that we were careful, and thus slow.

There was a large garage-like warehouse door in the very corner to our left and packing materials to our right. The place was packed with furniture of all shapes and sizes all waiting to be wrapped. There was a desk from which the paperwork was supposed to have been done, but it seemed to have been turned into a tool shelf. Some of the furniture had already been wrapped - obvious from the tight green 'jackets.' After a short silence while Mark and I got to grips with the work, Mike started to ask us questions. He was packing a large bookcase with Steve.

'So you're from England, are you?'

'Yep,' we both replied in unison as Mark tried to sort out some sellotape that had locked his fingers together.

'Both from London?'

'No, I'm from Brighton,' Mark said, standing at the table and attempting to hack through the sellotape with a dangerously sharp Stanley knife.

'Where?' asked Mike.

This was the first clue we received as to the extent of the warehouse worker's geographic knowledge of the UK. We would soon wise up to the fact that a complete explanation of the European continent would be needed each time we met somebody new, before they would understand where Brighton and indeed England were.

'Brighton,' Mark said slowly and purposefully. Mike looked at Steve and then back at Mark.

'Ain't never heard of it.' he said with a large smile.

The conversation continued in a similar vein - a question and answer session - so we were quite relieved when afternoon break came along at 3.00pm.

Afternoon break was taken in a small room, lit by one florescent tube. It contained a few chairs and an old table with refreshment provided by a drinks machine just outside the door. The room itself was situated under some stairs - which we hadn't noticed on the way in - just past Donna with the staple gun. Everyone kept themselves to themselves.

Our first afternoon's work in the warehouse continued until 5.00pm, by which time the others had all left. We had only met a few of the characters in the warehouse and had only just begun to get to grips with the packing material, but we were glad we had made our initial introductions that afternoon. Richard wasn't ready to leave at five, so Mark and I returned to the warehouse from his office and took a climb around the mountains of furniture.

'Ouch!'

'What's wrong?'

'Bloody cardboard is sharp,' I said, studying my first injury in the States and worrying about the possibility of contracting AIDS from cardboard. During our searches we found some beautiful furniture, most of it still wrapped in cardboard, having been shipped from factories in England. We soon got bored of our little climbing adventure though and took time to examine closely the wrapping materials and tools that we had been using that afternoon.

'Ahhhhhhhh!'

'What's up now?' Mark asked.

'I've cut myself again. I'll catch AIDS, Ahhhhhh!'

Mark started to laugh.

Bored with cutting myself to pieces, and with Richard nowhere in sight, I decided it was time to bring a bit of athleticism to the proceedings, in the form of 'warehouse tennis'. Mark was all for it. We made a ball out of tightly-packed masking tape and some tennis rackets out of thick cardboard. A piece of string was stretched between two piles of furniture, a small court marked out and warehouse tennis commenced. After no sleep at the YMCA, very little on the Greyhound bus and an afternoon's work, we still had enough nervous energy for a makeshift game of tennis and before long we were leaping and diving around. A shot that I thought was a definite winner would be spectacularly retrieved by Mark with a dive across the width of the court and a volley put away into the corner by Mark would merely set me up for a winning 'running volley forehand pass' - to quote a famous tennis commentator. Later we added our own commentary with the use of such expressions as 'Oh, what a crucial time to serve his one hundred and seventy first double fault' - to quote the same famous commentator.

The tennis lasted for almost an hour. It was truly excellent. With the game finished we took down the piece of string we had used for a net and hid our equipment, so we could have a rematch later in the week. We walked back the length of the warehouse to see if Richard had finally finished for the day. On the way we passed the area in which Donna, the upholsterer, had been working. As if drawn by a magnet, we both immediately ran for the staple gun that we had seen being used earlier. Our hunch about about this amazing piece of machinery proved correct. The gun was even more powerful than we had imagined. It could fire a huge staple through the air at such a speed that metal shelves thirty feet away made a loud clang when hit; fantastic. We spent the next ten minutes viciously attacking each other with it. As we were only dressed in T-shirts and shorts our arms and legs came in for quite a bit of grief. We both became quite accurate with the staple gun and if it hadn't been for Mark's lightening reflexes in dodging the lethal staples he wouldn't be alive today; well that's what he told me anyway.

We left the gun and went to Richard's office. He still wasn't ready to leave and so we studied the large colourful map of the US on the wall. We found Myrtle Beach. As this was the area that had been recommended to us by our 'friend' at the YMCA and was supposedly the place to earn decent wages as a waiter, we planned our route down.

Richard finished up and we were soon on our way from the office back to the apartment in the black Golf. It was such a relief to get back to an air conditioned apartment. Mark and I flopped down into the sofa, unwashed, unshaven. We were seriously tired puppies. Richard walked on through into the kitchen, then poked his head around the corner into the lounge where Mark and I were almost asleep.

'As you two pigs are here we need to get some more food in.' He looked at us and added 'A lot more food in.'

Mark and I showered and shaved and the three of us walked to the mall.

As some supermarkets in the US are open for twenty-four hours, there's never the mad rush that there is at the weekends at Tesco's or Sainsbury's in the UK, as people can shop when they like. It's half one on a Saturday morning, you've been out and need provisions as you're up early to go fishing; no problem, just nip down to your local supermarket and you'll find it just as accessible as it is during the day; piped music and all.

We managed to find all we needed quite quickly. A large case of beer was not on the shopping list but we managed to leave with one and ensured that it would become a regular feature of our shopping trips. We also left with a number of boxes of breakfast cereal, one of which was brought as a joke; besides the more 'normal' breakfast cereals, there were those that looked incredibly sickly and it was almost unimaginable that a human being could eat such brightly coloured nosh first thing in the morning. We picked out 'Circus Fun', a box of florescent coloured marzipan and crispy pieces in the shape of your favourite circus entertainers, which when mixed with milk at 7.00am would provide something really special!

The rest of the evening was spent getting accustomed to the apartment and chatting about our likely schedule for the trip. (A few pictures were also taken of Mark risking life and limb eating 'Circus Fun'.) We hit the sack early and after the hectic pace we had set ourselves slept extremely well.

The Dirty Dozen

The morning brought the beginning of our first full day's work at the warehouse, and a routine which we would become accustomed to over the next two weeks. We had thus far been swept off our feet. We hadn't stopped for a moment since finishing our industrial year jobs in the City, back in London. We didn't really relish the prospect of having to start working again. They say that a change is as good as a rest. Mark and I would have liked a rest for a change.

Richard drove us to work that morning. We said good morning to Carol and walked on through to the warehouse to start work. As we turned the last corner in the warehouse and headed toward and wrapping and packing area, we saw a few new faces. Mike, who we had met the day before and who had now taken to smiling an unusual amount every time he saw us walking toward him, introduced us to them. We first met Roland. He was a thin white chap, who looked to be in his thirties and sported a moustache. He appeard slightly more self confident than the others we had so far met.

Then we met another quiet black chap, Lee, who was curiously dressed in clothes that made him look as though he was off clubbing that night. He didn't say much and he didn't do much; in fact he said and did absolutely nothing at all while he was there, just sat on some boxes and watched everyone else work. We later discovered that Lee was actually the lorry driver and was a curious dude who talked as little as was possible and constantly wore night club gear. Roland, on the other hand, was quite talkative and not dressed well at all. In fact he didn't look as though he was off out for the evening, but rather that he had just come back from being out all night in a lot of rough bars.

As with the previous afternoon the usual question and answer session developed.

The radio was tuned to 'Kiss FM' and it worked away with us as we wrapped expensive reproduction antique furniture for our suspiciously quiet driver to distribute. We soon got the hang of the job and by eleven we were only breaking the odd piece of glass rather than scratching and breaking everything we touched.

Eleven o'clock in fact meant break time. This was announced by the arrival of the 'Chuck Wagon.'

'Chuck Wagon!' came a loud shout from the other end of the warehouse.

Mark and I looked at each other in horror. What did we have to do, hit the deck, dive for cover or was this a drugs bust by the cops which meant running out of the nearest exit?

'Hey, Phil, don't looked so worried, man!' exclaimed Mike as he shuffled past. 'It's food, man, crisps and coke, that sort of thing. Or don't you eat where you come from?'

We followed Mike out to the 'Chuck Wagon.' We had forgotten the intense heat and humidity and when we stepped outside it was like stepping into an oven.

'Jesus, it's hot,' I said.

'Yeah, man,' said Mike, 'Selling ice cold coke in this heat you can't go wrong.'

Our morning break was held in the same room as our previous day's afternoon break. Almost all the warehouse staff - including Mark and I - tucked into sugary food and drank a can of brightly coloured, preservative-filled drink. Now that we were all getting to know each other, the conversation picked up a bit.

'You know where Roland was yesterday?' Mike asked with a broad grin on his face. Mark and I looked at each other.

'Go on, Roland, tell 'em where you were,' he continued, still smiling.

'No man, it ain't nothing to be proud of.'

'Go on.'

'No, they don't want to know about that shit, man.'
Roland was becoming slightly embarrassed; a wry smile
crept in below his black moustache.

'He was in the slammer,' Mike said. They all started to
laugh. There was a pause. Then Roland spoke.

'That's right, boys, in the slammer. You know what
that is?'

'Yeah, prison,' I said.

'He spent his vacation in prison,' said Mike still grinning.

'What were you in prison for?' asked Mark.

'Well, it was a driving offense. I was unlucky. You see I
had been done for drinking and driving twice and third
time they stick you in the slammer.'

'How long were you in for?' I asked. I couldn't believe
this!

'Just two weeks. I've been in before for other things;
they just stick you in there to sort of dry out.'

'He had to take his two weeks summer vacation in the
slammer,' Mike repeated.

'Yeah, well at least I had a job when I came out. I deferred
my sentence a while so that it would coincide with my
holiday.'

The conversation switched - as most male conversations
do - to women.

'You married?' inquired Mike, who seemed to be making
most of the conversation.

'Me, no' I answered. 'I'm only twenty-two.'

'"Only twenty-two" - shit, man, quite a lot of people
are married at eighteen here.'

'I'm twenty-two as well and strangely I'm not married
either' said Mark, sarcastically.

'Why are people married so young out here then?' I
asked.

'Why not?' answered Cheryl, who had been quiet up
until now. 'We're all married, man.'

'How old are you then?' Mark asked.

'Twenty-three. I've got two kids too; been married since I was eighteen.' The conversation continued until everybody around the room had given their marital status and declared their number of offspring. We discovered that Roland (the jailbird) was on his third wife, but had been too drunk most of his life to actually produce any kids. Mike (Cheryl's brother) was also married. He had one girl and one on the way. They all seemed incredibly unhappy at having married so young, but we also got the impression that it was fashionable to get married young and then become really depressed about the whole thing and spend all your time complaining about your wife and kids. Life's too short for that, I thought.

We returned to our furniture moving and wrapping and the polishers returned to polishing. The work was becoming tougher; the furniture was heavy and became heavier as the day wore on. After a while we were told to follow Mike as he had to haul some larger pieces of furniture around.

'Come on, shift your ass,' Mike said to Mark with a smile.

'Come on, shift your ass,' Mark mimicked, and got a hefty kick up the backside from Mike.

As we climbed about the stored furniture in the warehouse Mike enquired further.

'You two been anywhere else then besides the good old US of A?'

'Yep,' I replied.

'Where?'

'France, Italy, Germany, Spain, Austria...'

'All right, so you've travelled a bit, man.'

'Well a bit, but most people in Europe have usually been to another country or two, on a summer holiday or something,' I said.

'Really? Wow, not so here, man.'

'Where have you been then?'

'Nowhere.'

'Nowhere?'

'Well I went to South Carolina this year.'

'But that's only the next state'.

'Yeh, I had never been out of the State until this year.'

'Never been out of the State?' I began to laugh with amazement. Mark couldn't believe his ears either.

'No, what's the point, man? I went to South Carolina, that's enough.'

'Don't you want to go anywhere else?'

'Nope. Everybody told me about how great the sea was before I went away and I discovered that it was vastly overrated man. Your body gets battered by the waves and your eyes are ruined by the salt, awful man, awful.'

Mark and I started to laugh. Mike was smiling.

'Is that usual then, for most people to stay in North Carolina?'

'Well, some people travel around the States, but most of my friends are like me and haven't been outside their home state?'

Mark and I were to discover many such features of life in North Carolina. You grew up, married, divorced, lived and died in your home state. To say that many smaller towns had a close-knit community would be the understatement of the decade.

We continued to work through the morning and took an hour for lunch with Richard, who took us to a sandwich bar. It was too hot to be hungry but we certainly drank a lot.

The afternoon passed quickly, with odd questions thrown at us about England and our lifestyles, before once again Mark and I were left in the quiet warehouse at the end of the day to resume 'warehouse tennis.' Richard came down to the end of the warehouse to pick us up.

'Do you want to go around to Diane's for supper tonight?' he asked as he stopped in front of us.

'Who's she?' Mark asked.

'One of the secretaries. The one who you first met as you came in to the offices. She lives just across the road from me. It was her, in fact, that found the apartment for me.'

'Why not?' Mark said and looked at me.

'Yes, sure.'

So that evening we drove back to Richard's apartment, had a swim in the complex's pool, and prepared to go to Diane's. It was a massive relief after a hot day's work to dive into the cool water. The swimming pool was situated just across from Richard's apartment and next to it was a long single story building which contained the launderette, drinks machines and other amenities. The complex seemed very well equipped.

Diane's apartment turned out to be larger than Richard's and was neatly furnished, with the added bonus of a small dining room, where we ate. We were entertained for most of the evening by Diane's daughter, Linda, who was sixteen. Diane was divorced and looked after her daughter during the week, while her 'ex' took Linda at weekends. Linda didn't stop giggling and seemed pleased to flash her expensive mouth braces at each of us in turn. We were fed with pasta and ate well. During the evening's conversation we were once again reminded us of the vast geographical knowledge that all the American's we had met so far seemed to be blessed with.

'Where is England; is it in the middle of Europe?'

'Well not really,' Mark answered with a smile.

'I'd like to go to London, I've heard some really neat things about London.'

There was a pause in the conversation before she came out with an absolute classic.

'Is England a communist country?'

This gave us a bit of a shock but we politely answered that it wasn't. Diane was a bit embarrassed at all the questions that her daughter kept on firing at us; not least because they demonstrated her very slight ignorance of certain aspects of general knowledge.

We returned to Richard's apartment having eaten Diane out of house and home. We drank coffee in front of the TV and started to think seriously about our future plans. It struck us that we had already reached our fifth day in foreign lands and that time and money were not on our side. As soon as Paul arrived from England we would have to leave for Myrtle Beach and make some serious money.

The following day we woke early. The trip to the warehouse seemed to be shorter than the previous day, and got shorter every time we did it. The work became harder and the summer sun hotter. Although the warehouse was air-conditioned we were still working in unfamiliar heat and humidity. We wrapped and stacked for the whole of the morning.

'You guys play golf?' asked our jailbird friend Roland as we worked.

'I do,' said Mark.

'I don't,' I added, 'But I could learn.'

'Yeh, its great fun. What about a game this weekend?' Roland asked.

'Yeh, why not?' I replied.

'Well I don't really know if you'd be up to my sort of standard,' joked Mark. Roland didn't understand English humour and said that he would try and keep up. We didn't bother to explain and let him talk on.

'We could take Jack too. Wait, you guys haven't met Jack yet have you? He's sort of in charge of the warehouse. Quite a good golfer too. Maybe Richard could come too.'

'Well Richard doesn't play golf, but I don't suppose he'd mind having a go,' said Mark.

'O.K. great what about Sunday?'

'We'll check it out,' I said in an American accent, another attempt at wit that passed Roland by.

The rest of the afternoon went slowly, our strength sapped minute by minute. The thought of a swim in the pool when we returned to Richard's apartment was the only thing keeping us going. Our swim was delayed though until we had been drunk under the table at a local bar by Diane, who had cooked for us the night before. This was something else we were to discover. Everybody drank beer, by the gallon. The hotter it got the more beer you drank; besides it was dirt cheap. Water was only to wash in.

We had now been working at the warehouse for a couple of days and, as is human nature, each individual started to open up to Mark and me. Conversation seemed to revert to the normal insults and bad language that probably took place before we arrived. We were no longer the centre of attention; our novelty value had worn off and Mike, Roland, Cheryl, Daniel and Steve now happily chatted to each other rather than spending the whole day asking us questions.

We spent much of this third day loading up the lorry for Lee, while he stood around and watched, in his night club clothes. It was like an oven inside the back of the lorry. Mike and Daniel (who we now called Danny) took turns to stack inside the lorry while the rest of us wheeled the furniture up to the doors. The warehouse was raised from ground level and the lorry was simply backed up to the warehouse door and the furniture loaded straight on to it.

'Shit, it's hot!' exclaimed Mike, as he emerged from the back of the lorry, sweat pouring off him.

'It's suppose to be near a record or something man,' said Danny. (Temperature records of over 100 degrees were to be broken throughout our entire time in the US and it didn't provide for a pleasant working environment!) Everybody was sweating profusely. Mark and myself, not used to the heat, were absolutely dripping wet. Mike looked at Roland who was sitting on some boxes watching the work proceed.

'Come on, Roland, do some work, man,' Mike ordered.

'It's too hot to work.'

'You're a lazy son of a bitch.'

'It's too hot, man. I need a beer.'

'Roland, you don't need another beer. Man, you drink so much God damn beer you already smell like the inside of a beer can.'

Mark and I laughed. Mike smiled at us, pleased that we appreciated his insult.

'Yeh and you've a dog's breath, man,' Roland said, trying to return the insult as quickly as possible, especially as it had come from a younger man. Mike's comment had been cruelly true. Roland didn't eat, he just drank beer; a fact that was to become the butt of many jokes. Every topic that Mark and I had discussed with Roland involved beer, or at least some sort of alcohol. He had just finished telling us of an excursion that he had taken on board a boat in Florida. According to Roland you paid $25 and the boat cruised out onto the sea with fifty passengers. The $25 paid for the trip and food and then you bought 'cheap' drink. When you had had all you could take the boat returned. At the time we thought the story might be leading somewhere, but it didn't lead anywhere at all. It was just another story about Roland getting absolutely plastered.

The insults and loading continued and the lorry was eventually filled. Afternoon break had arrived. Mark and I had taken to buying loads of drinks from the drinks machine that stood outside the rest room. But we soon became worried about the severe medical damage that the brightly coloured red liquid might be have been doing to our insides and so we started taking a large container of orange squash to the warehouse each day, which was probably just as bad for us but saved us an absolute fortune.

That afternoon we were joined by yet another warehouse worker, a character called Charlie. Charlie was cool. He was black, six foot three tall and built like a brick privy. He pumped iron and it showed; but he was one of the kindest natured people you are ever likely to meet. He spent the afternoon packing furniture with us and he didn't stop talking from the moment we first met him.

'So where you two dudes from then?'

Before we had a chance to say anything he answered for us. 'I bet you guys are from London ain't ya? I hear that's where it's happen'n man. Is that right?'

Again we didn't get a chance to answer.

'Yeh, an' I hear there's some pretty fancy women over there too. 'Yeah, there are some pretty nice women in England,' I agreed. 'But then there are some pretty nice women all over the world'.

'Yeh, you're right there, man.' There was a pause. 'But I hear English women are really, really good lookin', man!'

'Any woman's good lookin' to you, Charlie,' said Mike.

'I should say so, man. Any woman does me, man, I ain't choosy. But I could really do with some real English pussy, man. I hear the women over there are mighty, mighty, mighty good lookin', man.' Again there was a pause while Charlie caught his breath. 'You know I used to be real good lookin', man, real good lookin'. In fact I was so good lookin' when I was a kid even my grandma wanted me to suck on her tits.' The warehouse erupted with laughter.

'You're full o' shit, man,' said Mike, who was the only one not laughing too much to talk. Charlie continued.

'You married, Phil?'

'Nope,' I said. 'Are you?'

'Yep. An' I got two pretty little baby girls, and another kid on the way. An' I adore them all, man. I'm a really lucky guy.' Charlie then changed the subject and proceeded to tell us how much weightlifting he did and how much he could bench-press; the size of his chest and arms didn't give us any reason to doubt it. He also told us about his injury in Vietnam. He was almost crippled in a mine explosion and was lucky to be walking. His legs were quite thin given the size of the rest of his body, and he hobbled. He wasn't shy about his disability though, and even made fun of it, saying that we could punch him and run away and he wouldn't be able to catch us; but said that once he did catch us it was a one way bet.

We all continued to pack up the furniture, and Charlie continued to talk.

'...and you see the people here are basically crazy, man. You've got to get out, man, we're all crazy as a dog, man.'

He opened his eyes wide and turned to Mark.

'You crazy, man?'

But again Mark didn't have time to answer.

'Got to keep talkin' to you, man, 'cause you might let something out, man, and then we'd know you was crazy. If not then we might not find out that you're crazy and you could kill us or something, man, with this knife.' He held up the Stanley knife he was using to cut some packing material, and opened his eyes even wider.

Charlie provided the entertainment for the rest of the afternoon and was a great guy to have around. He tempted Mark and I to take him up on his bet and try to sock him and then run off and see if he could catch us and break both our arms. Not really something we wanted to try. Charlie was a gentle giant though and everyone liked him. The only person that was not too happy with him that afternoon was Mike who had become annoyed at the little work that had been accomplished.

Throughout our days at the warehouse the small radio, tuned to 'Kiss FM' had a habit of playing certain records to death and then dropping them flat. All we ever seemed to hear in our first few days was 'Do You Love Me' by the Contours. This meant that we sang the song in most of our waking hours, and were pretty sick of it by the time that they dropped it and began to play 'Animal' by Def Leopard.

That night Richard, Mark and I went to Greensborough - the town in which we had been dropped by the Greyhound Bus - and went shopping in the large Greensborough Mall. We bought provisions and had discussions about the lack of time we actually had to find serious employment somewhere else. Richard couldn't employ us for the whole of the summer.

The next day was Saturday, our first rest day in the US. What do Americans do at the weekend, we wondered? We discovered that a fair number of them play golf. We had agreed earlier in the week to play golf with Roland on Sunday but rearranged to play on Saturday. Roland suggested that Jack - the warehouse foreman we had yet to meet - joined us. We were up early to avoid the hot weather and drove out of Highpoint on a deserted wide road to pick Roland up from home. Home for Roland was actually a caravan, in a caravan park; he hadn't got round to buying a house, and anyway didn't really want one as he said that you 'weren't flexible and couldn't move around' when you had a house. The reality, though, was that Roland had never actually bothered sorting out a mortgage. It was probably also something to do with the fact that he was constantly broke and any money he earned was spent on beer. When we arrived at the caravan park Richard knew exactly where to find Roland's. As we pulled up and stopped outside the long green metal caravan Roland emerged from behind the broken door with a large elastoplast on the side of his head and stitches in his arm.

'What happened to you?' Richard asked as we all walked toward the caravan from the car.

'Listen, man, I had an accident. See that door, I tripped and fell through it,' Roland pointed to the broken door and fly screen. There were pieces of glass all over the damp dewy earth around the door.

'So you can't play golf then, Roland?' Richard asked, a bit tongue in cheek.

'No, man. I'm sorry, I got hurt quite bad.'

'OK, we'll go on and meet Jack then.'

'OK, man, sorry, man, we'll play another time, eh?'

'Yeh,' Richard replied as he turned back to his Golf. Mark and I smiled at Roland, who was still apologising, and headed after Richard.

'He is totally unbelievable,' Richard said as we caught up with him by the car. 'You know, he never makes it to the golf course: something always happens.' He started to laugh. 'What's probably happened is he's had a fight with his wife and she's chucked him through the door.' Mark and I laughed.

'It's true. He's always getting beaten up by his wife.'

We made our way to Jack's house and then on to a dusty bowl of a golf course a further ten minutes drive away. Upon arrival we were amazed to find the small course equipped with electric golf carts but were told that almost every course, no matter how small, had carts. We hired two and Mark and I spent the day successfully completing a series of 'handbrake' turns in ours, much to Jack's displeasure and that of the other occupants of the course.

My first impressions of Jack were mixed. He was approximately forty, six foot two tall, had a weathered face and his frame disguised his beer gut. On the day we met him he was wearing cut-off jeans, sneakers and a purple vest. (Although this may seem wholly inappropriate for a game of golf, the heat ensures that on a public American golf course, 'anything goes'!) Jack was friendly enough and being that much older than the others in the warehouse I imagined that he didn't have too much trouble keeping them in order. He seemed a tough character and the type of guy who would be quite at home in a bar-room brawl. Once again the thoughts of the movies came back when I met Jack. Here we were meeting another character in a film. With his tanned weathered face, large frame and vest, he could have just walked off a film set. He would be one of the guys leaning up against the bar when the camera slowly panned around a beer-drinking joint. He was from the same mould as John Wayne.

My overriding memory of that day with Jack though was the heat. We had not fully acclimatised to the heat and humidity and by the fifth hole that morning it was 98 degrees. Our golf was awful on that day, but was to improve throughout the time we were in the US.

We cooled off with a swim when we returned to Richard's apartment and then set off for another shopping trip. We revisited the shopping mall in Greensborough where we grabbed a bite to eat at the communal eating area. This is an area in the mall where you can obtain food of every possible description. You choose your food from a variety of service counters, situated in a large semi-circle on the outside and then sit in a communal area in the middle to eat. It was the first time we had seen such an arrangement and Mark and I thought it an excellent idea. The only trouble was that the choice was too great and once we had sat down we were constantly studying the food on the tables immediately around us and thinking 'maybe we should have tried the Mexican instead of the Italian, or perhaps the Greek.'

The day was finished off by taking in a movie called 'Betrayed'. The film was pretty good. Disappointingly though it didn't have any New York scenes in it, but it brought back thoughts of the city and thoughts of the movie scenes we had seen. I was sure I had been an actor while in New York, joining the massive cast in playing a role in New York life. The police cars, taxis and traffic, the buildings, the people and sights all seemed to have been constructed for a movie whose actors would all stop instantly at the call of the word 'cut' and return to somewhere else, to do something 'normal'. My role in the movies came back to me. All the people we had met, all the American cars we had seen, everyone a character or a prop in the making of a movie.

Sunday was a perfectly lazy day. We were up late and spent the day lounging by the pool. We took the opportunity to do our washing in the launderette, situated inside the long single-story communal building by the pool. Doing your washing becomes much less of a chore when you can wait for it by a pool, lying on a sun lounger in the hot sun. The pool itself was empty, the only others around were a couple sunbathing.

We had been there for about half an hour that morning when we heard the sound of loud music. It became louder and louder. Mark and I both sat up from across the clear blue pool and waited in eager anticipation, hoping that the classic American rock music was being brought in by two female Baywatch stars. The odds were stacked against such an event but there was no harm in dreaming. The ghetto blaster was in fact brought slowly around the corner by two blokes, both of whom looked as though they spent most of their time pumping iron and as though they had half a brain between them. One was carrying a cool box, presumably stacked full of cold beer and they were both wearing shorts, sneakers and baseball caps which had been put on backwards.

'Here come the pissheads,' said Mark in a disappointed manner. I nodded.

It seemed that resting further, or catching up on some sleep was out of the question, now that the meatheads and their rap music had arrived.

We larked by the pool for the rest of the day and in the evening relaxed in front of the TV with large cups of coffee and a frighteningly large 'family pack' of chocolate chip cookies, which we managed to scoff completely on that one night. Fat city.

Monday's work continued where Friday's had left off, packing and wrapping. Jack returned that day and took things by the scruff of the neck in the warehouse. Mike had been coping well but things were starting to get on top of him, especially the paper work. Having left school at sixteen he didn't exactly have a Ph.D. in 'Administration Techniques' and this led him to such comments as: 'Jesus man, what do you need all this paperwork shit for?' and 'I swear if I ran the world we wouldn't have paperwork, man, and it would save the God damn trees too.'

Lethal Weapon

That Monday in fact was the first time that Mark and I had to split. Mark worked in his brother's office feeding figures into a computer and I continued in the warehouse. I took it as more than a coincidence that we had been split on the very day that Jack returned to the warehouse. Our hand brake turns in the golf carts that Saturday probably had something to do with it. He guessed that Mark and I had been the focus of attention for the last week and that we had been larking around and constantly holding the others up in their work.

In the afternoon Mark and I swapped tasks. I was quite glad to be putting figures into the computer to get a seat for a while; moving from the hot packing and carrying jobs. While I was wandering through the warehouse, fetching some paper for the computer, I noticed Cheryl in the polishing area assembling what looked like a gun. I cautiously walked over to him. It was indeed a gun; a hand gun with a brilliant shine to it and a white enameled handle.

'Jesus, you got a licence for that thing?' I asked.

'Yeh,' said Cheryl as he looked up. 'No point in having one without a licence. They're quite easy to get and the cops 'll get you if you ain't got one.'

'Had it long?' I asked after a short pause.

'No, this is quite new actually,' Cheryl replied, putting the barrel back and closing the gun up with a flick of his wrist.

'Expensive?'

'Not really. But when you've got as many guns as I have the cost soon mounts up.'

'How many have you got then?'

'Well, if you count my machine guns, five.'

'You've got machine guns?' I was stunned. Was I speaking to the guy who would make the front of the local newspaper and the headlines on the national news in a weeks time by spraying his work colleges with machine gun fire? I chose my next words carefully, lest I be the one to light the touch paper.

'What do you need all those guns for, Cheryl?'

He looked up and smiled, then began to polish the shining handgun with a cloth.

'Well, this little baby is for my own protection, but my machine guns are for tournaments. Sort of like a sport.'

'Ah, sport, I see,' I said, with as much sarcasm as I dared. 'Are you a good shot then?'

'Not bad. I take part in machine gun competitions.'

'They have machine gun competitions?'

'Yep. I'm M16 champion of North Carolina.'

I stood in disbelief for a while. He looked up again and smiled.

'I'm also in the reserves. Sort of like joining the army at weekends, training and shit; so I do have quite a bit more of an association with guns than most people, I suppose.'

'Even so,' I said 'you seem to have one wicked armory.'

'Yep.'

I was still digesting the conversation as Cheryl produced the shining handgun from his polishing-cloth. He beckoned me to hold it. I did, it was heavy. I checked it was not loaded and whizzed the chamber around with the palm of my hand, the way I'd seen it done in films. It felt frighteningly good to hold. Cheryl, leaning up against the table, folded his arms and continued to talk.

'I know that nobody in England carries a gun, but out here you are at a one hundred per cent disadvantage if you don't, 'cause everybody's got one.'

'Well I suppose once a few people start carrying guns others feel as though they have to, and before you know it everyone's got a weapon,' I said.

'That's right.'

Besides a bit of clay pigeon shooting, I had never really used a gun and certainly hadn't held such a powerful handgun before. I was aware of the frightening power I held in my hand. It was a really awesome piece of metal

and I thought of all the gun fights that I'd seen in the Clint
Eastwood movies and how it was no longer surprising to
me that a handgun seemed to be able to blow a man off his
feet. This baby felt like it could blow a barn door off. The
warehouse suddenly seemed a perfect a movie set for Lethal
Weapon, or Magnum Force, and I could visualise guys
hiding behind furniture and running in and out of the
shelving waiting to be picked off.

'Does your brother carry a gun as well?' I asked.

'Well, I think he's got a shotgun in his car at the moment
but I don't think he usually carries any small arms.'

'Strewth, it's like an ammunitions dump around here.'

'Well it is if you include the guns that the girls carry.'

'Give me a break. The girls carry guns as well?'

'Yeh, man, they have to, for protection. Two of the
secretaries carry guns and that girl round the corner,
Donna, she keeps a gun in her sock.'

He took the gun back from me, turned around and stuck
it in the drawer of the table.

'Better get back to work.'

I walked back to Richard's office, mulling over the cost
of a three fifty seven Magnum.

Time passed quickly that afternoon and I was surprised
to see Mark enter Richard's office at the end of the day.

'Hi, Phil.'

'Good grief, is it the end of the day already?'

'Sure is, boy.'

'What have you been doing, Marky, you look a bloody
mess?'

He was standing in the doorway with his shorts and T-
shirt absolutely covered in dust.

'Ah, Mike got me climbing amongst all the furniture at
the back of the warehouse. Jack wants to sort it all out.'

On the way back to the apartment I thought of telling
Mark about the number of guns that were hanging around
the warehouse and the fact that Donna kept a gun in her

sock. But I thought, what the hell, let him get frisky with her and get his head blown off!

Our first official visit to the company showroom came when we were instructed to take some furniture there the following day. A few of the gang had loaded the lorry the evening before and first thing that morning we set off; Danny was driving, Jack was organising and Mark, Mike and myself were in the back with the carefully stacked goods. Danny backed the lorry onto the tarmaced courtyard of the smart, light brick building and we all helped to unload, being careful not to scratch the expensive wooden floor just inside the entrance hall. As we worked the heat became more and more intense. The inside of the lorry was like a sauna and the hot sun began to burn unprotected skin. Relief only came once we were inside the air-conditioned showrooms. We had all been told to take it easy by Jack, who was worried that we might keel over at any moment.

Inside the showroom, after all the goods had been unloaded, Mark and I took time to examine the displays of antique and reproduction furniture. I was carefully studying what must have been a very expensive antique desk at one end of the hall when Mike approached.

'Like one of these, Phil?'

'Sure would, boy,' I replied, unwittingly taking the mickey out of his accent.

'Have to work your ass off to afford one of these though, Phil.'

I remembered having seen similar antique desks in England and drawing on a combination of memories of my father's antiques and brute force, I managed to find the secret drawer that most large, well-made antique desks possess.

'Shit!' exclaimed Mike. 'You've broken that now, monkey brains?'

'No I haven't' I said purposefully. 'Most old desks have a secret drawer somewhere; and here is this one's.'

'Really?' Mike was genuinely impressed. 'Two years in the furniture business and I didn't know that, Phil.'

He took the small mahogany drawer from my grasp and studied it. Then he stepped closer to the desk and put it back in, concealing it once again.

'Impressed with my extensive antique knowledge, then?' I asked, smiling.

'Honestly, man, how did you know it was there?'

'Well, most of these antique desks have a hidden drawer somewhere; ever since knowing this I've looked for them in old desks I come across. They're usually quite small and usually disguised as decoration'

'Well God damn, Phil, you taught me something new today. You and Mark do actually have a use after all.'

We were all completely knackered after the removal job and Mike suggested we have our mid-morning break at Burger King.

At this point it is worth mentioning that we had only been in the US a few days and didn't mind a burger at every meal. We didn't realise however that we were in for a burger and fries for every meal for the next three months. By the end of our time in the States our bodies would be rejecting all other foods.

On the way to Burger King Mark and I were once again in the back of the lorry with Mike, but this time we didn't have any furniture to hang on to and Danny started to drive like a man possessed.

'Shit, this is a bit risky,' said Mark as we were thrown from one side of the lorry to the next.

'Hey, you God damn maniac, what are ya doing,' shouted Mike, starting to laugh nervously. He began to bang on the wall by the cab.

'Enjoying the ride, boys?' shouted Danny; we could hear him and Jack laughing in the cab. We arrived at Burger King, battered and bruised. We jumped out of the back and followed a smiling Jack and Danny inside. There was a bit of a queue. Mark and I were standing next to each other.

'Watch this, I'm going to order in Yank,' I said quietly to Mark.

He smiled. 'Go on then.'

'Could ya do me a large Whopper, fries an' a shake pleeeeeeese?'

Nobody had noticed my act, apart from Mark, who was now holding back his laughter as best he good.

'Nobody noticed, Phil!'

'I know. I risked life and limb for that escapade and nobody bloody noticed.'

The rest of the guys were almost finished by the time Mark and I had finished larking around and so we wolfed down our remaining fries and ran out to the lorry.

'Hey come on, boys' Mike said from the cab window; he was a smart enough kid not to travel in the back again. Mark and I leapt into the back of the open lorry just as it began to move off. Mike and Jack were quite prepared to leave anybody who hadn't finished and make them walk back to the warehouse. Mike was determined to get his own back for the drive to Burger King and the lorry drove off without Danny - who had been taking a quick leak around the corner. The lorry had to stop for the traffic at the Burger King exit. Danny appeared and we sensed he had been left behind before. He instantly started sprinting for the back of the open truck and literally had to dive into the back. Just as he did so the lorry screeched away, wheels spinning, onto the road. As the lorry straightened up, the view that greeted Mark and I from the back of the open lorry was that of a large black and white cop car. They must have witnessed the whole escapade. Fortunately for us though, they considered their stomachs far more important than the larking around they had just witnessed. They smiled at us, shook their heads and slightly further down the road cruised into the car park of the next fast food joint. Mark and I looked at each other with a relieved smile. We hadn't realised how lucky we had been; we discovered later in conversation, that nobody in the lorry cab had been wearing a seat belt; Jack had been drinking a beer while driving and that it is illegal to drive a lorry with its tailgate wide open!

The day had been hot, but a swim in the evening freshened us up and we ventured out later in search of some golf clubs. I picked up a set of Wilson Sam Snead clubs, a decent Spalding putter and a Wilson golf bag all for £150; considering that the putter alone in England would have been about £70, to say I got a bargain would be the second understatement of the decade. But this was my first set of clubs and I had actually made a mistake in buying 'blades', which only the better players use. I should have purchased some with a larger sole that would have given me a bigger 'sweet spot'. Nevertheless I was pleased with my purchase.

We then travelled on to a golf club on the outskirts of Highpoint where we could view clubs for the more discerning golfer - Mark. The clubs looked impressive and so did the prices, even though they were only about half of what you would expect to pay in the UK.

'Well I said I'd get some clubs out here, Phil, so I'd better take this opportunity to get some cheaply,' said Mark as he stared up at the neatly displayed club sets.

'Don't just buy some for the sake of it though,' I said. 'I bought some because I've never had any before and they were cheap; if your looking to spend heavy dosh then maybe think about it a bit longer.'

We continued to walk around the shop picking up the odd club to try.

'I'll almost certainly get some, Phil; it's just the thought of parting with all that money, it sends shivers down my back.'

'Tell me about it!' I exclaimed. Mark laughed.

'Hey, metal woods; never seen those before.'

'Yeh, there only just becoming popular in the UK, but they've probably been out here for quite a while.'

'Are they a bit of a gimmick?' I asked reaching to take one from a display.

'No I think they're quite good. I don't know if the ball goes any further but most of the pro's use them.'

Mark received advice about all sorts of clubs before eventually deciding on some serious RAM clubs. They were to be fitted with extra large grips to cope with Mark's extra large hands, so we would have to pick them up at a later date. As with my clubs, they were considered a bargain.

That night - just as Mark and I were having a competition in the living room to decide 'the greatest putter in the entire universe' - there was a call from Sonia, a friend of Richard's. Sonia worked as a waitress at a restaurant called 'Applebies'. Sonia met Richard when he was first out in the States and had rung to ask him to meet her boyfriend, who was apparently in a bit of 'trouble'. We all trooped around to Applebies.

'That wasn't far,' I said as we walked up to the door.

'Nope, that's why I used to come here, so that I could get home at night without getting lost, when I was blind drunk,' explained Richard.

Applebies was for the most part circular inside, well lit, with booths surrounding the bar and chairs and tables set further out, by the windows. The floor was pine and the booths were classically built with high sides and furnished with red leather. There were a few people eating at the outer tables and a few drinking in the booths. We took a seat in a booth and before long Sonia appeared.

'Hi!'

'Hi, Sonia,' said Richard. 'This is my brother Mark and this is Phil.'

Sonia was about five foot nine, with a good figure, curly dark brown hair and nice (albeit pale) skin. She was quite pretty but with slightly exaggerated features. She was obviously not working that night as she was casually dressed. She sat down and we ordered some beers. Her boyfriend joined us soon afterwards. I've forgotten his name but I won't forget him. He thanked us for coming and then told us his story and the 'trouble' he was in. He was English, had runaway to the States when he had failed medical school in the UK and had worked in menial jobs to earn enough to put himself through medical school in the US. He had completed all but one year of his course and had now run out of money. He waffled on for quite a while - an hour in fact - until we prised out of him the nitty gritty of the tale, that he basically wanted to borrow some money. I sat in disbelief as this chap that Richard had never met before and who was the boyfriend of a waitress that Richard had only known for a short while, asked him for large amounts of dosh. Mark's expression quite clearly showed he was thinking the same. What a cheek this guy had. Didn't he have anybody else he could turn to?

'Why don't you ask your parents for some money?' Richard asked.

'I can't. They'll only give me the money to finish college if I return to England to see them.'

'Well why don't you.'

'I just can't.'

'Why? Are you an international criminal or something then? Or are they going to arrest you at customs for not paying a parking fine in 1982?' This guy had been giving us earache for the last hour and Richard was beginning to take the mickey.

'I just can't return, man, I just can't. I ran away to get away from my parents; I don't really like my parents.'

'Why don't you pawn your watch?' I asked, having noticed his gold Oyster Perpetual Rolex.

'I can't, man. This was a present from my parents on my eighteenth birthday.'

'But you've just told us that you don't really like your parents,' exclaimed Richard, now starting to laugh.

'It's difficult to explain, but I just can't.'

This guy was probably the biggest bullshitter I had ever heard, and there was more to come.

'Haven't you got anything else to sell?' continued Richard. 'What sort of car do you drive?'

'Well I drive a Mercedes, but it's old and it's a really good car so I don't really want to get rid of it. It's my only transport man.'

'So you've got a gold Rolex and a Merc, and you say your desperate for money,' I said. 'Why don't you tone down your living expenses?'

'Ah. You don't understand. I just need five thousand dollars now to get me through college. I need it now, you see.'

'Well I can't help you if you don't help yourself,' said Richard. 'Anyway if you really wanted to, you could get the money.' He was now quite angry. The conversation dwindled so we gladly made our excuses and left.

'What a load of bullshit,' said Mark, when we'd got outside.

'I've never met such a idiot in all my life,' Richard said. 'What if I had lent him the money; how am I to know he's not going to run off and leave me five grand out of pocket? I've never met the guy before in my life.'

We about the poor chap all the way back. He was obviously quite clever to have made it to medical school in the UK, but he seemed to be very confused. He had probably been pushed too hard as a kid and pressured into going to medical school by his father, who he had mentioned was a doctor. He ran away to the States to escape it all and found that to progress from being a dish washer for the rest of his life he had to complete medical school. If he had a long hard chat with his bank manager he probably would have been leant the money. Doctors in the States are hardly strapped for cash.

The following day we took a rest. It had finally caught up with us. Practically no sleep for three days while we were travelling and then working in 100 degree heat since, meant that we could no longer go on and had to take a day off.

'What do you mean you want the day off?' inquired Richard. 'You had the weekend off a couple of days ago.'

'Yeah. But this heat is getting to us; I think we've been overdoing it,' smiled Mark.

'I don't know. The youth of today. All right, you are on a sort of a holiday, I suppose.'

We spent the day by the pool. We talked of our plans and once again realised that time and money were not on our side. Paul would be arriving from England in less than a week and we would probably be off to Myrtle Beach in search of serious money and a chance to see more of the States.

While we were by the pool some kids came to join us with their mother. One little kid was incredibly annoying and judging by his antics would probably be locked up before he was an adult. He couldn't have been older than six and was wearing swimming goggles and armbands. While Mark and I were swimming he would jump in on top of us and then resurface with a smile on his face. He was barely able to swim and after a lot of coughing, spluttering and kicking seemed to only just make it back to the side of the pool. After each attack he would climb out, get in again at the shallow end and lie in the water with his goggles and armbands still on and stretch out his arms over the top of the pool as though he owned the whole place, daring Mark and I to attempt to drown him while his mother was on hand. He had a real nerve considering he was so tiny.

This day off gave us our first chance to really look around the apartment complex. It was quiet during the day and the cul-de-sacs off the main road were free of cars. We hadn't seen anyone play tennis on the green asphalt court that was across the road from the pool and wondered why. The answer was that any serious tennis star would have given it a wide berth. Closer inspection revealed the lumps in the asphalt where it had obviously buckled and melted in the heat and in some areas weeds were growing to the surface. But what the hell, after 'warehouse tennis' this was the centre court at Flushing Meadows. Mark and I made use of it.

There were also a suspicious number of police cars parked on the complex during the day. We didn't know whether it was due to policemen doing night work and thus sleeping during the day, or whether they were all shirking off work. It certainly wasn't because there had been a crime wave; the place was quieter than a morgue.

That evening we went back to Applebies for a drink. We hadn't really had a chance to enjoy the place the previous night or to get drunk. Sonia came over to our table as soon as we had been seated; she was working that night. She was obviously embarrassed at first to see us and apologised for her boyfriend the night before. Sonia admitted that Richard had probably not been the best person to ask for a loan, seeing as her boyfriend had never even met him before. She was right. Richard politely dismissed the previous night's events saying that he understood. Sonia was happy that no permanent harm had been done and we were even happier, as she decided to give us a couple of rounds on the house as a gesture of reconciliation.

'Excuse the cliche,' I said, 'but what's a nice girl like Sonia doing with that nut we met last night?'

'I don't know,' answered Richard as he turned to watch her tend to another table.

'Is she engaged to him or something?'

'No, I don't think so,' he said. 'You know she's been married before, though?'

'Has she?' I asked, surprised.

'How old is she then?' asked Mark.

'She's about twenty-two or twenty-three; she was married for just three weeks and then got divorced.'

'Three weeks?' Mark and I exclaimed in disbelief.

'Only three weeks. It's not uncommon for people out here to get married in their late teens and early twenties. Most break up pretty quickly but I've got to admit three weeks is a bit of a record.'

'Good grief. Imagine your marriage only lasting three weeks,' Mark said. 'What a nightmare.'

'Mike and Cheryl at work were both married at eighteen,' Richard continued.

'Yeah, they told us,' Mark said.

'They all seem to marry the first girl they fancy and then end up regretting it. The divorce rate here is something ridiculous.'

'The divorce rate must be worse than Hollywood.'

'Hey, Tinsel Town has nothing on this lot when it come to completely ignoring your wedding vows,' I said.

Friends

'Where have you two God damn lazy assholes been?' inquired Mike on our return to work. 'Wish I could take days off man, but some of us have to work 'cause we have wives and kids to feed.'

'Ahh shut up, you God damn son of a bitch' drawled Mark. Mike smiled and slowly shook his head.

'Right, you two are gonna do some real work today. Come with me, both of you.' We followed him down the warehouse.

'Looks like you two been sittin' in the sun all day; gonna get yourselves a tan then while you're here?'

'Hope to, boy,' Mark said; he got a kick up the backside for his wise crack and was called a lazy son of a bitch. I then called him a lazy son of a bitch as well, ridiculing Mike but managed to run away before he had a chance to kick me.

Mike was a decent guy and larking around with him made the hot days pass more amicably. But taking the mickey out of Mike was probably not the wisest of ideas, as he had actually done a spell in the prison. We didn't discover this until later on and the offence was kept from us. So we now knew that there were two stars from 'Escape from Alcatraz' on the payroll at the warehouse and there were more surprises to come. Each day we learnt something new about one or other of the guys and the longer we spent in the warehouse the more amazing the stories became. Knowing someone for a day or two tells you nothing about them; but when they open up to you, then you discover their true colours. Charlie's comments to us on that first afternoon we had met him - when he hadn't stopped talking - about wanting to get to know us just in case we were 'crazy' and about to attack everyone with a Stanley knife, began to ring true. Who really gets to know anyone?

'OK, you two, we've got to sort out all this furniture on these shelves. Hope you don't have your best clothes on cause this stuff's covered in dust.'

Mark and I looked up at the vast shelves and then looked at each other.

'Lot of stuff on these shelves, boy,' Mark said. Mike had by now climbed half way up to the top.

'Far out, some climbing,' I said.

'Get about half way up here, Phil,' Mike said 'So as I can chuck stuff to ya.' I was already on my way. Mark was left at ground level and we spent all afternoon clearing and stacking furniture. Some of the pieces, such as solid mahogany table tops were outrageously heavy and Mike, although only thinly built, threw them down to me as though they were made of balsa wood. The heavier the piece the harder he threw. I was gradually losing my energy and Mark began to make me laugh.

'Don't drop that, man: expensive piece that,' Mike said, realising that one would soon be dropped. This encouraged Mark.

'Wehhhhhh hey, hey don't drop that, Phil.' The furniture kept coming down, with both the others eager for me to fall or drop a piece.

'I swear I'll drop one of these in a moment,' I called out. But they both kept encouraging a disaster.

'You drop this one, Phil and that's it, man, game over.' Mike said. 'Its coming out of ya wages.' He down threw another large solid table top. I couldn't hold it. It fell on me and I fell off the shelves along with the table top. I could hear Mark and Mike howling with laughter as their destructive efforts had finally succeeded. I had hurt cut my leg slightly but wasn't really hurt and I looked around for the table top. It was wedged amongst the stack of chairs that had broken our fall, and I could see the wrapping had been torn and the polished top was now heavily scratched.

'You God damn crazy son of a bitch,' said Mike. He hadn't had so much fun in ages. He looked down at the table top.

'We'd better get that top to Cheryl. He'll sort it out; get rid of those scratches in a second. Be as good as new.' I climbed down to ground level.

'Hey your work ain't done.' called Mike.

'Never mind me then' I said. 'I could be injured.'

'I'll injure you if ya don't get back up here.'

Mark's laughing stopped suddenly when Mike called him up to replace me on the mountain of furniture. He didn't fare much better and dropped nearly everything in hysterics. Mike climbed down when we had finished.

'You two are worse than useless, man,' he pronounced.

That evening we once again relaxed in front of the TV with large cups of coffee and chocolate chip cookies. It was our longest look at American TV. Although we had watched it previously, we only really seen the music channel, MTV. We had a total of thirty-six channels to choose from and rather than a thin magazine containing the week's programmes a thick booklet the size of two Reader's Digests was available with the local paper. But by the time you had studied it thoroughly, the programmes you wanted to watch were over and the next booklet was available; there was a bewildering amount of TV viewing. We didn't bother trying to find out what was on that evening, or that week, and we wondered how many people actually did. Maybe all the reported hours spent in front of the telly by American kids was simply due to them switching channels to try and find the one they wanted; or trying to fathom out the TV guide. One thing we did notice though throughout our viewing that evening, as we flicked between channels, was that channel twenty-seven's programmes didn't change much. They were all about sharks and carried interviews with intrepid divers who had spent their entire lives diving with sharks. No comedy, no drama, no Daffy Duck cartoons, just sharks, for four hours.

'Ahhheeeeeeeee,' cried Mark, after switching to channel twenty-seven for the umpteenth time. 'This must be the shark channel.' He looked at me with a strange expression.

'Maybe there are so many channels that one is entirely devoted to sharks!'

'I don't think so guys,' laughed Richard. 'I think it's called the Discovery channel. They must just be having a shark evening or something.'

'Oh, just a shark evening,' Mark said. 'They're gonna run out of animals if they have an animal evening every night.'

In between watching telly and drinking buckets of coffee we managed to book up our accommodation in Myrtle Beach. Paul would be arriving from England on 26th July and we would then be off to search for work there. Restaurant work with fat tips - we hoped.

The next day at work I received the first sign that I was at last considered slightly trustworthy. The warehouse guys obviously didn't think that we were complete morons, even though we spent most of our time generally mucking around.

'Hey, Phil, can you drive?' asked Cheryl.

'Sure can, boy,' I replied.

'You're a cheeky son of a bitch!' Cheryl laughed.

'You being cheeky to my brother, Phil?' asked Mike as he walked passed us in the warehouse with Mark in tow.

'Good morning, Mark,' I said.

'Good morning, Phil,' Mark replied.

'Hey, never mind that polite shit,' said Cheryl 'You gotta do some work.'

'Now, do you have a driving license?'

'Yes. An international one,' I answered.

'Right, well you have to go out and pick up a chair. I'll draw a map for you.'

'What am I going to drive?'

'The company van.' There was an ominous pause.

'Come on, spill the beans,' I said, 'what's the "company van" like?'

'It's awful, Phil. It's a ten year old Chevy with a V6 that's been round the clock at least twice.'

'Oh neat. Then there's a pretty good chance that it will pack up on me is there?'

'No, those things go on forever, man, but the ride might be a bit jerky. Oh, and by the way there's no air-conditioning, so if the van actually gets you there in one piece, chances are you wil have fried on the way.' He laughed.

'Oh thanks, I won't last a minute out in that heat and humidity without air-conditioning.'

'You'll get used to it, Phil. Just don't drive with the slide door open 'cause the air will seem like an oven when it hits ya and you'll be fried even quicker'

Cheryl drew me a map and took me out to the van.

'Well, boy, this is it,' he laughed.

It was a classic 1970s American van; the type that the criminals always drive in films, where the hub caps come off as it squeals around a corner. The sort of van that Jim Rockford would be chasing in the Rockford Files, or that the Dukes of Hazard would persue around Hazard county to apprehend a couple of third-rate criminals. It was tatty but not falling to pieces. I hopped in and was given a quick tour of the instrument panel. Cheryl wished me luck and I drove off.

'Hey, you'll be in serious shit if you stop for a burger, man,' Cheryl, waving a finger.

I ventured out in the dark green van, sure I'd get lost. I was right. A trip that should have taken half an hour took an hour and a half. I spent the time tearing up and down different roads driving like a maniac in the powerful, automatic V6 van, looking for the small company shack from which I was supposed to pick up a reproduction antique chair. The trip also took slightly longer than anticipated due to the short queue at the Burger King Drive Thru'. I was dripping with sweat when I finally returned; it was 98 degrees, with oppressive humidity.

'Find the way then, Phil?' asked Cheryl.

'Just.' I threw my burger wrapper really obviously into the bin by Cheryl, but he continued laughing.

'Hot enough for you was it? You get a real luxury ride in that machine, man. Better not have damaged the chair, man: that's an expensive piece of furniture.'

'Never mind the God damn furniture, I need some water,' I said as I pushed passed Cheryl.

I spent the whole day with Cheryl and was unfortunate enough to have to take another trip in the van with him that afternoon. We had to pick up some large dining chairs that were being changed. We travelled out to a large house on the outskirts of Highpoint

'Each house here, Phil, backs on to the golf course,' Cheryl told me as we drove up a shaded private road towards the house.

'What does the guy do for a living then?' I asked as we swept into the gravel drive of a large house.

'He's got a large car dealership in Highpoint. But I'm not sure which one.'

'Wow, trade must be good.'

The house was massive and very well kept. It was very symmetrical, white with dark wood covering the front in mock Tudor style. We admired it, and then walked around to the back. A small Mexican chap came out to greet us. I thought he looked somewhat old to still be working at a large car dealership, but all was soon explained.

'Phil, this is Alberto, he's the sort of butler here.' I smiled and shook Alberto's hand. He guided us in and we quickly collected the chairs from the large dining room. We carefully loaded them into the van and then had a short chat to Alberto, who complained about the time it took to keep the large house tidy.

'Hey, ask for a pay rise, Alberto,' joked Cheryl.

'Yeh, maybe I will,' said Alberto solemnly. We left him contemplating the thought and drove off back to the warehouse. When we returned our shirts were soaking in sweat. It really was stifling hot and it even took a hardened Cheryl an hour to recover from the short trip.

The next day was Saturday; a lying by the pool day. The weather was still unrelentingly hot. The three of us decided to play golf again. For the first time we played on the 'smart' course, although we had been to the shop there before, when Mark had bought his clubs. It was a public course, but kept in supreme condition. The fairways and greens were lush and well watered and the surroundings idyllic. A few of the holes were by small lakes or ponds and even the foliage was neatly trimmed. The good weather naturally helped to show it off, but the course really was in fantastic condition. To cap it all, electric carts were available. But not the older ones we had used when we had previously played. These were new and gleaming white with plenty of room for your bags on the back and a canopy overhead. I remember thinking, as we hacked our way down the first fairway, that it was a shame our golf didn't live up to the surroundings.

Being a Saturday the golf course was quite full but it only looked as though we had a few moments to wait before we drove down the first fairway. As we approached the tee, though, a golf cart pulled up and a really fat chap got out. He was wearing a huge white T-shirt and a pair of fawn shorts, which finished below his knees. He was accompanied by a small chap wearing thick glasses and both of them were sweating and smoking fat cigars. They walked up to us and the fat chap stuck his tee in the ground and looked down the fairway to play. This was queue jumping of the highest order we thought and 'being British and all that' we looked at each other in amazement. Richard was about to say to him 'look here, old chap, this isn't really on' when he turned to us.

'You playing through?' he asked. We stood silent and a slight depressed looked started to cover Richard's face. Oh no, here was another American custom we had yet to appreciate. The fat chap repeated his question and then noticing our puzzlement informed us that the course was only nine holes long and that if you were 'playing through' i.e. eighteen holes, then you had right of way over those just starting their round. We all smiled politely and stepped back off the tee to let this 'walrus' and his friend 'play through'. Having been only moments from teeing off we eventually had to wait another twenty minutes while two more sets of 'golfers' screeched to a halt in their buggies, jumped out and started before us, claiming they were 'playing through'. We were eventually wise to the situation and when the first buggy, that had not seen us waiting at the tee, raced around the corner we were ready.

'Are you playing through?' asked one of the buggy's occupants.

'Yes,' shouted Richard 'We're playing through!'

Much of the rest of that day was spent back by the pool, in the sun, although we did venture out later to pick up some more Budweiser beer.

On Sunday we played golf again, on the same course, where a women's golfing tournament was being held. All the participants, about sixty middle-aged women, were nattering and collecting their buggies. Some had already made it to the first tee. We collected our tickets and buggies and raced around to the first tee to beat the rest of them. Richard jumped out of his cart.

'Playing through,' he shouted loudly. Mark followed him up to the tee and I raced out of my buggy, smiled at the now silent gathering of ladies and prepared to tee off. The Ladies didn't seem to care, or inquire as to how we managed to be 'playing through' when the course had only just opened; they just nattered away enjoying the social side of the golfing day. What an excellent idea of Richard's I remember thinking, while attempting hand brake turns in my buggy at the end of the first fairway.

The sport continued later in the day when we made use of the tennis court that stood opposite the pool. Although it was rarely used due to the bimps in the asphalt and weeds growing up at various intervals, this didn't bother us. We borrowed two rackets from Diane and proceeded to have an excellent game of tennis at an incredibly high standard. Having fought our way through the crowd of keen tennis spectators and signed a few autographs we returned to the apartment.

The second week brought the return of Charlie; our big, black, cheerful ex 'Nam veteran. He had been helping a friend move house and it was good to have him back as work was beginning to become mundane. Charlie kept the warehouse lively and laughing, much to the annoyance of Jack and Mike, as it meant that work proceeded very slowly. Everybody in the warehouse came in for abuse at some stage or other, Charlie didn't care. Everybody in the warehouse was 'a lazy son of a bitch' and 'God damn asshole' and he told us that he was the only real red blooded male among us as he was the only one who dreamt about pussy all day, every day.

That morning Richard received a call from Paul in his office. He had arrived last night and had stayed in the YMCA in New York, as Mark and I had done. We were amazed that he had made it and that he had remembered Richard's telephone number. Richard told him how to get to Highpoint and hoped to see him the next day. All seemed to be going according to plan.

On that Monday Mark and I managed to sort out our social security numbers. These allowed us to work legitimately for the rest of the summer. We already had documents from BUNAC to present to future employers, enabling us to work in the US, but we needed social security numbers to make sure that we were registered as non-tax payers. Those waiting in the large social security office were typically desperate individuals; the sort you would probably find in any similar place in any country. They all looked as though they had been waiting for at least a year to see someone official and looked as if they didn't really care whether they eventually did or not. The social security offices were just like those anywhere else: unwelcoming, with hard plastic chairs and a lino floor.

That evening Mark and I got a lift home from Diane, as Richard wanted to stay on and work. As usual we went for a swim. We were now setting records in the pool for underwater swimming. We could only manage a single cross length of the kidney shaped pool when we had first arrived, but now two and even three were not out of the question.

Much of Tuesday I spent working with cheerful Charlie. This was due to Jack's philosophy of keeping Mark and I apart so that we did some work and didn't just muck around. Charlie was always making stupid comments that made me laugh. I was supposed to be helping him take furniture to and from different businesses in Highpoint. We spent quite a time in the truck while we were transporting the stuff and Charlie used the opportunity to tell me a tale or two.

'You probably noticed, Phil, being from university and all that, that I can't walk too good. I got a bit of a limp. Do you know how I got it?'

'Yeah, Mike told me; you trod on a land mine in Vietnam or something.'

'That's right. I was God damn lucky not to lose my legs, man. That was an awful experience, man. Sort of makes you realise how lucky you are to be alive and kicking, if you know what I mean, Phil.

'You know we are so lucky you and me man, being healthy and mobile. There's a lot of people out there who ain't as lucky and can't really get around like we do man'. I looked out of the front, solemnly listening to his words.

'That's why I try and get as much pussy as I can, while I'm alive man.' We both burst out laughing. Just when you thought Charlie was turning to serious subjects he would come out with such a statement.

'You married, Phil?' he asked, once he had stopped giggling.

'Nope.'

'Oh yeh, you told me before. I'm married man. I've been really fortunate, Phil, I got myself a beautiful wife and two little beautiful daughters; and we're expecting another kid in a couple of months now.'

'Congratulations.' I said. 'Do you want a boy?'

'I don't really mind, Phil, you know. But I've gotta say keeping three women already costs me a lot of money. A boy would probably be cheaper, you know.' He laughed.

As we reached the different destinations the tables and cabinets we were delivering seemed to get heavier and heavier. Charlie was talking continuously and we were both sweating profusely in the intense heat.

'Hear you're gonna try and get to Florida while your over here, Phil,' Charlie said as I carried a heavy shelf and a cabinet door from the truck.

'Hope so,' I said, struggling with my load.

'Florida's a really nice place, man: beaches and stuff and all that sun and all those women. You'll have a real swell time down there, man.' He pointed to the shelf I was carrying. 'The only thing you'll find as heavy as that in Florida, man, is a bucket of orange juice.' I burst into laughter and staggered with my load. The statement 'working with Charlie' was a paradox.

Much to our amazement Paul managed to arrive in Highpoint that day. Mark took the call in Richard's office. We all happened to be in the office as the phone rang. After a brief conversation of 'yes' and 'no' Mark put down the phone and turned to Richard and myself.

'You'll never guess what,' he said with a broad grin.

'Don't tell me, Paul's missed a connecting bus and has lost his wallet and is stuck in Philadelphia.'

'No,' said Mark. 'He's stuck in New York; he missed the bus because of some mix-up over tickets or something.'

'I knew it was too good to be true,' I said.' He'll probably get down here on Monday week!'

'No, only joking, he's at the Greyhound bus station in Highpoint.'

'Well, that's absolutely amazing,' I said. 'He's travelled three thousand miles and is only,' I looked at my watch, 'twenty minutes late. I've known him be twenty minutes late for a lecture at university that was taking place just two hundreds yards from his room on campus.'

'Well, the boy's made it, I suppose we had better pick him up.'

'Yep. Is it OK if we take the van?' I asked.

'Sure,' said Richard.

It was good to see Paul and there were greetings all round. He was pleased to see us and chucked his belongings in the back of the van. He told us about a guy he had met on the way over who had guaranteed us all a job in a restaurant if we went down to Texas. Poor old Paul probably would have gone. He was still on a high, as we had been when we first arrived, but Mark and I had by now come down to earth and were fortunately sober enough not to think that travelling all the way down to Texas to try and find a chap who had promised us a job over a drink was a good idea.

We spent the evening showing Paul around the complex, playing cards and going for a quick swim.

'This is the life, eh lads!' exclaimed Paul whilst we were sitting by the pool.

'It's not all beer and skittles you know,' Mark warned. 'Phil and I have been working our butts off these last couple of weeks.'

'How did the wedding go by the way, Paul?' I asked.

'You'll never guess what happened.' he began. Knowing Paul as we did, something was bound to have gone wrong and Paul explained how the car in which he was travelling to the wedding reception had had a puncture and he had to get out and change the wheel in his top hat and tails, whilst smiling politely to all the other wedding guests passing by. Paul's knack for 'mishaps' is unsurpassed.

Later, at the apartment, we told Paul of our plans to reach Myrtle Beach and to find jobs as waiters. Paul had also heard that this was a decent way of earning a fortune and was all for it. We all needed to earn as much as possible in as short a space of time.

Now that Paul had arrived the sleeping arrangements in the one bedroom apartment started to get difficult. It was always going to be a squash, but we sorted out a system which we stuck to for the rest of our time in Highpoint. Mark and his brother Richard slept in the bedroom, while Paul and I took turns to sleep on the floor and on the sofa bed. With three month's luggage in tow as well, the place was cramped.

Our final two days in Highpoint were spent working at the warehouse, waiting to leave for Myrtle Beach. We were leaving on the Friday and because we planned to spend the rest of our time there we had to pack everything once again into our rucksacks. Our golf clubs we would pick up on our way home. We had booked accommodation in a small motel, by phone and now simply couldn't wait to leave and set about exploring the States.

Our last day at work, the Thursday, was spent messing around as usual and saying our farewells, promising that we would be back at the end of our trip to say our real goodbyes. All the secretaries envied us going to Myrtle Beach.

'Oh you are just so lucky to be going. I promise you it will be great. Everybody is sort of like in holiday mode and really relaxed, and its hot and...oh you're just gonna have such a great time.'

I also spent much of that last day talking to Mike about cars. Both he and his brother Cheryl were heavily into cars and Mike told us that he had rebuilt about nine engines, having done his own recently. On this last day he was keen to show me his car - well, just the engine, really - and the new stereo that he had just fitted. The fact that I could hardly hear the stereo over the roar of his supercharged V8 didn't seem to bother him.

'Neat, eh?'

'Yeah,' I shouted back. The stereo was turned off and the engine left to idle. It sounded mean. 'What's the nought to sixty time in this baby, then?'

'About five seconds.'

'You're joking?'

'Nope. This is a performance car, Phil; a finely tuned supercharged V8, constructed by my own fair hand.' He smiled.

'I'm impressed.'

'That's nothing,' he continued. 'Cheryl's got a car he takes to drag meets. The car has to be street legal and we've got it pretty hot. He only uses it to drive to the meets. It's the fastest street legal drag in North Carolina.'

'Cool, why doesn't he drive it to work?'

'Well it's not the easiest thing to drive from day to day, even though it is technically street legal. You know, the car is so powerful that if you stuck it up on the pavement and put your foot down you'd bald the tyres. Yep, put your foot down in first and you would not move, man.'

Mike rattled out some more facts and figures to me; it appeared that what he didn't know about cars wasn't worth knowing.

I climbed out of the car and Mike, realising that we had now wasted an hour studying his car, called me a lazy son of a bitch and said we had to get back to work.

Mark and I continued the day by saying our goodbyes and taking the mickey out of anyone we passed. Our jokes weren't cutting though. Since discovering that Mike and Roland had been to prison we were cautious with our comments; and it was a wise thing too. We had been taking the mickey out of Steve, a large black guy who, since being introduced to us on our first day, had only uttered about three words. But we discovered later that he was yet another member of the crew who had been 'inside'. He seemed docile and friendly but amazingly had been sent to prison for G.B.H. and armed robbery. He apparently also boxed when he was younger and was quite useful. Being completely oblivious to the fact that we were working with the entire cast of Death Wish 3 was probably not a bad thing. If we had known at the beginning of our time at the warehouse what we knew now, it surely would have inhibited our fun. The thought of working in a warehouse with three ex-cons - at least one of whom had been done for GBH and armed robbery - and where almost everybody carried an automatic weapon was hardly the dream job as outlined in the BUNAC handbook. We were also later to discover that Richard had been as ignorant of Steve's past as Mark and I had been. Richard told us some months later how he had wised up to the fact after Steve had been given extended responsibility.

Steve had been asked to drive the company lorry up to New York to distribute some furniture. Nothing had been heard from him and he was late returning. The first Richard knew of his whereabouts was when he received a call from the New York police. They were holding him in a police cell. Apparently he had been found in the New York offices of 'Readers Digest' with a number of sharp steel 'Ninja Death Stars' and a six inch knife and was attempting to open a drawer with a crowbar. When questioned about it by the police he said he had been looking for the toilet.

We looked for Roland on our last day to say goodbye. We found him in the polishing area talking to Cheryl. He seemed to be in pain and was holding his back.

'You all right, Roland? What's wrong?' I asked.

'Ohhhh. It's nothing really, man. I just had a coke and all that sugar is sort of sitting on my kidneys, man.'

Roland was trying to kid us that his body was such a finely-tuned machine that a little more sugar and his vital organs would start to play up. The reality was his poor old kidneys were at last starting to give way, on account of all the alcohol he had consumed. Either that or they were now so used to seeing nothing but alcohol that they rejected any other sort of liquid. Roland once boasted to us that when he was on holiday the year before for a week, there wasn't a moment in the day when he didn't have a beer can in his hand.

So that was it. The first part of the movie was over. A new scene was about to be acted out. What did the script hold for us in the weeks to come - situation comedy, horror movie and action adventure all rolled into one?

True Lies

We had made it through the first two weeks of our trip and set off for Myrtle Beach, with Richard taking a day off work to drive us down. Ahead of us lay a life of sun, sand, sea and, we were reliably informed, certain employment. We sped along the wide American roads that stretched out to the horizon, the end of time in the distance.

Twenty miles outside Myrtle beach we were struck with the thought that this paradise might not be all that it had been cracked up to be. Even from this far out large billboards appeared by the roadside advertising everything from fairground attractions to T-shirt shops. The roadside was littered with small shops selling inflatable sharks, buckets, spades, waterwings and other holiday trappings. When we passed our first shop we looked at each other in amazement. What was a beach shop doing in the middle of nowhere by the side of a dusty roadway and so far away from the sea? The answer was that there was nowhere else for it. Every square inch of land closer to Myrtle Beach was packed with identical beach shops. Myrtle Beach, we discovered, is the Blackpool of America.

By the time we drove slowly down the wide road that led into town it was nearly dark. Our eyes were dazzled by the lights from the shops that lined the route. Supermarkets, tourist shops, burger joints, the lot. We turned into a road in an attempt to find our accommodation. Guesthouses, motels and small hotels were everywhere, displaying their neon signs in the heat of the night. It had been a long journey and Richard wanted to get things sorted as quickly as possible, so we returned to the main road to search for a phone box.

'There's one, Rich,' called Mark.

'Good.' We stopped and got out. 'Now we need to give them a reference point so that they can give us directions.' We all looked around and then up at the massive illuminated shop sign above our heads.

'Piggly Wiggly!?' Richard said, with a laugh. 'I can't tell them that we're standing outside Piggly Wiggly's.' The rest of us started to laugh, catching peculiar glances from people passing by. 'I'll be arrested or something.'

'Well at least they'll know where it is.' Mark said.

'Well do you want to do it then? Where are you? Well we're actually using a telephone outside Piggly Wigglies.' We were all laughing and had trouble finding a volunteer for the phone call but Richard relented. Perhaps it was because we had spent all day in the car that we suddenly found the situation so funny. When Richard was finally given directions to our accommodation, we took another five minutes to pick ourselves up off the floor after he had mentioned that he was standing in a phone box on the main road into Myrtle Beach by Piggly Wiggly's.

By the time we reached our motel Myrtle Beach's nightlife was in full swing. We got out of the car and unloaded our gear. After signing in at reception we were taken to our room. We had taken a room (for all of us, we weren't rich enough to afford one each) at a classic American motel with about twenty rooms per floor over three floors. We passed holiday revellers at every corner, from the car all the way to our room. Having dumped our luggage we stepped out onto the balcony and looked out over Myrtle Beach. Bright coloured lights illuminated the night sky in every direction. Four hundred yards from our landing was a fairground, with a ferris wheel and a large roller coaster, the screams from which were only too audible.

'Wow! Got to have a go on that,' I said.

'Yeah, bit close though isn't it?' said Richard.

Taking our valuables with us, we set off to explore the town. Our first stop was Wendy's burger joint, but after a hot day travelling we didn't really feel much like eating and only managed a salad and a coffee each. We sat at a table by the window and watched what for many people seemed to be the highlight of the day: 'cruisin'. Anybody who was anybody - or thought they were somebody - spent the evening cruising around the town in open top Mustangs and Corvettes. At ten at night there were traffic jams around Myrtle Beach. We watched this spectacle for a time and then decided to walk the streets to try and get to know a bit more about the place and to try and convince ourselves that it had been a good idea to come to Myrtle Beach. Maybe the secretaries back at the warehouse been talking about somewhere else?

We walked along the main street, by the fairground. Each car that passed us was packed with at least ten people all waving and screaming at those passing by on the other side of the road. Dodging the traffic and trying to politely acknowledge the waves we received, we walked the length of the road. Blackpool now seemed more and more inviting and would have been like a haven of peace compared to this place. Amusement arcades and gift shops, all of which were still open, beckoned customers. There were so called 'T-shirt Shops', which sold towels, swimming costumes, T-shirts and every other conceivable item needed for a day at the beach. We entered one and took a look around. The merchandise was cheap and cheerful and opposite the main counter in a small corner an artist was using a paint-spray gun to spray a T-shirt with the design of your choice. All good stuff!

Eventually the bright lights and noise became all too much. After a long tiring journey it was enough to give a night club DJ a migraine, and we decided to make our way back to the motel, via the rollercoaster. The rollercoaster ride turned you upside down twice and was extremely expensive, but it turned out to be the only thing that had been worth doing that night.

After buying some Budweiser, we were making our way back to the motel down a side road when a Delorean sports car suddenly turned the corner and stopped just a few yards in front of us. The neon lights of the amusements reflected off the windows and and the exhaust fumes surrounded it in smoke. We all stopped and instantly had the same thought: Back To The Future was really happening. The gullwing doors opened and we half expected to see Marty and the Doc appear and rush to ask our help. But out clambered something a lot better looking, a stunning blonde girl wearing cut off jeans and a bikini top. She was ideally dressed for the heat; well as far as we were concerned she was ideally dressed, period. Unfortunately her boyfriend stepped out of the other side of the car. There didn't seem to be a shortage of decent looking women around but they were all accompanied by guys who scraped their knuckles on the ground when they walked.

We stood out on the balcony and drank literally gallons of Budweiser.

'So this is the great Myrtle Beach.' Richard sounded really tired.

'Well, it is slightly more of a tourist spot than I had imagined it to be,' said Mark.

'Slightly more! It makes Southend-On-Sea look like a ghost town. Are you sure you want to stay?' Mark shrugged his shoulders in reply.

'I suppose so, now we're down here. We'll look for work tomorrow and see what comes up. Maybe it's a good place to work.'

Our air-conditioned room provided a good night's rest and relief from the almost unbearable heat. The following morning we 'checked out the beach, man'. The employment side of things could wait. The beach was situated right next to the main road and about four hundred yards from our motel. It was large, clean and the Atlantic ocean was refreshing. There were only a few people around when the four of us arrived and for a while all was peaceful. The sun was hot and we all managed to burn, even though by now we were quite brown.

From ten o'clock the beach began to fill up and with the punters came all the traders. There was no escaping the commercialism of this place. Boats with small cabins

motored up and down a few hundred yards from the shore
with large electronic advertising boards flashing messages
telling us to 'Eat at Dino's'. But there was more to come.
When the population of the beach was at its height, we
suddenly heard a buzzing overhead and all sat up in time
to catch sight of a single-engined plane fly by, trailing a
large red banner proclaiming that 'Arnie's Hot Dogs' were
the greatest. Soon planes littered the sky, trailing banners
advertising everything from plane rides to T-shirt prices.

'This is unreal,' I said, shaking my head.

'Who suggested this quiet little coastal resort to you
anyway?' asked Richard.

'Some little know-all we met on the plane,' answered
Mark. 'And again at the YMCA. And I'd like to meet him
again.'

'It could be worse, chaps,' said Paul.

'Oh yes?' said Richard.

'Yeh, it could be pissing down with rain; and anyway
we haven't even started looking for work yet.'

'I suppose you're right. Let's just hope there's
compensation in the way of a decent job with massive tips.'
I said. Our conversation was interrupted by yet another
vehicle. This time it was the Beach Patrol. Two guys in
open-necked blue shirts, light brown shorts, Rayband
Aviator sunglasses and displaying gleaming gold police
badges rode by on red quadbikes with fat black tyres.

'Cool.' I exclaimed. We all watched them ride by, kicking
up sand. I almost found myself looking for the cameras
that were recording the next episode of Baywatch, or
perhaps Police Academy 7. The sun was so bright it lit the
film set completely, with every colour exaggerated. Not
only in New York did America remind me of the movies;
each new location seemed as though it had been built for a
film set. I could have been on one of those quadbikes
patrolling the beach with the Baywatch team while the
camera circled us, getting those action shots against the
perfect backdrop.

We were at one end of the beach and half a mile further along a pier split the beach in half. It looked quite new and as befitted Myrtle Beach there seemed to be a restaurant at the end of it. Shops and hotels backed all the way down onto the beach and food from any spot was no more than a few metres away. We were tempted to buy a drink at a ridiculously high price from a chap carrying two 'cool bags' over his shoulders. We thought about the three of us doing the same thing to earn money during our time in Myrtle Beach; at the prices he was charging and the public demand, we would be millionaires. But the idea was knocked on the head by the appearance of three more similarly clad 'travelling salesmen' within the space of the next five minutes: a saturated market.

With empty bottles of sun cream we headed back to the motel to prepare for an evening of job hunting. Equipped with our BUNAC papers and as neatly attired as we could be in dirty jeans and unironed T-shirts, we headed out. We began by trying a number of restaurants along the main street and left our names, having been told to return once the manager was around. Perhaps there was a restaurant managers' meeting for every manager in Myrtle Beach that night. Or perhaps it was a polite way of telling us to 'sod off'. We called into a small hotel and filled in a couple of forms, told them that we were registered to work in the States and left our motel number. The hotel said that there wasn't any work there, but there might be at a restaurant that was affiliated to it. We were pleased with our evening's work, seeing as we had only called into a few of the many restaurants that littered the resort. We returned to our motel, viewed the 'cruisin' from the balcony and retired to watch TV.

The air-conditioning was a godsend. The night air was so muggy that it was almost impossible to breath normally. Every now and again you had to inhale deeply, so that your body wasn't starved of oxygen. We all sat in a drunken haze in front of the TV. Items kept appearing on 'The

Lizard Man'. Various members of the community appeared, claiming to have seen this creature, usually just as it had its back to them and was escaping. We were intrigued and were not sure whether to take it seriously or not. Was it an animal that had escaped from a zoo or perhaps a laboratory experiment gone wrong? Certainly, the whole of South Carolina seemed absorbed by these sightings. T-shirts with 'I've seen the Lizard Man' were selling like hot cakes. At the end of one programme an elderly man claimed that he had seen the Lizard Man.

'Yea. I seen him all right; as clear as day. He was walking down the road, hand in hand with Elvis Presley.' That settled it: we had to take it seriously.

Mission Impossible

The following day was spent looking for restaurant work. We began by trying the restaurants along the main road into town, on which Piggly Wiggly stood. Most wanted us to fill in application forms and then kept us waiting for half an hour before they told us that they had nothing to offer. We tried about thirty restaurants along the main road without any success. Perhaps finding employment in Myrtle Beach was not going to be so easy or lucrative after all.

Richard, who had been travelling with us on our searches during the morning, left us at 2.30pm to return in time for work on Monday. Neither Mark, Paul or I really thought about returning with him. As bad as Myrtle beach was, we all believed that something decent would eventually turn up. Richard told us afterwards that he was puzzled as to why we didn't come back. We all wished afterwards that he had persuaded us to, as this was certainly the turning point in our trip.

Most of the restaurants said that we had arrived too late and that they had all the help they needed for the summer. Part of our problem was that all three of us turned up on the doorstep of these restaurants, hot and dusty from our travels and with rucksacks in tow and asked for work. Given this sight, interviewers for jobs as toilet cleaners in the French Foreign Legion would have had reservations about our appearance. Most of the places that we tried only had about five people on their entire staff anyway and would hardly have three waiters' jobs going all at the same time. These finer points on the art of seeking employment seemed to have escaped us!

Exhausted and worried about ever earning any money, we returned to the motel, having walked miles and spoken to over a hundred different people. We would have to find alternative accommodation for the following night, at a much reduced rate. But our spirits were lifted when we opened our motel door and found a note from the small hotel we had visited on the previous night. The note was neatly written in blue biro and said that we should turn up at 9.00 a.m. as there might be a job for at least one of us at their restaurant. We sank what remained in the way of beer in the room to celebrate.

We cleared out of the room completely the following morning. With our Union Jack covered rucksacks the three of us set off for the restaurant in high spirits. The main street was just coming to life. It was as hot as ever and the smell of doughnuts and takeaway fried breakfasts was nauseating. As we walked passed the souvenir shops and restaurants we encountered two English students, a boy and a girl, obviously BUNACers, handing out leaflets on the street; we stopped to talk.

'Hi, BUNACers?' asked the chap.

'Yes,' replied Mark. 'I suppose the three stuck-on Union Jacks on each rucksack gave it away,' he continued. They laughed.

'Have you just arrived?'

'No, we arrived on Friday and have basically spent the last two days looking for work, unsuccessfully.'

'Most of the jobs have been taken for quite a while now. We only have one more week and then we're off. We've been down here for about five weeks already.'

'How many of you are there?'

'Four, but there are about another ten or so BUNACers down here at the moment, all doing different jobs.'

'So what have you been doing while you've been here?' I asked.

'Well we worked in a restaurant for a while, part time sort of thing, but we've mainly been handing these out.' He gave us a long thinish card and pointed to a tall building about two hundred yards away.

'See that building? Well, we hand out these things in the street to passersby and it basically invites them to go and look around the condominiums, or holiday apartments, in that building. All they have to do is turn up and they get forty-five dollars, or a gift, just for turning up. It gets them along to view the place and there are a surprising number of sales from it.'

'So you get paid by the number of leaflets you hand out, do you?

'No, we get paid by the number of people that actually turn up to view the condominiums. We get ten dollars for everyone that turns up and fulfills the conditions on the back of the card here.' He turned one of the long cards over and pointed to a list of eligibility conditions.

'And if somebody that you sent actually buys a condo,' he continued, 'then you get twenty-five dollars.'

'How long have you been doing this, then?' I asked.

'More or less the whole time we've been here and we've not done too badly. The thing is not to spend the money once you've made it. We've saved a fair bit and at the end of the week we're off travelling.' At this point the girl, who had up until now been accosting every passerby, came into the conversation.

'Why don't you go and ask if they need any more people? They know we're leaving at the end of the week,' she said, her eyes invisible behind a pair of black Ray-bans.

'Is it worth it?' I asked.

'Yeh. OK, you probably couldn't do it all day every day because there aren't as many people around as there were at the beginning of the summer, but you could do it part time, perhaps with some restaurant work.'

'We could do, I suppose. Not really much to lose at the moment, we haven't got a job at all.' I smiled.

We decided to give it a go and they told us who to ask for and where to go.

'Where are you staying, by the way?' asked the bloke.

'Well we've just left our motel and haven't really got anywhere for tonight, but we'll book into a motel if we get stuck.' Mark said.

'If your looking for a room that's cheap, Mildred, the lady that we're staying with, has one.' He quoted us a price of seventy-five dollars a week for a room.

'How much?' Paul exclaimed. 'We could probably get a motel room for that.'

'You'd be surprised, there aren't really any motels around that are cheap, especially in town.'

'Yeah, our motel cost twice that,' Mark said to Paul, realising the financial difficulty we were now in.

'Anyway, if you're interested you can find Mildred in the "Gay Dolphin".'

'The what?' asked Mark. 'Is that a pub or something?'

'No,' the guy said with a straight face, 'it's a gift shop along on the other side of the street.'

'OK, well we'll remember that if we need the room,' I said nonchalantly. We said goodbye, thanked them for their help and continued on our journey to the restaurant. It was only a few metres further, in between the BUNACers we had just talked to and the building which housed the condominiums that were for sale. The restaurant turned out to be a let down. The owner explained to us that there was only work on a part time basis for two of us and that we would have to wait another two weeks for permanent employment.

We walked out, down the restaurant's wooden steps, into the bright sun again. What a disaster this was turning out to be. The selling of condominiums looked to be our only way out and we headed for the tall building a few hundred yards further down the road. It was a tall modern-looking building, rather like a hotel, and upon reaching it we descended some steps and knocked on a door labelled 'Offices.' A tall chap dressed in a suit came out. He took one look at us with our rucksacks and in a moment decided that he didn't want to know us.

'Yes,' he said abruptly.

'We've come about the condominiums,' I said.

'Didn't they explain when they gave you a leaflet, you have to fulfill certain conditions.'

'No, what conditions?'

He pulled the tall card, I had earlier been given, from my hand and turned it over.

'You have to be married, earn over twenty-five thousand dollars a year, etc., etc.' We realised instantly that he had the wrong end of the stick. He thought that we had come along in the hope of grabbing the free dollars for simply viewing the condos. Students had probably tried it on before.

'We don't want to buy one,' I explained, carefully omitting an insult. 'We want to hand out the leaflets and try and sell them.'

The chap's stiff expression changed.

'Ahhhhhhhhhhh,' he said with a broad smile. 'Of course, of course.' He was now as nice as pie. 'Why didn't you say so. Come in, come in.'

It was difficult not to laugh at this creep's sudden change of character. He was used to employing BUNACers and took our details and employment papers in the office.

'Now you guys need solicitation permits.'

'Need what? We're not supplying any other services are we?'

'Noooo, don't worry,' he grinned, 'it's just the term used for the handing out of leaflets on the street. Basically we take you down to the local police station and they check you out, make sure that you don't have a criminal record back in England and then issue you with permits which allow you to hand out leaflets.'

'How long will that take?' asked Paul.

'Well, we'll take you down now and your passes will be ready tomorrow morning.' So, leaving our rucksacks in the offices and with passports and papers in our mucky paws, we set off for Myrtle Beach Police Station.

The police station was a low modern building and the policemen were friendly and efficient. We had our pictures taken, which went on the front of our identification; and then had our thumb prints taken, which were to be displayed on the back. It all seemed extremely serious. We finally walked up to a large desk and handed in our passports to a policewomen at a computer terminal.

'OK, you guys can collect these in the morning. Just going to find out a little more about you,' she said with a smile and a wink. Despite her reassuring attitude, I was becoming quite anxious about all the information that was being gathered on us. I pointed to the computer.

'What sort of information can that thing pull up, then?'

'Well, this little baby tells us everything about you,' said the policewomen. 'We key in your passport number and a few other things and we get to know where you live, what you are supposed to look like, your parents names, where they live, your brothers and sisters...'

'Frightening,' I said.

'Sure is.' She smiled. I looked at the others with a nervous expression. They obviously also thought it unnerving that so much information about us was available to so many people all over the world.

We were driven back to the condo office and told we could pick up our cards in the morning, along with our passports. We could then start work. We sat confused and drained in the heat. It had all happened so quickly.

'I think we should go back to Highpoint,' said Paul suddenly.

Mark and I laughed, but we sort of agreed with him. We had spent a lot of time and effort looking for work in Myrtle Beach, and had only secured a commission-based job that gave us no guarantee of any income whatsoever. We were all tired. Paul then suggested we sat in the cool with an ice-cream at the parlour along the main road. It was an excellent idea and we staggered wearily along the road with our heavy packs. When we arrived we fell in the door and into three chairs at a table by the window. There was nobody else in the ice-cream parlour. I approached the counter where there was a teenage girl waiting to take my order. I ordered for all three of us in a very slow, tired manner.

While she was preparing our ice-cream, it suddenly hit me like a bolt: we were in Myrtle 'Toilet', with no jobs, no money and nowhere to stay, save the chance of a 'cheap' shared room in a house owned by Mildred, who worked at the suspicious sounding Gay Dolphin amusement shop. I turned and looked at the other two and shook my head despondently. Mark and Paul both suddenly woke up to our dilemma and we all started laughing. We were soon in fits of laughter. I could hardly stand and the poor girl behind the counter didn't know what to do. She giggled nervously and tried not to look embarrassed. I couldn't even raise the energy to take our ice-creams from her. Any mention of the name Myrtle 'Toilet' as we now called it, or Mildred, simply set us off again. Paul suggested that to cap it all we would probably be arrested for riotous behavior in a public place. Here was our worst and greatest moment of the Myrtle Beach trip so far.

We eventually came to our senses and tried to discuss our future seriously. Although we wanted to return to Highpoint, we felt that we had to give Myrtle Beach at least a day or two more as we had already invested so much time in the place. The rest and laughter had done us a world of good and we set off in search of permanent work yet again, our spirits rekindled.

Leaving the ice-cream parlour we headed back toward our old motel and began to try restaurants 'off the beaten track'. But the story was the same everywhere, no work was available; we were either too late to take the summer jobs or too early to take over from those that would be leaving after Labor Day - the national holiday signalling the end of summer.

One of the restaurants told us that there was a Hilton hotel about two miles out of town where they had a high turnover of staff. We had nothing to lose and started to walk out of town in the ninety degree heat, with all our possessions on our backs. This was the end of the line. No work at the Hilton would be the last straw.

From a distance the Myrtle Beach Hilton looked like any other, tall, neatly kept and pale in colour. It appeared to be in the middle of nowhere, surrounded by what looked like desert. We approached gingerly as it loomed larger and larger at the end of the long road down which we were now walking. We didn't really want to enter the grounds or the building as it might mean further rejection. We had learnt not to build our hopes up. At the door a porter was helping a couple unload their luggage from the boot of a taxi. We walked into the lobby and accosted a uniformed lady behind the reception counter. I asked to speak with the manager.

'He's upstairs. Do you have an appointment at all?'

'Do we have an appointment, boys?'

'Nope, we simply forgot to call him as we left,' answered Paul. The lady behind the counter repeated that he could be found upstairs and then continued with some other work. The hotel foyer was impressively large and completely saturated with marble and plants. A large red carpeted staircase further along the foyer led up to a balcony. As we climbed it we noticed a number of satellite rooms, which appeared to be a variety of different restaurants, off the balcony area and when we reached the top of the stairs a chap in a black suit approached. He was the restaurant manager. He was really quite courteous, considering our appearance, and left us admiring the decoration as he walked off to talk to the general manager about our request. We said we would do literally anything and felt hopeful that we would be able to help out in some way in the large hotel. The man reappeared about ten minutes later and gave us the bad news; they had more than enough hotel staff at present, but thanked us for calling by. Once again we had been rejected.

We got lost on our way back into Myrtle beach centre. We were all so disappointed we didn't really care where we ended up. After walking for about an hour on long roads, surrounded by vegetation, we suddenly came across a caravan site. We walked along by the outer fence, it seemed quite large and was certainly well kept.

'Let's stop here, I've just got to have a rest,' Paul said.

'Yeah, me too,' I added. Mark was too tired and distraught to care. There was a young chap standing by a hose at the entrance to the caravan park. He looked at us oddly out of the corner of his eye pretending not to notice us. I approached him.

'Would it be possible to get a glass of water from somewhere please?' I asked.

He stood bolt upright as though he had been startled by our presence.

'Errr, sure,' he said. 'Thought you were gonna ask if we had anywhere to pitch tents, with your rucksacks an' all.' He smiled and told us to follow him. He took us into a large brown caravan to the left of the entrance. My request must have sounded more like a desperate plea, as he seemed to take pity on us and invited us in. Inside, the caravan had a microwave, TV, video, every conceivable luxury.

'You want something else besides water, Coke or something?' he asked. He didn't really need an answer and pulled a large bottle of Coke from the fridge. He had noticed our English accents and we got talking as to how three guys from different parts of England ended up outside a caravan park on the outskirts of Myrtle Beach in America. Suddenly the door swung open and a lady, the chap's mother, came in. She started at our presence in the caravan and gave us the suspicious look that her son had done upon our arrival. He explained who we were and before long we were all chatting away happily. The time flew by; before we knew it we had been there for almost an hour and had finished the large bottle of Coke. They were very friendly people and our little conversation restored our faith in the States once again. Everywhere else we had been we had been rejected; here we had been made to feel welcome. We thanked them profusely as we left and completely refreshed, physically and emotionally, we walked on until we saw the extremely familiar sight of the main road into Myrtle Beach, where we had tried at so many of the restaurants for work. We all sat on our rucksacks in the searing heat by the side of the wide road.

'Well, what the hell are we gonna do now, boys?' asked Mark.

'We could go back to Highpoint I suppose?' Paul said.

'Yeah, could do...' said Mark slowly. 'But then who's to say we would get any jobs there? We were all extremely tired.

'First things first,' said Paul, 'before we decide what we're gonna do later we have to find some accommodation for tonight. How much money have we got?' We all emptied our pockets. We had enough for about three nights cheap, very cheap, accommodation.

'Mildred.' Mark shook his head. 'Mildred in the Gay Dolphin.' That it had come to this: having to go and find Mildred, the lady whose room we had once scoffed at. I shook my head too.

'Cheer up, guys, could be worse' said Paul.

'Oh yeah?' we answered.

We decided that the only way we would find the Gay Dolphin would be to order a taxi to take us back to the centre of town and go on from there. We would worry about the fare later. So having rung from a public call box, and having given our location as 'not outside Piggly Wiggly's', we set of in a taxi in search of Mildred.

The Gay Dolphin was actually situated along the main boulevard in the centre of the town. The taxi dropped us outside. Having argued with the driver for five minutes about the extortionate fare, we bade him an unpleasant farewell and received unpleasant hand signals in return.

Inside the Gay Dolphin were dolphin souvenirs in every size, shape and form you could wish for: plastic dolphin models, dolphins in glass bottles, and even dolphins in snow storm bottles. There was a large variety of other plastic items available as well, such as souvenir bottle openers and brightly coloured and highly ornate Myrtle Beach clocks. Having surveyed the merchandise, Mark expressed his considered opinion.

'What a pile of junk. The only thing missing is a dolphin turd in a bottle; I'm sure people would buy it if they made one.'

Paul approached the counter and gained the attention of an old lady.

'Wonder if you could help, we're looking for Mildred, we were told she had some accommodation, a room or something to let.'

'Well she's not here at the moment, but I can call her at home if you want,' answered the old lady. 'Think I've got her number here somewhere.' She fumbled around amongst some papers to the side of the counter, and then disappeared around a corner. We were all leaning up at the counter now and peered around an old wooden partition to see her talking into an old phone.

'Hello Mildred? It's Ester from the Gay Dolphin. There are some lads here who want somewhere to stay, I think they're English, do you still have that room available or...Oh you do, so...OK, right. I'll send them over then, is that all right?'

Heat

Mildred's was easy to find, just a short walk along a wide avenue, heading the opposite way out of town to the Hilton. It was impressive, built in a typical southern states style; large, white and made of wood.

Mildred herself was also white, but not large or made of wood. She was in her early sixties, short and had gingerish hair and a very pale complexion. She had obviously been waiting for us as she came out to greet us and invited us in out of the late afternoon heat. She asked a few questions of us and then showed us to our room upstairs. It was small for three lads, and there was no air-conditioning, but we were happy that we had somewhere to put our heads down that night. There was a small communal fridge situated just outside our room that was used by other BUNACers staying in the house. We were told we could keep any food we wanted in the fridge, but having seen its grubby interior we simply smiled at her kind offer and decided against it. The whole house, in fact, was far from spotless. It was a large place for a single old lady to keep clean and the only place that seemed to get star treatment was the living room downstairs.

We were given a key by Mildred and informed about the house rules for coming in late at night, which were to be as quiet as mice and lock the door when we came in. Actually Mildred informed us about anything and everything; she hadn't stopped nattering from the moment she had come out to greet us. When she eventually left us to our own devices we left our packs and headed out to the beach for a refreshing swim in the sea in the late evening sun.

This was great. Because most people had by now gone home, we practically had the beach and sea to ourselves. Mark and Paul carried on mucking around in the sea for a while after I had gotten out. It was now dark and I sat on one of the tall life-guard chairs situated at various intervals

along the deserted beach. The high chair had been roped
off was adorned with notices about life guard use only. But
there was nobody about and no life guards needed its use. I
climbed up and sat regally watching the sea. It all seemed
rather spooky. The sea, now as black as the night, reflected
the moon and all its beams. It was all too quiet. In a flash it
struck me. The lull before the storm; this was a great film
set for 'Jaws'. Mark and Paul splashing around in the water
would suddenly each in turn disappear, without a sound;
and I would be left to run up and down the beach calling
for them, in vain.

As the warm night air blew up small amounts of sand
beneath the life guard chair, my gaze followed the coastline
and I noticed for the first time a series of yellow flags all
along the beach and I wondered what they might be for. I
looked at the vast expanse of sea in which the others were
still swimming, its black colour only broken intermittently
by a stretch of white as each wave broke. Was the sea rough
enough to warrant yellow flags on the beach? I didn't think
so; perhaps it had been rough earlier I thought. When Mark
and Paul eventually finished I pointed out the yellow flags,
but like myself they thought them insignificant.

The swim had given us all an appetite. We hadn't eaten
a decent meal all day and as we walked into Wendy's
hamburger joint we knew we had little chance of getting
one!

We arrived back at Mildreds and, as quietly as possible,
used the key she had given us let ourselves in.

'Ah, you got in OK then?' said Mildred, popping her
head around the corner of her ground floor bedroom. Poor
old Mildred was a bit of a lonely soul and would accost us
at every opportunity to chat.

'Yes, thanks. Just been swimming,' said Paul.

'Ah, its nice to swim in the evening.'

'Yep; it was refreshing.'

We were walking on through the lounge to the stairs when Paul stopped to continue the conversation with Mildred.

'I don't suppose you know what the yellow flags are for on the beach, do you?' he asked. 'The sea didn't seem that rough and we wondered what they were for.' I had forgotten about them.

'Yellow flags?'

'Yes, there were quite a few on the beach while we were swimming.'

'Ohhh!' yelped Mildred. 'You shouldn't have been swimming when they were out.'

'Yeah, we thought it a bit odd, there was nobody else at all swimming along the whole of the beach. What do the yellow flags mean then?'

'They mean "Beware Sharks"!'

'Ahhhhheeeeeeee!' exclaimed Mark after a few seconds of shocked silence. We all looked at each other and then back at Mildred.

'They feed in the evening and in the morning,' she said 'some must have been seen quite close in, so they raised the flags.'

We all stood in shocked silence.

'Wow, we could have been the sharks' evening meal,' Mark said. 'Frightening!'

'Oh yes, people have been lost to the sharks before now,' continued Mildred. 'Every so often they come right in; have even seen some myself quite recently.' We were still silent. Mildred smiled. 'So now you know not to swim when you see the yellow flags out.'

'Yeah!' we all said.

We were relieved to have escaped the sharks. Twenty minutes later, Mark and I were relieved at having finally escaped Mildred. From the subject of sharks Mildred had, with years of practice and skill, managed to turn the conversation around to her life story, and poor Paul, who was not unknown to chat a bit himself, was in deep conversation. After an hour he was in a deep coma.

The following day lifted our spirits. The restaurant that had written to us before telling us that there would be jobs in two weeks' time, came up with the goods; they now wanted us to work part time immediately. We were pleased with the news and to add to it we collected our 'Solicitation' permits and passports from the condo' office. We could now start handing out leaflets on the streets. At last things were looking up. We wouldn't start earning money for another day, though, from either the restaurant or our leaflet work, so we continued to look for steady work. We had now been reduced to calling in at fast food chains, but even here there was little joy. Our very last port of call for the day was one such fast food emporium. We were tired and sat down on green moulded plastic seats to await a reply - as usual - from the manager. While we were waiting a plump blond-haired girl ran up to us in a very unflattering waitress uniform.

'Hiiiii!' she exclaimed. 'I noticed your accents, you're from England, aren't you?'

We didn't think that there was anything special in that, since it wasn't difficult to find an English student in Myrtle Beach.

'Yeah.' I was too tired to say more.

'Wow, what a coincidence,' she continued. 'I'm also from Europe, I'm Danish.' That was even less amazing, but she really couldn't believe that she had bumped into other Europeans.

'Small world,' I said to humour her.

'Sure is,' she said with sincerity. 'Wow, I heard that you were looking for work, I'll go and see if I can do anything for you.' As she waddled off we all looked at each other with pained expressions. What a handful to have her working for you; if there was one way we were sure not to get a job, it was through her recommendation. We were right.

We decided to spend the rest of the day on the beach. The system had finally beaten us. We had scraped together what little work there was left in Myrtle Beach and on the way to the beach we discussed the following day.

'I'm really not looking forward to work tomorrow,' commented Mark. 'Working all the hours of the day and night just to survive; there must be an easier way to make money.'

'There is,' said Paul. 'There's that guy who's selling "I've Seen The Lizard Man" T-shirts and he's making a fortune; why don't we do the same?' Mark and I both looked at Paul, puzzled. 'There's no way he can have sole rights to that merchandise, or any sort of patent. You saw how popular the item was on the news down here; it was on every channel.' Mark remained silent. I'm not sure whether he thought that it was so stupid it wasn't worth commenting upon, or whether he was contemplating the idea.

'I've an idea,' I said. 'Instead of selling T-shirts, why don't we say we've seen the Lizard Man himself. We could make a mask and take a picture of one of us coming up out of the sea wearing it.' Mark and Paul laughed. 'It would work, the press would jump at it and in one step we would have all the money we would need to travel.'

'Do ya think so, Phil?' asked Paul.

'Yeah. The TV and radio stations would lap it up; especially as we're English and we can say that we were unaware of all the stories on the monster.'

'But can't we get arrested or something for making false statements. You know what they're like over here, Phil, someone would probably say they were the Lizard Man and sue us because they weren't there when we said they were.'

'Who cares. By the time they find out that we're completely unscrupulous students we'll be long gone.'

I was really keen on the idea and thought we should give it a try, but the others didn't. Here was our chance to get in on the movie scene. The Creature from the Black Lagoon, Jaws and Jurassic Park all rolled into one. We could entice a young blond American girl to be in our shots, being supposedly attacked by the monster, if we were ever fortunate enough to meet one! All the ingredients for a perfect blockbuster movie; and in the States. But my neat idea was rejected out of hand. Mark was still feeling dejected as we walked toward the beach and although he cheered up momentarily, his dejection returned when we finally reached the beach.

'I'm thinking of going home,' he said as the three of us sat in a small wooden shelter at one end of the beach. Paul and I looked at each other. Mark continued.

'I would just prefer to spend the rest of the summer playing golf in England rather than trying to scrape a living over here.' Paul was thinking along the same lines, I could tell. I said that we should stay and give it all we had as this was probably the longest we would get to spend abroad as we would all be out of university and working in a year's time. The discussions were all very serious. Paul and I could both see Mark's point of view and although it was a difficult situation, Mark was eventually persuaded to stay. But it was touch and go. The trip could have easily fallen apart there and then.

That evening we ate fast food again. The food was by now starting to seriously affect our health. We would all be hyper one moment and down the next; we had all gained masses of weight; we regularly had chronic indigestion and none of us were able to sleep within two hours of eating a burger. All healthy, we were sure.

Also that evening Mildred, in an unavoidable chat, told us that if we were looking for work, it might be worth trying some 'T-shirt' shops. We had noticed these 'T-shirt' shops each time we walked down the main boulevard, you couldn't really miss them; their exteriors were covered from top to bottom in bright neon signs in every lurid colour imaginable. They would give anybody with a hangover or headache a justifiable excuse for suicide. So we decided to give them a go the following day.

We were up bright and early looking forward to our first day's work. After a very quick lesson in how to attract a customer and the prime areas to stand when handing out leaflets, Paul and I took opposite sides of the main street and tried to entice 'Joe Public' to take leaflets from our grubby little paws. It was frustrating work in the heat. We started at about ten and worked through until about two in the afternoon. It didn't take long to master the job. In fact, the first ten minutes suggested that I was worse than useless; and Paul didn't seem to be doing much better on the other side of the street. It was no good, I had discovered, timidly walking up to a passerby, mumbling about the condominiums we were selling and hope that they would take a leaflet. What was needed was a forceful and direct approach. Once I had studied the individual to check that they were married and looked like they fulfilled the other conditions on the card, I walked up to them and thrust a leaflet into their face; they had to stop.

'Let me give you one of these, sir. All you have to do is take it to that large glass building up on the right and take a few moments to look around the condominiums, and you will be entitled to forty-five dollars or a free gift, provided you fulfil the criteria on the back of this card; there's no obligation to buy and it will only take a few moments of your time. Must be worth it just for the free gift. Thank you for your time, sir.'

It was a successful ploy. I was told at the end of the week that I must have got the chat right as I had plenty of visits and my first visit actually resulted in a sale. Handing these leaflets out on the street was called OPC, or OPCing; but I can't remember why.

Before Paul and I actually started our OPCing that day we took Mildred's advice and went to a T-shirt shop to ask about work. Much to our delight we were taken on instantly. All three of us were to start work that evening in the shop and because Mark had first stint at the restaurant he would join us there later. We were pleased that we now had more work than we could handle, and began to think that things at last were going well.

After the OPC work at two, Paul and I wandered over to the T-shirt shop which was situated about a hundred yards from the fairground on the high street. The place was run by a couple of Arab guys with various helpers scattered around the shop, whose job it was to persuade people into buying T-shirts or beach towels, using the usual selling techniques of chatting and laughing with the customers and persuading them that each shop item was essential for the perfect beach holiday. There was also a tall blond-haired chap with a moustache in the shop who seemed to be the chief assistant, ordering the floor guys around from time to time. He seemed to have a lighthearted side to his character when we were first introduced, but this was kept suppressed throughout our time at the shop.

We started work at about 2.30 and were told by one of the Arab guys standing behind the counter to help anybody that appeared lost, and to generally get people spending as much cash as possible. There was no training or a look around the shop, that was it. So we went to work. We were put under the watchful eye of the young guy who ran the floor. He told us where to stand and the price of various items. He then asked us if we had ever done any T-shirt shop work before.

'I didn't know it could be identified as a specific profession,' I said sarcastically. The guy had no brain and didn't really understand the irony, but Paul and I smiled at the fact that we had answered our boss' question and had managed to take the mickey out of him all in one sentence.

The work turned out to be incredibly boring and we were relieved to see Mark arrive after his restaurant stint so that we had an excuse to chat. We had in fact already been told off twice for talking by the floor manager, but we told him where to go. Mark lent against a rack of T-shirts, he was knackered.

'Well how much do you think I made in tips?' he asked. Paul and I opened our eyes widely in eager anticipation.

'How much?' I asked. Mark smiled.

'Seven dollars.' he replied.

'Seven dollars!' But we had been told that if you worked in a restaurant with an English accent, it was your licence to print money. There was a stunned silence.

'I can't believe it,' I said, 'Seven dollars. Were there many people there?'

'Oh yes, the place was full and we had two sittings as well.'

'So much for restaurant work as a way to make travelling money.'

'What are we going to do?'

'Well, I'll do my breakfast stint at the restaurant in the morning and if we don't get much more in the way of tips we'll just do OPCing and work here.' I said. We were all dejected. By now the floor manager had had a word with one of the Arab managers about our general conduct. He made his way over. He was a small, miserable, wiry chap.

'You guys are paid to work, not talk. And why are you late?'

'I'm not working tonight; I've just called in to see these two,' answered Mark.

'Well, now you've seen them. You two get on with your work.' He motioned to Paul and myself.

'I'm finishing now.' I said cheekily. The chap's face turned sour. 'Don't worry, Paul's staying.' I continued with a smile. Mark and I left.

Paul actually worked until 2.30 am. Apparently the shop stayed open twenty-four hours. If there were people on the streets then there was money to be made and the only time that they would close was when it turned completely dead. Paul arrived back at Mildred's with various bangs and crashes which unfortunately woke me and kept me awake for the remaining few hours before my early breakfast stint at the restaurant.

We had noticed, upon taking an obscure route back to Mildred's from the beach, that a particular restaurant was advertising as much breakfast as you could eat for $2.99. So that morning I gave it a try before my own breakfast work and walked to the large mustard coloured building that housed the restaurant. It was full of labourers. The food was filling but under-cooked and was the last thing that I really wanted on the dawn of another hot and humid day. But it was so cheap and the place opened so early that I couldn't pass up the opportunity.

I arrived for my restaurant work at 7.30am and was greeted by the owner as I walked in the door. He was a small chap with short black hair and was wearing jeans and a red jumper. He introduced me to the two others that would be working with me that morning, a French guy and an English girl. He briefly explained the ropes and the American terms that I might not have been used to. The restaurant itself was a single story affair with bright blue canopies over the front windows. It was quite a smart place with the tables looking out onto the street and the kitchens at the back. There were about twenty tables in the wood-lined interior of the restaurant and another five or so outside. It took a while to get used to the pancake and syrup orders but the work was not taxing and my two fellow waiters gave me help. This was my first at restaurant work and I was nervous and made a few mistakes, but I soon felt confident. Halfway through the morning, just as I was delivering some eggs, done over-easy, and some hash browns, I began to realise that the work was not going to be lucrative. This was for two reasons. Firstly, the place was far from full; and secondly, who tips at breakfast?

The cooks at the restaurant were two black women who did nothing but laugh and make fun of me, the English girl and the French guy. Throughout the morning the owner sat at a back table reading the paper. He looked up from time to time to smile at the customers who came in. At about nine, a blond women, who I took to be his wife, came in and sat opposite him. At first their conversation seemed tame, but once they moved onto the subject of the restaurant all hell was let loose. Their voices were suddenly raised and she was almost in tears complaining at his lousy book-keeping which was costing them money and his insistence that they keep the place on. The customers were a little put out by this heated personal discussion, but none of them left. Eventually the wife ran out leaving the owner to look down at his morning paper once again, slowly shaking his head and pretending not to notice the agitated looks from the punters.

'Hey, Phil,' he whispered to me as I walked by with a tray of eggs, sunny side up.

'Yes?' I replied calmly, drawing closer to hear him.

'Just want you to know, Phil, you're doing a real great job,' he said.

'Thanks.' I walked on with the eggs. How on earth did he know whether I was good or bad, I thought, but then saw that he was praising all the staff, simply really to settle us all after the embarrassing argument with his wife.

At 11.00 we started to prepare for the lunch crowd; this involved making side salads.

'Ever made a side salad before?' asked the French guy in the kitchen, in a heavy French accent.

'Nope,' I replied.

'Well, there's absolutely nothing to it. This is the main ingredient.' He produced a lettuce. 'Every side salad is nearly all lettuce. Next time you're in a restaurant take a look. All you do is fill the bowl with lettuce, which is cheap, and then put a few tomatoes, peppers and cucumbers on top.' With his hand gripped firmly on the top of the lettuce he brought it down on the chopping board with a crash. The two cooks turned round slowly to see what all the noise was about. He lifted the lettuce, turned it upside down and pulled out the core, leaving just the leaves. He looked at me expecting a round of applause.

'Neat trick,' I said with a smile, but I didn't overdo the praise.

The salads were prepared, the tables laid and the glasses polished. Time came for me to go. The morning had passed quickly. The owner called me over.

'Hey, you've worked really well this morning, Phil,' he said as I took my standard issue blue apron off and handed it to him. The procedure had a final air about it. I knew I wouldn't be returning; he seemed to sense it as well.

'Well, see ya tomorrow, Phil,' he said as I walked out the door with my wages and a total of just five dollars in tips.

'Sure,' I said under my breath as I walked out into the bright midday sunlight. I walked to the T-shirt shop where Mark and Paul had just started work for the day. They both smiled as they saw me walk in. I briefly looked at the guys behind the counter who had spotted me instantly and would soon be over to chuck me out for talking to Mark and Paul.

'Well, how did you get on?' asked Paul with a smirk.

'Well, let's put it this way, Mark earned considerably more than I did in the way of tips.'

'Oh shit.'

'Yep, five dollars is the total I received. Restaurant work is a complete waste of time.'

'We'll have to do OPCing and T-shirt work then.'

By now one of the thin Arab chaps behind the counter had started to make his way over to us.

'Hi there, I'll be back to work this evening,' I called out as I headed toward the door, before he had a chance get close enough to tell me off. The other two made themselves scarce and the wiry chap was left standing where we once had been, with an angry expression. I walked out of the shop and straight down to the beach, passed hordes of holiday makers ambling along the promenade. I felt tired at the beach and I desperately need a swim to wake myself up but I couldn't be bothered to go back to Mildred's for a towel or swimming gear. But what the hell, I thought, and I walked down to the sea and plunged straight in with my jeans, T-shirt and sneakers still on. I got some curious looks at first but those around soon became accustomed to the idea. It was so hot that I was dry again in a little over an hour; I brushed the sand off my jeans and was ready for my OPCing that afternoon.

I did my OPCing in the same spot on the main street where I had been the day before. I was kept entertained by a clown, who was standing only a few feet away. He face was heavily covered in white make-up, exaggerating his other brightly coloured features; he wore a bright orange wig and his costume was an all in one harlequin affair in blue and orange. He was trying to attract people to a burger bar. Kids loved him, but the adults found him a tiresome pest, trying to entice them into somewhere that they didn't want to go. I spent quite a time watching him literally cling on to the adults' clothes, trying to drag them into the burger bar with their kids. The adults fought back and the clown was often hit several times on the arm before he finally gave up. It was the sort of scene that you might see in a Naked Gun film, with Leslie Neilson working under cover as a clown, and trying to keep up the pretence of doing the job. It often caused me to laugh out loud, much to the annoyance of the clown who would make various defeatist gestures. After a while he approached me.

'What a way to earn a living, eh boy?'

'Yeah,' I said. 'You must be hot in that clown get-up.'

'Hot ain't the word. Last year I had lost two stone by the end of the summer season.' I looked at him curiously and for the first time, under the heavy make-up, I noticed his age; he was sixty if he was a day.

'How long have you been doing this, then?' I asked.

'Well, this job only for about five seasons but I bet there ain't a job in Myrtle Beach I ain't done,' he responded, tipping his hat back to let the air to his face. Given that the place made Blackpool look like the cultural centre of the universe I dreaded to think of some of the occupations with which he had been blessed. And this was the pinnacle of his career, dressed in a heavily coloured clown outfit, covered in make-up, getting physically abused by the public. I chatted to him for quite a time that day; although, from time to time, each of us would have to suddenly walk away to entice Joe Public to take our wares, returning to pick up the conversation exactly where we had left it. The guy often made the kids laugh and now and again the adults would smirk. Clowns had never really made me laugh before; I had always considered them as quite sad characters, hiding a heavy heart or a hurting soul behind make-up and slapstick antics. This clown had made me laugh, but it had been for the wrong reasons and I felt sorry for him.

I continued my OPC stint until my T-shirt shop work at five, joining Mark and Paul. I had been on my feet all afternoon and wasn't relishing the idea of the spending the rest of the evening and most of the night continuing to do so. The work at the shop was again boring spiced up intermittently by the odd chat to British tourists who would wander in, aimlessly looking around at the merchandise. The three of us also made the evening interesting by talking to each other for extended periods, waiting for one of the guys to come out from behind the counter and then dispersing around the large shop floor before they could reach us. They became wise to this though and on one occasion set up a pincer movement. One came toward us, while another, who we hadn't notice go missing from the counter, waited behind a T-shirt rack. We all bumped into him making our escape. We stood motionless trying to hold back the laughter as he began to shout at us for generally treating the job as one big joke.

The next day we were all up late. Mark and I went straight to the restaurant and handed in our notices. Having originally said we would definitely work part time for three weeks, the owner was livid. We felt no remorse, the wages were lousy and the tips even worse. We wanted to earn money to travel, not pin money. Much of that day was similar to the last, OPCing and chatting to my new friend the clown during the morning and working with the other two until midnight at the T-shirt shop. That night after work, we shuffled along to a bar a few doors down. We sat at a large round table and chilled out deciding to spend the little money we had earned on getting completely legless. It was dawn when we made it to bed, and we crashed out until midday.

On our fifth day in Myrtle Beach life was beginning to get tough. I again met Paul and Mark in the T-shirt shop after my OPCing. Neither of them particularly liked OPC work and had subsequently given it up, spending all their time in the shop working incredibly long days and becoming increasingly frustrated with the paranoid management team. We were supposed to be experiencing the States and enjoying our time, but it felt to all three of us as though we were in The Great Escape with all our freedoms and enjoyment stifled by prison guards constantly hovering over us. The more time we spent in the shop the more irritated we became, and the more petty the owners seemed to get. Even talking to an English couple in the shop about where they had come from etc., was not considered a selling technique and I was instructed to move on to other customers if there was no sign of a sale within the first two minutes. Mark and Paul had had similar run-ins with the management, making as loud a scene as possible to embarrass them in front of customers. The shop was still busy at midnight and we worked on, but by 2.00 a.m. we had had our lot. Mark and I were leaving, we were shattered; Paul though wanted to work on to earn as much as possible.

'No, you can't work on,' Paul was told by the thin Arab chap.

'Why not?' asked Paul, 'I'm helping out and want to earn more money,' he added, clearly annoyed.

'If you want to earn more money come in tomorrow, at eight in the morning.'

'But that's hardly worth going to bed for, and anyway I'm used to the hours now and wouldn't be able to sleep.'

'Listen, you can't work tonight, cause I say you can't.' Voices were now raised. Mark and I smiled, and looked away awkwardly; if Paul had seen us he would have started smiling as well and would have lost all credibility in the argument. We had been difficult employees ever since we had started, but only in protest at some of the ridiculous rules we had to endure. Now this guy was trying his best to get his own back. He seemed to think all our larking around had been a personal insult to him; he was steaming up.

'You work the hours I say you work!'

'OK, then if I can't work the hours I want simply because you say so, out of spite, then I quit!' exclaimed Paul. The Arab chaps face turned sour. This was a surprise move.

'Listen, that's stupid,' he said, on the retreat.

'No it's not. You can stick your job. I'll collect my wages at the end of the week.' With that, Paul walked out.

The whole management were now staring at Mark and I. Mark answered their question before they asked.

'We'll be in tomorrow afternoon.' We walked out of the front doors without looking back and caught up with Paul. We all had another laughing fit on the way back to Mildred's, making jokes about Myrtle 'Toilet' and would have attempted another drinking session had we had any money. We tried to creep into Mildred's but were caught.

'Ah, you're back then?'

'Yes, Mildred, we're all back.' Paul said loudly. 'I told the T-shirt shop guys where they could stick their job.'

'What was that?' Mildred asked, finding Paul's northern accent at three in the morning a little difficult to decipher.

'I said the T-shirt shop guys are a bit odd!'

'Well they seem all right to me. We work quite close to them and we don't get any trouble from them, you know.'

'Night, Mildred,' we said, one after the other, not stopping at all in the living room.

'Night, boys.'

We had been eating breakfast at the 'eat as much as you can for $2.99' place each morning and what with more grease during the day our digestive systems were playing up. So we bought some high altitude alpine cereal the following morning and ate it back at Mildred's. Burgers, hash browns, eggs, sausages and pancakes each and every day were all very well in the movies, but did Arnie really keep his physique eating such calorific food; we didn't think so. Mark went off to the shop to start work while Paul accompanied me to the condo' office where I officially quit our OPCing.

Escape From Alcatraz

Paul, now jobless, went to the beach and I met Mark at the T-shirt shop. The previous evening, on our way back to Mildred's, we had all decided that enough was enough and that Richard's air-conditioned apartment back in Highpoint was paradise compared to the hot small room we were squashed into, work or no work. We would lose that sense of adventurism that BUNAC is supposed to encourage - but what the heck, sitting by the pool at Richard's complex was what the trip was all about. Even if we never worked again we could at least enjoy our time and, if it came to it, borrow money from Richard to live on and send money back over once we were home. So Mark and I had intended to work as late as possible in the shop that evening before handing in our notice; but when 11.00 o'clock came I'd had enough. I was standing at the other end of the shop floor to Mark; I looked at him and smiled. He knew exactly what I was thinking and followed me up to the counter.

'We're quitting!' I said.

'What?' came the reply from the small, miserable chap Paul had argued with the night before. He looked at both of us with a sour face; Mark and I grinned.

'Why don't you just work on for a few more hours? We'll probably close at one tonight, it's a bit quieter.' He hadn't understood.

'No. We quit. We're not just quitting for the evening, we're quitting for good. Fineto, kaputt, finished!' His face dropped. The others working behind the counter had noticed the sparkling relationship that we had built up with him in recent days. They all looked on to see what he would do.

'You can't,' he said.

'We can quit any time we want,' I said, annoyed that we had actually bothered turning up that evening. 'We'll pick up our wages tomorrow with Paul.' We left and felt relieved of a great burden as we walked out of the shop into the warm night air. We walked back to Mildred's laughing and joking. It was all over, we could travel back to Highpoint and start once again enjoying our trip.

Cashing our cheques for our OPC and T-shirt shop work involved a trip out to a shopping mall on the outskirts of Myrtle Beach. We had seen advertised that the mall contained the largest clock in the world.

'Now why would anybody with half a brain build the largest clock in the world in a place like Myrtle Toilet?' asked Mark.

'Maybe it was built a long time ago,' said Paul 'and these tourist excesses have been built up around it.'

'Maybe.'

He couldn't have been more wrong. The clock fitted perfectly. It was in the ceiling of the mall and was made of three consecutive circles of different coloured balls of light. Every five seconds another red light would illuminate around the outside of the clock and then another. Every five minutes another, differently coloured ball, would illuminate further inside the structure. And every hour yet another differently coloured ball would illuminate, further in. It took a while to sort out what the time was, and you soon felt sick craning your neck to look up at the brightly illuminated balls. It was actually quite awful and hardly the traditional sort of mechanical clock you would imagine as having the prestigious title of largest clock in the world.

The rest of the day was spent eating yet more fast food at Wendy's, on the beach and walking to the Greyhound bus shelter to find out times of buses back to Greensborough. It was while we were on our way back from here that we passed one of the many tourist attractions in the main street that we had passed daily but hadn't really given a second though to: a wax works. We wouldn't have dreamed of spending any money on any sort of entrance fee but as we passed we noticed people slipping in the back door for free. They were being let in by a girl who seemed to work there and must have known them. We quickly joined the group and followed them; given our financial state we couldn't miss the opportunity of getting something for free, and it was something to do while we waited for the Greyhound the following day.

Inside, it took a while for our eyes to adjust to the bad light. The exhibition itself was very small, with dusty scenes that looked as though they hadn't been cleaned or changed for years. In fact it was so bad that even though we hadn't paid an entrance fee we still felt cheated. And because we hadn't paid we felt comfortable laughing at the displays that had pieces of their anatomy missing. One scene brought together a collection of wax works of different characters that had no connection whatsoever, all standing around or sitting at small tables. Closest to the glass in this particular exhibit was a wooden table with a women who in no way resembled anyone famous; there was a very poor wax interpretation of Napoleon and one of Queen Elizabeth I, sitting bolt upright at a table. Opposite her the seat was completely empty; it was labelled as 'The Invisible Man'; we fell about with laughter; what a con, charging people to look at an empty chair. Thank goodness we hadn't paid!

That night would be our last in Myrtle Beach and we spent it walking around to say farewell to all the sights that we didn't wish to see again until the end of time. Although we had little money, we were in better spirits, dreaming of an air-conditioned flat in Highpoint instead of our curent accomodation where the temperature never seemed to fall much below eighty and the humidity much below ninety; where there was no need to use the hot tap as the cold water always came out lukewarm.

We packed our belongings the following morning and paid Mildred the rent we owed and thanked her. She had really been very good to us, providing us with a room and suggesting we try T-shirt shop work when we were desperate. We took a couple of snaps of Mildred's large, white classic house, and then made our way to the beach to sunbathe; we would be travelling over-night by bus. While we were on the beach, and having just brought our cameras out from hibernation to snap Mildred's place, we tried to take some action shots. But our Pentaxs were soon full of sand and as the waves were such 'nippy little blighters' as Mark called them, we didn't actually manage to get too many action shots in which a large wave and one of us both appeared at the same time.

When we had finished, Mark was still in the sea, diving into the waves, I was on the beach sorting out all the rubbish that we were carrying around with us and Paul was standing around doing nothing in particular. Paul decided that this was the perfect opportunity to drown an unsuspecting Mark and ran down the beach toward him. Paul jumped on Mark heavily in the water and they both came down with a crash into the sea. Even though Mark was big he was taken by surprise and they both fell underwater. They both surfaced smiling; but Paul for some reason looked different, a lot older. What had happened? It took me a few seconds to work out what it was, but as soon as I had, I ran down the beach shouting to him.

'Paul, your tooth'. He couldn't hear and kept smiling gappily as I approached. Eventually he heard me. He stood up in the sea and felt the front of his mouth with his tongue; he had lost one of his front teeth completely, leaving him with a large gap at the front of his mouth, and looking nearer forty than twenty.

'Oh shit,' he said just as I reached him. He looked at Mark, who laughed.

'Did you knock your tooth out just then?' I asked; there didn't seem to be any blood.

'No, it's me bloody cap. My tooth was capped and it's come out, I've lost it.' He began to search the water.

'I didn't know you had a cap,' said Mark.

'Well, you see those dentists up north are so bloody good they can cap a tooth and you don't even know its been done!' Paul smiled, showing off his toothless grin.

We helped Paul look but it was the proverbial needle in a haystack and our searches were in vain. Paul was the one who finally called of the search and we all walked up the beach.

'You know what this means, guys?' said Paul as he sat down on a towel.

'Yeah, our chances of pulling any birds with you around are practically zero!' answered Mark.

'It means I'll have to go back to England.'

'Why?' Mark asked.

'Well, I might get an infection or something if I don't get it seen to.'

'You can get it done over here; your insurance will probably pay for it.'

'Yeah, might do. Didn't think about that.'

'Anyway I'm sure you'd be OK if you gargled with TCP or something every day, to keep any infection away.'

'TCP, Top Cat's Piss, that stuff is disgusting,' complained Paul. 'I'd rather lose all me teeth than have to swallow any of that stuff.'

'Antiseptic mouth wash isn't supposed to taste like honey,' I said.

'I'll give it a go for a while. But I'll check to see if I'm covered on insurance for it all the same.'

Paul was genuinely upset and was quiet for some while. It really was the icing on the cake for our disastrous trip to Myrtle Beach. It had been the pits.

While Paul was thinking through his options and wondering whether dental surgery was covered by his insurance, Mark started to get impatient; our bus was not due to leave until late that night and having previously travelled on a Greyhound bus for an extended period of time, he wasn't relishing the prospect. He began to voice doubts about the journey. Would we perhaps meet the mental patient again who had accompanied us on our first trip? Would our luggage be taken off at the wrong town, to be left, unclaimed for six months in a Greyhound depo? We decided to inquire about hiring a car.

From the beach we walked up back toward the 'Eat as much as you can' restaurant, to a phone booth. In New York, after about a dozen phone calls, Mark and I had found hiring a car practically impossible, unless we were willing to fork out a ridiculous amount of money. But here in Myrtle Beach, after just one call we found that if we got a taxi out to the airport, we could get a car immediately, for a similar amount as it was going to cost for the three of us by bus. Mark put down the phone, turned and looking up at the heavens, exclaimed, 'We were destined to leave this place.'

We called a taxi and told the guy to race to the airport, we just couldn't wait to leave and once there dispensed with the formalities as quickly as possible. It was as though we were taking part in the Cannonball Run as we screeched out of the hire car park and onto the long wide roads. Being the only one of us with an international driving licence I was to drive the five hour journey.

'Don't fall asleep at the wheel, Phil,' laughed Paul as we set off from the airport in our burgundy Ford Tempo.

'Yeah, wake us when we get there will ya, Phil?' added Mark, with a smile.

'Oh, neat. Well if you two think you're sleeping all the way to Highpoint you've another thing coming.' I threw the map book at Mark. 'You're the navigator,' I said. Paul laughed from the back and Mark said that if Paul fell asleep we would leave him by the side of the road. As it was, it was such a boring journey along straight wide roads at fifty-five miles an hour that all three of us fell asleep at one stage or another.

We reached Highpoint late at night. Richard was asleep and not expecting us until the following day but our homecoming celebrations soon woke him.

The Good, the Bad and the Ugly

We spent the next day swimming, playing golf and generally resting after our momentous week in Myrtle Toilet. We laughed about our experiences: turning up at restaurants with a total of two staff and asking whether they had three waiters jobs going; our run-ins with the managers at the T-shirt shop, Mildred's luxury accommodation, the invisible man at the wax-works, the shark flags and the ice-cream parlour where we had sat and cried with laughter for over an hour.

That evening we all watched telly; the first time Paul, Mark and I had seen television since the Shark Channel. The Shark Channel was still around, but we skipped that and watched a film on one of the three film channels.

'This is awful,' I said after about twenty minutes.

'Yeah, it is really I suppose,' said Richard. We had all been watching it for the sake of watching something and nobody could be bothered to change channel.

'I tell you what, this isn't as bad as some of the films I've seen,' said Paul.

'Oh yes,' I said 'what's the worst film you've seen then?'.

'The worst film I've ever seen...' said Paul, making us all laugh as he built up to it, 'The worst film I've ever seen,' he repeated, 'is....How Santa Claus Beat The Nazis!'

'What?' I exclaimed.

'Yeh, it was about these guys who were in the trenches during the First World War and in trouble. Then Santa arrived and helped them out. He was lobbing handgrenades and all sorts. And later Santa went up and over the top of the trenches in his red suit with a machine gun, and gunned down all these Nazis.'

'It must have been a comedy or something, Paul?'

'No. It was all dead serious. The guy in charge shook Santa's hand at the end of it all as well, and thanked him for his help. It was such a pile of shit.'

'It would be great to see, what a laugh. Can you get it on video?' I asked after a while.

'Who would want to see that on video?' Paul was amazed we found it so funny. He was obviously still bitter at having spent hard earnt cash on going to see it.

'It could become a cult movie,' I said. 'Those things do, maybe we should get a copy and market it.'

'Honestly, Phil, it was so bad that all trace of it has probably been destroyed.'

Richard was good to us on our return. He can't have relished the prospect of three student animals returning to ruin his peace and quiet. Three unemployed guys, who were by now so darkly tanned that they looked like beach bums, hanging around the apartment complex completely ruining any credibility he might have had. To make us feel even more guilty he was the one that found us work; in fact Richard found his brother a job the following day, working on a building site for a local construction company, Golden Triad Construction. Paul and I played tennis and swam while Mark was at work, which was all very relaxing but we would need money shortly, or need to talk to Richard about a loan.

Mark returned that day saying that the work had not been too bad, despite the heat. Richard landed me a job with the same company the next day and I was naturally very grateful. Richard drove me the short distance to their offices.

'Good luck!' he said, as he threw me out of his Golf and sped off. I walked into the offices and saw one of the bosses. He was a short chap, dressed in a checked shirt and jeans and was extremely nice to me. He made sure that I had filled in the appropriate tax forms and then kindlly drove me to one of the company's building sites - unfortunately not the same one that Mark was working on. I had noticed from our previous time in Highpoint that anybody who was anybody in the building trade drove a flash pick-up truck. The make didn't matter; GM, Ford or the like, they just had to be huge and brightly coloured. The engines in these pick-up trucks seemed to range from 17 million litres upwards and the chap that drove me to the site had one such beast. We were only in it for a few moments before we arrived at the site and all the while the engine did little more than tick over.

When we arrived we went in search of the two guys I would be working with and who had the general responsibility for the whole site, Danny and Benny. The site itself was large and consisted of some twenty bungalows in various states of completion; some were yet to have the brickwork finished on them and others just needed their final coat of paint. We moved in and out of each bungalow searching for Danny and Benny; each different set of workmen suggested another bungalow and we eventually found them at the back of the site sorting out a wiring problem with an electrician.

'Danny, been lookin' all over for ya. This is...What did you say your name was, son?'

'Phil.'

'Yeh, this is Phil, and he's gonna be workin' with ya for a few weeks just helpin' out on the site and things, OK.' Danny looked pleased with this; there are always a thousand and one jobs on a building site, such as carrying and sorting out, that nobody really wants to do, and it looked like I had arrived just at the right time. Danny and Benny greeted me with a smile. Danny was about five foot eight with a round face and thick grey hair swept to one side. He looked to be in his late thirties and had a kind air about him, as far as you could see through the thick layer of dust. Benny was taller, probably five foot eleven, with thick black hair and a thick black beard. He appeared to be slightly more reserved than Danny but friendly nevertheless.

With the introductions over, the boss left me on the site with Danny and Benny and they instantly began chatting. They started to ask the usual mix of questions about where

I came from. The first job that I was to help them with was a water drainage problem. They had been looking for a burst, or incorrectly fitted, water pipe which was under the tarmaced road that ran to the back of the site. They were tired by the time I arrived, having been digging all morning before the electrician's problem had arisen and instantly set me to task with a pick and shovel at the front of one of the bungalows. I had been informed by Mark, who had already been working for a day or two, to wear the tattiest clothes that I possessed. I consequently blended in well, looking as though I had been working there all my life.

While I was digging in the 90 degree heat, Danny and Benny took the opportunity to rest in the porch of one of the bungalows. I didn't mind, as I was keen on my first day and felt full of energy, driven on by the need to earn some hard cash. They told me a little about the large bungalows we were building. They were owned by the local church and were being built for older people as retirement homes. The church was not giving them away however, they had to be purchased. It was considered a privilege to own one of these bungalows, but I presumed it would hardly be Christian to charge more than the going rate. But it was worse than that. Because these homes would be bought by elderly people they would stay there until they died; the bungalow would then become the property of the church again to re-sell. Your family weren't allowed to inherit it and you weren't allowed to sell it, even though you had bought it up-front with cash. When this was all explained to me I found it hard to believe. It would be the biggest con imaginable, even if executed by a cowboy property outfit; but for such a scheme to be run by the church was almost unreal. Danny and Benny thought the same, but said that some people were so religious they would do anything to get their hands on one of these properties.

Religion, I was to discover, was big business in the States. Danny and Benny told me that there were a number of religious radio stations in the area that were dedicated to reciting passages from the Bible and playing hymns and that they had some of the largest audiences in the whole of the state. The church was wealthy in North Carolina, it appeared.

I finished the digging during the morning and having located and fixed the pipe with Danny and Benny it was time for lunch.

'What you doin' for lunch, Phil?' asked Benny.

'If there's a shop nearby I was going to get a snack; perhaps eat it back here.'

'Well, there ain't no shops near by and workin' out here all day you'd do best to come with Danny and me to get some proper food inside ya. Come on now.'

'Thanks.' We all walked to Danny's new pick-up, which was a shiny green and cream colour and which, like all the other pick-ups in the county, was powered by an engine more usually fitted to an ocean-going liner.

'Hop in back there, Phil.' I jumped in and instantly burnt myself.

'Shit.'

'Oh, be careful there, Phil. The truck's been roasting in the sun for the whole mornin.' said Danny. 'You'd better sit on that wood there in the back.' Danny and Benny both laughed. We drove to a greasy hamburger joint, just by the shopping mall near Richard's apartment. But this wasn't a large modern fast food joint; it was an independently run, homely sort of place. There were checkered table clothes on the wooden tables and the whole of the inside was wood. Everybody in the place was a labourer and almost all of them were wearing checked shirts and dirty baseball caps: the perfect set for a film about someone returning to the small American town in the south in which they grew up.

The food was classic American burger and chips with the only real choice on the menu being the size of the burger and the relish required; The food tasted good, all home grilled, and went down well with hungry workmen. Danny and Benny seemed to know quite a few other guys at other tables and shouted greetings around the place with mouthfuls of food. They also seemed to know most of the waitresses.

That afternoon we filled in the hole we had dug that morning and tarmaced over. To level it we used a pneumatic hammer. It stood upright and had a large pad at its base and packed literally tons of pressure. Danny handled its weight and powerful thumping easily, guiding it around with ease.

'You ever used one of these, Phil?' he shouted above the deafening noise of the thumping and petrol engine.

'Nope,' I shouted back.

He stood to one side and beckoned me to have a go.

'Watch your toes now, Phil, this thing can crush bones to powder in no time,' he shouted in my ear. I grabbed the bar and took it from him. The weight of the machine was tremendous and it started to veer off the new tarmac. I used all my weight and strength to try and control it, but it had by now found a life of its own and was out of control and falling. Danny rushed over. Even though he was smaller than me he was skilled at using the machine and brought it upright. Benny was laughing.

'You got to treat it like a woman, Phil,' Danny shouted. 'Firm and at the same time smooth, use its own power and weight to take it along; you should just be here to balance it and let it go its own way a bit, don't fight it all the time, OK?' I nodded. He was right, there was no point in fighting it, it had to be guided gently and there certainly wasn't any point in trying to move it quickly in a direction that it didn't want to go; just like a woman, indeed!

We finished close to 4pm and then took another hour to pack up. All the shovels, cables and other tools were kept in the back of a large silver articulated trailer, kept on the building site. It was huge inside and housed every conceivable construction site tool imaginable.

I was pleased with my first day's work and that I got on well with Danny and Benny. It was going to be tough work in the heat and humidity, I thought, if I was to work there for a while; especially as I would probably be given all the heavy manual jobs to do. But it was the sort of work we should have looked for as soon as we arrived in Highpoint: the pay was good and the hours sociable. Danny drove me home in his pick-up. It was Friday and as he said he would see me Monday I assumed I had done OK.

That evening we all went out to Applebies and met Sonia. Although we hadn't seen her for about three weeks, she was still embarrassed about the episode with her boyfriend and his request for cash. She introduced us to another waitress and we all sat and talked a while. We were all happy to be back in Highpoint and it wasn't long before all four of us had sunk far too many Budweisers. We sat round with Sonia and her friend until we were chucked out at closing time at two in the morning. We staggered home completely knackered.

Richard was up early the next morning, as he had to go into the warehouse to sort out a Saturday morning delivery. Mark, Paul and I were all up late and helped ourselves to a feast of breakfast cereal and toast. We spent the day playing tennis and swimming. It was tough playing tennis in the heat of the day and any running around was strictly limited; you would hope that the ball was on its way out rather than make any attempt to run for it. Each day seemed to be getting hotter and the TV weather channel told us that there was no break in sight. North Carolina was constantly covered with a red hue on the weather map. We were all a deep mahogany colour by now.

Every day in Myrtle Beach had been repetitive, struggling from day to day to scrape a living. But back in Highpoint the weekends would again be something to look forward to. The general messing and mucking around by the pool had to become more spectacular and more dangerous each time to keep us entertained. Our finale came in the afternoon when we seemed to be playing, 'Who can break their neck first.' A ball was thrown into the air and each of us in turn had to jump as high into the air and as far across the pool as you could to catch it. We ended up crashing into the water from a very great height, either on our sides or backs. The ball was thrown across the pool for the last time and it was my turn to retrieve it. As I left the side and leapt into the air I thought 'this is all going to end in tears', somebody will get hurt if this continues.

It was a premonition: I got hurt. I crashed into the water from higher than ever, the first point of impact being the right side of my head. Coming into the water with such speed and with all my weight behind it meant that water was forced up into my ear with such might that my eardrum burst, and the ampulla (the small piece of flesh that stands up in the inner ear and gives you balance) started to swing uncontrollably.

The instant I hit the water the pain was unbearable. I screamed underwater and then struggled for the side. The world seemed to be spinning and I screwed up my face in pain and tightly closed my eyes. I clung to the side of the pool, not daring to move. After a while I opened my eyes and realised that I had done some serious damage to myself. I pulled myself out of the pool but I couldn't walk. The swinging ampulla had made me lose all sense of balance. I called to the others who were packing up and leaving the pool area, oblivious to what had happened. I wasn't aware of the extent of my injuries at the time and told the others that I was having trouble walking. Although I regained my sense of balance after a short while I couldn't hear anything with my right ear and like the others I assumed that there must have been large amounts of water trapped deep inside my ear. We all walked back to the apartment slowly and although sympathetic, the other guys had no idea of the pain I was enduring and as my balance had returned somewhat, assumed that all was now well.

That evening we had arranged to meet Sonia again at Applebies. I kept shaking my head while I was getting ready, almost until I was sick, to try and dislodge the water that I thought was probably lodged in there. The pain hadn't left and I was getting worried, but went out with the others. We met Sonia and ordered our drinks. By now the pain in my ear excrutiating, I thought I was going to collapse and after a further five minutes I asked Richard to take me to the twenty-four hour supermarket to find some drops for my ear, to dislodge the water. Richard kindly obliged, leaving the other three to chat on. We found some drops that claimed to dislodge any water in your ears and then Richard took me back to the apartment where I said I would stay, while he returned to the others. I applied the ear drops according to the instructions; but the chemical drops simply fell onto my torn eardrum. The pain was unbelievable, and I had to hold on to the sink in the bathroom to stop myself from falling to the floor. I breathed deeply to stop myself passing out and began to shake my head to try and move the water once again. Nothing moved and I could still hear nothing. I looked up into the mirror and slowly turned my head to look at my ear; there was now a steady stream of blood coming from it. This was more serious than a blocked ear.

I tried to watch some TV, but my senses were being constantly overwhelmed by the pain in my ear. When the others eventually returned I told them what had happened and Richard called around in an effort to find a twenty-four hour clinic, but in vain. It would soon be morning, so it was agreed that I should get to a doctor as soon as I could that day.

Brief Encounter

That Sunday morning we spent searching for the nearest medical centre in the phone book, wondering whether I would have to pay five thousand dollars up front before they even looked at me. We found the nearest hospital and decided I would take a trip out there on Monday, as the pain was subsiding and I felt guilty at having to ask Richard to take me there on his one day off. The rest of that Sunday was spent worrying whether I would regain my hearing at all in my right ear.

Monday morning, and Mark and I went to work on our respective building sites. Paul had yet to find work though as Golden Triad Construction didn't need any more help at present. When I got to work I found the site foreman there and was immediately introduced to him. His name was Mark and he was a young chap of about twenty-eight. Danny had told me on the first day about Mark and how he had civil engineering qualifications, putting him in quite a senior position in the company. Mark was sitting under one of the bungalow porches at the back with Danny and Benny. He didn't say anything when introduced, just smiled and sat back, looking up.

'Mark had four wisdom teeth out only yesterday, so he ain't feelin' too good right now, Phil,' said Benny, apologising for Mark's shy greeting. Mark's face had struck me as rather fat in comparison to the rest of his body and this explained why. Danny told Mark that he was no good to anybody sitting around with a fat aching face and said he should really go home. So Mark obliged. Danny was left in charge again.

We spent the day on road repairs, and travelling to the small town movie set once again for lunch. The heat was unreal. My pace of work soon slowed to accommodate for it; digging and moving building materials in 90 degree heat needs to be done at a steady pace or you literally pass out. On that Monday I was also briefly introduced to a couple of plasterers, a couple of brickies and a couple of electricians, all of whom were working on the site and all of whom I would get to know a lot better in the coming days.

Danny gave me a lift home again that evening and on the way chatted about his son. In fact he always talked about his son, who was eight and his pride and joy. Danny was divorced, which he seemed to greatly regret.

'I went through Vietnam you know, Phil; but I tell you having your parents divorced must seem just like a war when you're so young; I wouldn't have liked it.' There was a pause.

'You were in Vietnam, then?' I asked.

'Yeh, an' I lost a lot of friends out there too. And what's it all for, Phil? Nobody knows.'

'Was it as bad as they said it was?' I asked as we stopped outside Richard's apartment. Danny looked at me.

'It was worse than that. Night after night without sleep. You knew you couldn't sleep or that might be the end of you and your buddies. Your mind starts playing games with you after a while. It's like one long nightmare; you feel like crying.' He went quiet for a while and looked away. Then he turned back to face me. 'But the worse thing is losing so many friends; some stood on land mines, others died from their injuries but most I knew just seemed to disappear. Then word would come to us that they had died. After a while I lost so many good buddies I thought that I was going to be next and you know I really didn't care. I would do crazy things. But when we moved away from the front line and rested I would come to my senses and it would make me shake to think about how close I had been to death. It was horrid, Phil.'

'You still suffer at all?' I asked as delicately as I could.

'No, not really. Not any more - it was such a long time ago. But when I do think about it, it's usually when I'm just daydreaming and my mind wanders. I usually end up looking at my medal and remembering my buddies.'

'You got a medal?'

'Yeh, was decorated when it was all over. But hell what does a piece of metal mean at the end of the day?' He seemed to snap out of his mood 'Anyway, come on. Got to get on and collect my boy.'

'OK, see you tomorrow; thanks for the lift.'

That evening I was taken to the hospital by Richard to have a doctor look at my ear. The pain had dulled but I wanted to check out what exactly had happened, and whether I would be able to hear again in my right ear. The hospital was crowded. There was an open area by a reception desk where at least twenty people were waiting. I approached the desk.

'I damaged my ear about forty eight hours ago and wanted a doctor to take a look at it; would that be possible?' I asked the receptionist.

'Well, there is a bit of a wait,' she said indicating the other patients in the waiting area with her yellow pencil. I looked at them briefly. They all looked in a sorry state and amongst them there were two policeman accompanying a black youth, who had a head wound that seemed to be bleeding profusely.

'Is it an emergency?' she asked. I turned back to the receptionist.

'Well, I suppose I could come back another time, or make an appointment perhaps.'

'This is only for emergencies really, you see. You'd be better off going to a medical clinic.'

'Is there one nearby?'

'There's one about two miles away but it will probably be closed now, you'd be better off arranging an appointment for tomorrow night with them.'

'OK, thanks for your help,' I said, disappointed at the prospect of having to take another trip out the following evening.

'You couldn't order me a taxi then could you?' I asked, realising that Richard had just driven off.

'Sure. Just sit over there and when it arrives I'll let you know.' She smiled and picked up the phone.

'Thanks.'

'You're welcome.'

She had been very helpful; perhaps the medical system in the States was not as bad as it was made out to be. I remembered seeing countless documentaries on how in the States real medical care just didn't exist unless you were able to pay for it. Perhaps all those documentaries and reports had been misguided, I thought, as I walked over to a chair in the hall to wait for the taxi.

Then something happened that completely changed my perception and shook me. I had only been sitting down for a few moments when, to my right, the electric doors slid open and a man came rushing in looking as white as a sheet. He was carrying a girl of about five or six; she was screaming with pain. Everybody looked up. It was instantly obvious what was wrong with the little girl: she had broken her arm. There was bone sticking out of her forearm and the whole arm had swelled to the size of one of her legs. It was truly an awful scene. The chap ran up to the reception,

'My daughter's broken her arm, we need a doctor right away.' The receptionist looked up slowly from her paper work.

'Do you have insurance for her?' she asked. I couldn't believe what I had heard. My image of the receptionist changed in an instant. She waited until she had a reply from the father before acting further.

'Yes, yes we have insurance,' he said hurriedly. Only then did she move and rush to show the father through a door and out of sight to 'Emergency' to find a doctor. What if he hadn't had insurance for her? What an awful state of affairs when in such an emergency such a question has to be asked. Obviously there are advantages with private health care, but it seemed to have been taken too far in this instance. Would the father perhaps have had to stump up a couple of hundred dollars before the girl was treated? The incident played on my mind for the rest of evening.

Rocky

The following day was another very hot one at work and everybody on the building site was wearing the bare minimum of shorts and sneakers. I began the day with Benny, clearing bricks away from the porch areas of the bungalows at the back. How Benny survived with his thick black hair, beard and baseball hat in all the heat I'll never know and was just about to question him on the subject when Danny called us over to some bungalows nearer the front of the site where the brickies were working. Some plain wooden interior doors were being delivered by lorry, about fifty of them, and they needed us to help unload. As we strolled over, the lorry driver was grabbing his paper work and jumping out of the cab, joining Benny and I as we walked toward Danny.

'Benny, come with me, I want to see where we can stack these doors and how many we need in each place.'

'Sure thing, Danny.' Benny followed Danny over the site's rough ground and I was left with the lorry driver. He looked at me.

'Can you sign these papers for me?' he asked.

'No. I've only been here a couple of days I'm afraid.'

'You from Europe, son?'

'How did you guess?' I asked, sarcastically.

'From your accent. Where about's you from, England?'

'Yeah, London.'

'Hey, I've heard of that, that's just about the biggest place over there isn't it?' Someone else with a degree in geography!

'Yes, something like that,' I said. There was a pause.

'Do you have Benny Hill over there?' he asked. I was completely unprepared for the question and taken aback.

'Yes we do. He's English.'

'He's just the greatest. I don't know how he gets away with so much on TV, he's amazing, man.' This chap was obviously an ardent fan. 'They put it on really late over here, 'cause its considered quite rude you know?' He paused. 'Is that the case in England too?'

'Well, he's not on at the moment but when he is, he's not on that late. He's considered quite tame in England. Some things are much worse.'

'Yeh, I heard Europe was pretty liberal!' His intrigue grew. 'Tell me is it true you have a daily newspaper over in England where page three is always a picture of a topless woman?'

'Yeah, we do.' I started to smile.

'Wow.' I was beginning to wonder whether the U.S. was an incredibly conservative society when it came to nudity, or whether this guy was simply a pervert.

'But you must have magazines and that over here for men?' I ventured to ask.

'Yeh, of course, but they're quite strict about who's allowed to buy them and it's all sort of secretive you know. We certainly don't have topless women in daily papers, man; don't you think that's just fantastic?'

Humouring him I said, 'It's bloody great; sort of starts the day off well.' I was all for having a really perverted conversation about women with this guy when Danny and Benny returned. They had decided how many doors were needed in each bungalow so we all walked over to the lorry and began unloading the doors. After five minutes of trudging across the muddy site with our heavy loads, Danny and Benny were called away by the electricians to look at a problem, leaving myself and the driver to continue unloading in the heat. It wasn't long before the driver too had skillfully managed to drift off to chat to the brickies. That left me to move a further thirty doors from the lorry into different bungalows around the site. I was dripping with sweat.

Outside one of the bungalows the two ceiling blasters were sat on upturned buckets. They were a couple of specialist guys who sprayed the ceilings of the bungalows with a thick white paste from a powerful gun to give it a textured finish. But whenever I came across them throughout my days on the site they never seemed to be doing any work and were usually only on site for a total of four hours a day, which included a suspiciously long lunch break. Unlike the rest of the guys on the site they were exceedingly overdressed for the heat, wearing classic American labourers clothes of dungarees, checked shirts and baseball caps. They also both had long beards. They looked exactly like the two bearded guitarists from ZZ Top.

'Looks like hard work,' said one, as I struggled passed carrying a door.

'Sure is,' I replied. I left the door inside and went to collect another from the lorry. I carried a second door passed them.

'Yep, sure looks like tough manual labour that,' said the other.

'Yep,' I said. I continued on inside, struggling under the weight of the door.

'Ain't anybody helping you, then?' the first chap asked as I passed them again on my way out.

'Nope.' I didn't stop. As I passed again with another door he said,

'That's outrageous, man, nobody helpin' out. I bet they're just sittin' around on their backsides somewhere.' They both looked down at the ground and shook their heads. I continued on inside with the door. I realised that these two jokers were taking the piss and smiled to myself. When I walked passed them on the way out they looked down at the ground again and began to shake their heads.

'Ohh man, nobody helpin' out; and in this heat as well,' the first said as I passed. This made me chuckle to myself and by the time I returned with yet another door I had to put the door down to steady myself. Just the sight of the two ZZ Top lookalikes was setting me off. As my load hit the ground one of them got up and sauntered over to me.

'You manage there, boy?'

'Yes thanks,' I said still laughing.

'Let me give you a hand there.' I thought he was going to take the door for me but he just lifted it slightly so that I could grip it and once I was loaded up he winked and walked away. I had to let the door drop again and laugh. The two of them just sat smiling, and watched me laughing.

Danny and Benny returned to find all the doors unloaded and the lorry driver asking me whether we had Playboy in England.

'Well done, Phil, all unloaded,' said Danny. He then signed the lorry driver's papers and sent Benny and me back to the bungalows at the rear, to continue clearing the porches. I looked back and saw the ZZ Top duo still sitting on upturned buckets. They were now drinking cans of coke and one of them raised his can to me. I smiled and waved back. Benny saw and said,

'Those two are great guys but they're the laziest God damn buggers you'll ever meet, Phil.'

'Tell me about it, Benny!'

In the afternoon we continued doing odd jobs around the site but rested often from the tremendous heat. My ear hadn't bothered me all day but I was still deaf.

When Danny dropped me home that evening I found Paul back there.

'Thought you were working today for the construction company?' I said.

'They didn't need me,' he said. 'Things are getting bad, Phil, I'd better get some work soon.'

'Ah don't worry Paul, they'll give you a job on one of their sites soon.'

'Yeah well maybe, but I'll look for something different anyway.' He was quite depressed.

Mark and Richard returned later and headed straight for a swim. Paul spectated, he had been swimming all day and I gave it a miss, still too painfully aware of my injured ear. Richard then suggested that to kill two birds with one stone they could go shopping for provisions while I visited the

medical centre. We all ventured off in the Golf. I was careful
to take my medical insurance certificates. Richard dropped
me off outside a red-bricked building and then drove off
with the others to the nearest mall. I stood outside for a
while and then made for the big glass doors, entered and
walked up to the receptionist. She was younger than the
receptionist at the hospital but similarly dressed in a blue
nurse's uniform.

I had already made an appointment and so I didn't have
to wait long on the padded plastic chairs. In my jeans and
T-shirt I was the best dressed and cleanest guy in the entire
surgery; every other patient looked like they had just come
from a building site and some were still wearing hard hats;
most had blood on some part of their anatomy. The health
and safety executive had obviously missed a few potential
accident hot spots on their latest building site tours, I
thought. A smartly dressed young doctor soon appeared
wearing a long white coat; he had a stethoscope around
his neck. He looked down at his sheet of paper and called
my name. Clutching my insurance documents, I followed
him along a corridor. The place was quite high tech, with
the low lighting giving it that movie set look. We passed a
number of doctors and nurses all in immaculate white coats;
a classic soap scene. I wondered when a voluptuous nurse
would run by crying, because her love for Dr Kildare was
not reciprocated and because, anyway, he was more
interested in a patient he was treating for a hysterectomy,
who's husband was mixed up in arms dealing but who had
seen the error of his ways and was now racing to the
hospital for one last moment with his wife before the police
caught up with him and took him away! But we made it to
the treatment room quite uneventfully.

The doctor told me to sit up on the long high couch and
asked about my ear. He seemed to know of my ailment
even though I had only mentioned it briefly to the
receptionist when I phoned to make an appointment; quite

efficient I thought. He took a look into my ear and let out a little yelp.

'Oh yeah!' There was a pause. He looked at me 'You've burst your eardrum.' This was confirmation of my first ever serious injury and confirmed my worst suspicions. As my medical knowledge was limited to what I'd learnt doing my first aid badge in the cub-scouts, I began to worry.

'Will I ever hear again?' I asked, as he continued to peer into my ear.

'Yeah, of course, don't worry.' He put away his little instrument and took out a piece of paper and a pencil from his top pocket.

'Now this is what you've done' he said. He drew a picture of my inner ear and described the damage to my eardrum and how it would heal. His drawing was of a typical medical student type, elaborate and scientific but expertly proportioned. He probably wanted to be an artist; in fact if I hadn't told him that I understood perfectly, I'm sure he would have gone on to draw a complete cut-away diagram of the human head.

'Anyway,' he said 'your hearing will return but it will never be quite as good as it was. It's like when you break your arm, it's never as strong as it was and you will always have a weak point where it was broken.' He prescribed me a course of antibiotics, told me not to get my ear wet and we spent the next ten minutes filling in insurance forms. How would I survive without a swim in all this heat I wondered. But it was a relief having finally been diagnosed and reassured of a successful, if not complete, recovery.

The others had had a fruitful shopping trip while I was at the clinic and they collected me with Richard's car full of groceries.

The next day was Paul's first at work. The construction company had finally called to say they needed him, which was a relief to us all. They stuck him with Mark, which obviously meant that work for the two of them now was going to turn into a bit of a lark.

As usual, Richard gave me a lift to work that morning as the site was on his way to the warehouse. We set off from the apartment and had just reached the shopping mall at the end of the road, when Richard started to look concerned. We pulled out into the main road and after thirty seconds Richard took another look in his rear view mirror.

'Shit, what do they want?' I turned around and saw a huge black and white police car, with lights flashing, almost touching the car's bumper.

'They followed us from further up the road,' Richard said. 'You didn't see me jump a red light or anything did you, Phil?'

'No. And you certainly weren't speeding.' We pulled into the car park of a fast food joint further along the road and got out. Wish I had my camera with me I thought. Stopped by a real 'Black and White' in the States, fantastic: movie city! Richard was anxious. The police followed us into the car park and remained in their car for a few seconds before getting out and putting their truncheons into their holders. They put their hands on their guns to straighten them up and approached.

'Do you know why we've stopped you, sir?' asked the smaller and younger looking of the two.

'I haven't a clue,' Richard replied.

'Well sir, at the junction back there, there is a clear 'Stop' sign and you failed to stop.' The junction he was referring to was half way down the road adjacent to the apartment. It was only small and as there was a clear view to either side to slow down seemed quite sufficient.

'There was nothing coming and I didn't feel the need to stop completely. I slowed down and made sure it was clear both ways,' Richard explained.

'Nevertheless there is a stop sign there, sir, which means you are legally obliged to come to a complete standstill. Do you have your driving licence with you, sir?'

'Err yes, it's in the car.' Richard and I walked back to the car.

'Did you see the young chap? He was shaking,' I said quietly to Richard as he sorted through his glove box to find his licence.

'Yeah, this is probably his first booking. Anyway I'm going to contest it no matter who dishes out the ticket, there's no way it's necessary to stop, nobody does; they're just behind on arrests for the month.' I waited in the car as Richard talked to them further. He returned and slammed his door closed.

'That young guy was still shaking when I left,' he said 'if I take it to court there's no way he can make that stick.' We left the police in their car at the car park and Richard spun his rear wheels as we left, making a short screeching sound. I was unsure whether it was a good idea to metaphorically sticking two fingers up at two cops who were packed with more weaponry than Rambo and who would have no problem catching up with us without taking their fourteen thousand litre car out of first gear. But they didn't give chase.

When I arrived at work Danny told me that he had been assigned to another site; he informed me I'd be going with him because leaving me with Benny would be 'a holiday.'

'Goin' to work on a church, Phil,' he exclaimed in his pick-up truck on the way over to the site. There was a pause.

'Does the Church have a monopoly on this company's work or something?' I asked cheekily.

'Well, we do a lot of work for them that's for sure, but one of the reasons is that they are one of the largest property owners in the area. And one of the most active institutions in the building game at the moment.' Danny paused while the realisation of how much the company relied upon the Church sunk in and then he added that we were in fact going to work on a church school.

When we arrived Mark, the boss, was there (minus his wisdom teeth). His face had now returned to normal and he managed a smile when he greeted us. He was standing on a grass bank spraying the large sloping roof of the church school with a powerful hose.

'You see the problem, Danny?' He asked. We looked up. The roof was so large that when it rained the drainage system was unable to cope with the huge amount of water that ran off it and the walkways and basement area around the school were flooding. The school had been officially completed six months ago but they had only discovered the problem after a recent freak downpour one afternoon. We certainly hadn't seen any rain.

'We need to dig down beyond the wall there and increase the piping for the drainage.' Danny frowned, it looked like a lot of hard work. Mark turned off the hose and we walked down a steep grass bank to the basement area of the school. Our attention was diverted by the arrival of a massive dumper truck, that looked like something made by 'Tonka', towing a trailer with a JCB digger on it. The driver parked on a large grass area in front of the school and as the air brakes hissed he jumped out; this was Larry. He walked over to the three of us and greeted us with a broad smile. 'Pipes are blocked,'was his professional opinion.

Once he felt confident that Larry, Danny and I knew what we were to do, Mark left us to drive to another site, he said he had other work to do. But Danny later informed me that Mark had just moved house with his new wife and sneaked off now and again to do his own DIY and to make sure that any decorators he was employing weren't skiving off - like him!

The weather was scorching and we had to start digging further drainage around the basement with spades before we could use the JCB. Larry didn't talk much, he just dug but I slowly got to know him throughout the day. He was a really decent guy and his slight build disguised the fact that he was as strong as an ox, having worked on the roads for the past fifteen years. This also later explained his driving skills in the JCB and the speed with which he was working. We were digging directly downwards to discover where the pipes lay.

The JCB was eventually brought in, but Larry had great difficulty driving down the steep slope with the giant machine. We stood and watched as he used his skill to try every angle in order to inch the JCB closer to the basement. He finally reversed the mighty yellow vehicle back up the slope and jumped out.

'No good,' he said 'We'll have to do the last bit ourselves.' Danny, who had found the hours of digging in the morning particularly tough due to his previous night's drinking session, looked at me and rather resignedly.

'Well, another hours digging. You up to it?'

'Sure am,' I replied with a smile.

'You're a cheeky son of a bitch,' he said and tried to slap me around the head.

'Come on, Danny, back to work,' I called. Danny smiled broadly, muttered something under his breath and followed me over to the ditch. We had to dig through a mixture of wet earth and gravel in this next session and each shovel-full felt like a ton weight. When we reached the pipes we discovered that not only were they blocked, but they had also been crushed in places by the weight of earth on top of them, which meant that almost all the pipework had to be replaced, which meant more hard digging. There was no way that we could dig up the whole basement area without mechanical assistance; it would have taken a week. But the JCB had already had trouble with the slope. Larry looked at Danny and said he had to give the JCB another go.

Larry edged the JCB forward very slowly, but then it suddenly began to slip down the steep slope toward the school. The massive treaded tires at the back were spinning in reverse but the slope was too steep. The JCB's bucket was raised and looked as though it was going to crash through the church school roof. Larry, realising what was happening, rapidly lowered the bucket as the massive machine slipped uncontrollably down the slope. The bucket came down just in time to miss the roof but ploughed straight into the wall. There was a loud clang of metal on brick and the wall held, stopping the JCB. There was a moment of silence as Larry cut the engine. We all smiled with relief; Danny put his hand over his heart.

Larry restarted the engine and slowly tried to move the machine back up the slope at an angle to gain any grip he could; but the huge wheels were constantly slipping. He motioned with his arms and as I approached he held up both his hands toward me indicating he wanted a push. I walked around to the front of the JCB and was about to give it a go when he leaned out of the cab and shouted above the noise of the engine, 'No no, only joking!' He laughed.

I felt a bit stupid, thinking that a push from a human might help a ten ton JCB get back up a steep slope. Larry was still chuckling as he jumped from the cab.

'Don't worry, Phil,' he said, 'it's just a cruel joke, had it played on me when I started in this game.' But I had already seen the funny side. Larry stood next to me with his hands on his hips, studying the scene.

'That was a bit close.'

'The company would have had another construction job on its books if the roof had collapsed,' I said.

'Yeh, we wouldn't have been around though, Phil. Would have had to find jobs with a demolition team.' Larry sighed with relief.

'We need the Bobcat,' Danny said. This was the first time I had heard its name, but the Bobcat was to become one of the greatest toys I have ever played with. It would make my days on the site a lot more enjoyable.

'Yeh, the Bobcat would do the trick,' agreed Larry. 'Think it's over with Steve at the moment, I'll pick it up when it's free.' I recognised Steve as being the boss at the site where Mark and Paul were working.

Our next task was to pull the JCB back up the slope, out from the bottom of the gully. For this Larry suggested we use the 'Tonka' lorry that he had arrived in. So we unhitched the JCB trailer and Larry reversed it into position. We didn't want to risk the lorry slipping down the slope as well so we used heavy chains to pull the JCB up, keeping the lorry on flat ground. The process was awkward with Danny and I both cutting our hands badly as we pulled the chains vertically upward to try and keep them from ripping up the grass bank. We eventually succeeded and spent another hour sorting out the site and packing away; there was little we could do without the Bobcat.

Much of Thursday was spent with Benny. There were odd jobs that needed doing around the site and Benny and I got lumbered with them while Mark and Danny sorted out a major construction problem.

'You been in the building trade all your life, Benny?' I asked as we cleared out bricks from a large balcony area.

'Nope. Done a lot of things in my life, Phil. Ain't none been too flash though.' He paused. 'I didn't have too good an education you see, Phil, so I can't read and write too good; so that's sort of hindered which jobs I can get, you know.'

'Oh,' I said. 'Sorry to hear that, Benny. What sort of things have you done then?'

'You name it and I've done it. Everything from working in packing factories to building sites and restaurants. You see, everybody was more interested in getting out of school and getting a motorbike when I was younger, so you took a job quickly you know, just to get a bike without thinking of the future. I've had some good times though, Phil, but I would have liked a better education, you know?'

'As long as you're happy, that's what counts.' I didn't really know what to say and felt a bit stupid, but Benny wasn't listening. Smiles began to appear across his face as he continued moving bricks and I knew I was in for a trip down memory lane.

'Yeh, when we left school all we was interested in was a bike, and I sure had a bike. Hand built, you know.' He

paused to reflect, with that glassy look of reminiscence.
'And do you know what happened to that bike, Phil? Some
God damn son of a bitch goes and steals it from right under
my very nose. We were in a bar and suddenly there was a
noise that was just so familiar to me, my bike being started.
Well, I ran out the door but it was too late: the guy was
riding out of sight. I was with my girlfriend at the time
and I tell you she loved that bike as much as I did. I tell
you if I ever caught the guy that stole my bike…well it just
wouldn't be right to tell you what I'd do to him.' Benny
paused for a while, screwing up his face with hatred,
imagining all the evil he'd inflict upon the guy that took
his bike. He looked at me.

'Best job I had though, Phil, was a "Bus Boy" in a
restaurant in Las Vegas'

'A waiter?'

'Not really, a "Bus Boy" is kind of different; just really
clears up the tables when the customers go and puts out
the cutlery and plates and things ready for the next person.
It was a really swell joint and we used to get all the stars in
there, I tell ya. Burt Reynolds used to visit all the time and
you know he used to chat to me and after a while we became
quite friendly.'

'Really?' I exclaimed.

'Yep. He used to tip good too, far as I remember.'

'Anyone else famous become a fan of yours then, Benny?'

'Well most of them kept themselves to themselves but
Victoria Principle used to sort of talk to me now and again,
you know.'

The conversation continued in a similar vein for the rest
of the day. As Benny and I were the only ones on site for
much of the day we took the opportunity to keep out of
the sun as much as possible and took long breaks with the
cold drinks that we periodically drove off to buy.

The Deer Hunter

On Friday Benny took the day off, so I was left following Danny around the site in the early part of the morning, inspecting work done and planning the schedule of work for the next few days. Later we were joined by Larry, who arrived in the 'Tonka' truck towing a trailer supporting the Bobcat. Here it was, the greatest building site 'toy' ever invented. It was basically a miniature chunky JCB. The bucket at the front was large in proportion to the rest of the vehicle and the driver in the enclosed cockpit could reach and touch it as it rested directly against the front of the machine. The arms of the bucket came back to be attached at the back, by the engine, as if it were hugging itself. Its low, sturdy look made it look like a rescue vehicle from Thunderbirds. Since my return to the UK I have seen these creatures everywhere, but this was my first experience of one.

The Bobcat was maneuvered using two joysticks, one in each hand, with each controlling the two wheels on that side. Pushing them forward set the machine off in a forward direction and pulling them back took you backwards. Since they were independent, one could be pushed forward and the other back turning the wheels in different directions and enabling the Bobcat to turn in its own length. The bucket was moved using floor pedals, raised or lowered using the right pedal and the bucket tipped using the left pedal. Larry undid the chains and drove it off the trailer; he moved the little machine as though he had been born in it.

'Managed to get it from Steve,' he said proudly as he jumped out of the front. 'You can use it here for a while before we take it to the school to finish up there.'

'Wow, it's really neat.' I wandered around it, spellbound. Larry got back in and drove the Bobcat to the back of the bungalows to clear a build-up of rubble; Danny and I followed. I was anxious to have a go at the controls, but

Larry was using it so efficiently that for anybody else to take the reins would be inefficient; the rubble was cleared in no time.

We took a break from the searing heat for lunch and returned to our usual 'film set diner' where we ate again burger and chips. Larry began talking about his family and homelife. He lived in Virginia (the state below South Carolina) and drove up all the way each Monday for the week's work.

'Why don't you live here in Highpoint, or closer at least?' I asked as we tucked into our greasy lunch.

'I like it down there. There is just the most fantastic scenery and I love goin' huntin' in the mountains. Besides my kids and wife are settled down there.'

'Why don't you work down there, then?'

'Well, there isn't the sort of work I want down there. There's not much in the way of building goin' on at the moment.'

Larry went on to talk about the love of his life, hunting.

'You ever been hunting, Phil?'

'No, can't say I have actually. I know quite a lot of people carry guns though over here so..'

'Well, I tell ya there's nothing like a good hunt. Tracking a deer and catching it to eat - and we don't always use a gun, I usually use a crossbow. I always take a gun though when I go with the kids, in case something goes wrong.'

'Do your kids like hunting?'

'Yeh, they love it. How would you like to come and stay with me for a weekend? We could go hunting.'

'Yeah, love to.'

'You could bring the friends you came over with as well.'

'That would be great.'

'I'll talk to the wife and one weekend you can come down.

'You know,' Larry started, 'once, I put a bolt right through a buck's eye, poor thing ran a mile half blind. I

had to catch it to finish it off, boy what a chase that was.'
Suddenly the burger in my mouth didn't taste that good.

'It's such a thrill, man, havin' a decent chase.' Larry reeled
off story after story. 'Another time I remember I started to
skin a deer and it started to move off on me, damn thing
wasn't dead.' Danny looked at me; he was feeling as ill as I
was.

'And another time...'

'Er, don't you think Larry that the huntin' stories can
wait till after we've had a bite to eat here?' Danny said.
Larry realised he had begun to get carried away and
apologised. Mark, Paul and I never did get to go hunting.

After lunch Larry moved on to work at another site
and left us with the Bobcat. Danny, who had obviously
driven the thing before, started using it to clear rubble
around the site, but could see how keen I was to have a go.
He stopped it and jumped out of the front.

'Go on then, Phil,' he shouted above the noise of the
Bobcat's engine, 'let's give you a go'. Fantastic. Life's too
short not to go completely mental in one of these things, I
thought. I climbed into the cage and strapped myself in. It
didn't take long to get used to steering with the two
joysticks and the pedals which controlled the bucket were
not that difficult either. Before long Danny left me to it,
motioning to me to clear the area of rubble while he talked
to the brickies at the other side of the site. I spent a couple
of hours clearing the area, knocking into the bungalows
from time to time when I became overeager.

Occasionally I got out to load the bucket by hand, as
some of the rubble was awkward to 'scoop' up, and a lot
was stuck in undergrowth on the fringes of the site amongst
the foliage. As I was loading the bucket on one such
occasion I lifted up an old plank, which had obviously
been in an area of weeds for quite a time. As I did so, a
snake, about three feet long, shot out. It moved like a flash
between my right leg and the plank of wood. I shouted in
shock and dived back into the cab of the Bobcat. I was
breathless with fright. The snake had darted into the

undergrowth and was now nowhere to be seen. Had it bitten me? I didn't think so; but if it had, and was deadly poisonous, I was for it. Danny was talking to a couple of electricians a short distance away as the incident took place and they all suddenly looked around when they heard my shout. Danny instantly realised what had happened and started to smile.

'What's up, Phil? Ya see a snake?' he called.

'Yeah,' I called from the cab. I was still in shock. Danny and the electricians started to laugh. I wasn't particularly frightened of snakes, but the incident had happened so quickly I would have been completely helpless if the snake had chosen to bite me and that shocked me. I had been warned about poisonous spiders and snakes when I first started to work on the site and I had, in fact, glimpsed a Black Widow spider when we moved some bricks one morning, but had thought no more about it. Danny and the others all walked over to try and find the snake in the undergrowth.

'He's well gone,' Danny said, after he had been poking around in the weeds for a while. 'That your first sighting, Phil?'

'Yeah, it was so unexpected.'

'Ain't nothing further from your mind than a snake when one appears; suckers frighten the hell out of me I tell ya,' said one of the electricians. Then there were the usual fun and games as the electricians threw pieces of rope at me and pretended they were snakes. I never lived that moment down, actually. Even guys on the site who I had never met before began asking if I wanted to see their snake collections, or whether I was in the market for any snakeskin boots that they could get hold of.

I remained in the Bobcat for the rest of the afternoon, struggling to scoop everything up with the bucket this time, lest the snake should reappear. Once almost bitten twice shy. So by the end of the day I was a real whizz with the Bobcat.

Backdraft

On the way back to Richard's apartment that evening, in Danny's fourteen thousand litre pick up, Danny told me of his trucking days. He had driven lorries for quite a while, it turned out, covering most of the States.

'I tell ya there were some real events out on the road there, Phil. Once we were in convoy in California and we all got a call on the CB from the back to check out the chick cruisin' our way in an open top Mustang. Well I tell ya I ain't seen nothing like it, she was wearing a little white number up top but nothing underneath; no skirt, no panties, nothing man, an' she was waving at us all as she passed by.' He paused to laugh out loud. 'I tell ya you could have heard the noise coming from those trucks about ten miles away: all blastin' their horns! I tell ya she was one pretty sight.

'Wow, did we have some times and see some sites.' Danny said, and then suddenly broke of his reminiscences.

'What's that there, Phil?' He pointed into a wood by the side of the wide road. Just by a fenced off area in the woods containing electricity equipment and pylons, smoke was rising out of the trees. We continued down the road a short while longer and looked into the trees as we passed. Danny suddenly did a U-turn and we drew up by the side of the road with a screech. Everybody else was looking at the smoke from their cars but nobody was stopping. We rushed from the truck into the trees. Just a few yards inside the bushes we saw that an area of the very dry vegetation had caught fire. The weather had been very hot all month and it hadn't rained in ages; bush fires were reported regularly on TV.

'We got a bush fire here, Phil! Quick!' We ran out back to the road and Danny looked hurridly around for perhaps a phone or some water. About a hundred yard away, further down the road, there was a row of builder's merchants tucked in from the road and easily missed if you didn't know they were there. Danny started running in their direction as I followed. Amazingly, one of the builder's merchants had a large hire shop attached which had various machines out on its large forecourt. As Danny and I ran quickly toward it I noticed that one of the machines on display on the forecourt was a Bobcat and I was sure that Danny had the same thoughts as me. Danny ran into the offices.

'I need to borrow your Bobcat.'

'Yes, what would...' Before the assistant had finished his sentence Danny asked for the keys and thrust forward his open palm.

'Well the keys are in it ..but...' Danny was out of the offices like a shot, chased by two assistants

'You can't just take it, sir!' one shouted after him. In the meantime I had grabbed a couple of shovels from just outside the office door. The two assistants had caught up with Danny and one stood stubbornly in front of the Bobcat, his arms raised, as if to say that there was no way Danny was going to take it without entering into a hire agreement. Danny had started up the machine and shouted to him.

'There's a bush fire you idiot!' He pointed toward where the smoke was rising profusely and the two assistants turned to look. Danny drove at the assistant in front of him, who had to literally dive out of the way, finishing up face down on the floor. I ran after Danny with the shovels.

'Call the bloody fire brigade!' Danny shouted back to the two bewildered assistants. When we reached the fire Danny started to clear an area of small trees and bushes in an attempt to contain the fire. I shovelled earth at a furious rate onto the flames but I was soon aware that the fire had crawled all around me like a pack of wolves circling before the kill. I panicked slightly and decided that as it was the first bush fire of my life, experience was not on my side. I threw earth onto a small area and raced out of flames. The fire was spreading at a frightening rate. I ran out of the undergrowth to get some air, passing Danny in the Bobcat who seemed to be doing well in creating a fire break. By now other cars had stopped - out of necessity, as the smoke lay across the road like a wall. I stood for a while on the edge of the wood, just being able to make out Danny as he beavered away in the Bobcat. It wasn't long before fire engines were audible in the distance. Danny was only just keeping it all at bay, their arrival would be in the nick of time.

The fire brigade instantly unloaded their equipment upon arrival and headed into the fire where Danny was still at work. He moved the Bobcat back to the roadside once they were there in numbers and we watched as they flooded the entire area with water. There were two fire engines and two large white cars with 'Fire Dept.' written on the side. Out from one of the cars stepped what looked like the senior fireman and he approached us for the full story and praised Danny and I for our work and quick thinking. He explained that such a fire spread at a frightening pace; he didn't need to tell me!

The two assistants from the hire shop were standing by the fire engines, anxiously looking out for the Bobcat. Danny had been anything but careful in his driving and bits of trees and shrubs hung from all areas of the vehicle, with the seating cage almost completely covered with branches. I saw them watching anxiously and smiled and they smiled painfully back.

The bright red fire engines were classic American beasts, just like they were in the movies: long, low, bright red, covered in spot lights with the front cab detached from the long trailer that it hauled. They were straight out of the Towering Inferno or Backdraft. The firefighters wore thick charcoal jackets and yellow helmets with gold badges on the front. Where was the Director, the camera? The senior fire officer had taken the place of Robert De Niro in Backdraft and the guy in charge of the engines could have been Steve McQueen. But as my gaze was drawn away from the fire engines and back to the woods, I somehow felt that I wasn't in this particular film, not even as an extra; the cameras had only begun rolling when the fire crews arrived. This time I was watching from the wings.

When the fire was well and truly out, the surrounding area dampened down and the hoses were being packed away Danny said, 'Well, I think we did our community bit for the day there, Phil.'

'I think we did more than our fair share,' I added. 'I was almost burnt alive in there.'

'Well I tell ya, you should never underestimate how quickly fire can spread and the damage it can do.' He paused. 'Perhaps if I'd been a bit more cautious and thinkin' a bit straighter we wouldn't have gone in there, Phil; just called the fire brigade.' As he was speaking the two hire shop assistants approached. They looked the Bobcat up and down and then looked us up and down. They couldn't complain: we were heroes. They took the shovels back and one of them jumped into the Bobcat to drive it back.

'Thanks!' Danny said cheekily.

'Let's hope that this doesn't happen too often,' said the chap with the shovels, with more than a hint of sarcasm. They left without another word.

'Quite a day, Phil, what with the accident we almost had back at the school and the fire.'

'Yeah,' I said as I got out in front of Richard's apartment. For the first time I realised how absolutely filthy I was; covered from head to foot with dust and mud from a hard day's work, overlayed with black charcoal from the fire.

'You make sure you don't turn up to work like that Monday morning,' Danny laughed.

'No, I won't.'

It was late and the others had all been back for some time and had showered; so when I stood in the doorway covered in every form of dirt they all looked in horror.

'What the hell have you been doing?' Richard asked.

'Yeah I'm one dirty puppy and it's a long story but I've been auditioning for Backdraft and doing my bit for the area.' I proceeded to relay the days events to them.

'Hey, might be on the local news,' said Mark.

'Think it's on at the cinema,' I said and went to get showered.

Saturday had come around again and that meant golf and shopping; well, golf and Budweiser. For the first time I was introduced to Steve and Brian - the two guys Mark and Paul were working with. I had heard various stories about each of them and they seemed to be just as characterful as my Danny and Benny. Steve was a likable guy who constantly cracked jokes. Brain, on the other hand, was extremely religious; he listened to the religious radio stations, spent his breaks at work reading the Bible and all his spare time converting non-believers. Apparently he had 'seen the light' after a spell at a rehab' centre for junkies and in the nick. He didn't talk much while we played golf, he left that to Steve.

Sunday was much the same. Roland, from the warehouse, had at last sobered up and managed to give his violent third wife the slip just long enough to play a quick round of golf. We hadn't seen him since leaving for Myrtle Beach but he hadn't changed, his conversation focused entirely on alcohol. It was a hot day and he managed to put away a six pack within the first nine holes.

Later we went swimming and then Richard asked us if we wanted to do a bit of an E.T. and phone home, as we hadn't been in contact with our parents since we first arrived about two months ago. We travelled to Richard's office at the warehouse to make the calls and we all felt guilty about the length of time it had been since we had spoken to our respective parents. I was happy to hear my parents' voices and to know that everything was as it had been when I had left. They were also relieved to hear from me; but I was reprimanded for not having called earlier, and for having burst my eardrum. The parental phrase 'I told you it would all end in tears', seemed appropriate.

'Amazing,' I said to Mark. 'If you had told me a year ago that a year from now I would be calling my parents from a phone in a furniture warehouse in the States having just played golf with an ex-con, I wouldn't have believed you. I didn't play golf then.'

'Fact is often stranger than fiction, Phil!'

We were early to bed on that Sunday. Paul had to work with Larry the next day and was due to be picked up at seven.

'Ohhh. That's it for you. No more larking around with Steve,' I said, that evening. 'Larry works really hard, you'll be lucky if you get away with a fourteen hour day.'

'Get off.'

'It's true,' added Mark. 'He's got a reputation for really hard work.'

'Yeah,' I continued. 'He lives in the mountains in Virginia and gets up at three on a Monday to get into work.'

'Yeah, and that's for the following week's work,' said Mark, raising a smile or two.

'But he does seriously have this reputation, Paul,' I said. Paul went to bed earlier than anyone but he needn't have as Larry didn't turn up the following day and Paul went to work with Mark as usual. For me, that Monday was the easiest of the most recent days I had spent on the site, as I was once again in the Bobcat. Benny hadn't been present when the Bobcat had first arrived and so hadn't yet driven it. But unlike me, he didn't have any wild desire to be let loose on it and was quite content to chat away, loading up rubble into the front bucket by hand, while I drove.

The site boss, Mark, was in high spirits that day. He had fully recovered from his wisdom teeth operation and seemed to now take every opportunity to take the mickey out of poor Benny. I assumed that this was how it had been before his operation. The banter started when we were all working in an area at the back of the site. Danny and I were relaying our fire fighting activities to Mark and Benny and the look on the assistants' faces as we fled with their Bobcat.

'Why weren't you there then, Benny?' asked Mark with a smile. Benny looked at him expecting some sort of rude comment. Mark didn't disappoint.

'You could have sat on the flames, Benny,' he said, 'and what with your size an' all, they would have been out in no time.' Danny and I were laughing. Poor old Benny was smiling and knew he was regularly ridiculed because of his size and slow ways.

'No, wait a minute,' continued Mark, 'that would have been disaster, Benny boy, there would have been an explosion, you're always fartin'!' Danny and I laughed and Mark almost died at his own joke. Benny stifled a laugh and continued to load the Bobcat pretending to ignore Mark's games. There was a pause while Mark recovered from his hysterics and gathered his thoughts before he began to wind Benny up once more.

'Moved into my new house just the other day, Benny.'

'That's nice for you, Mark,' said Benny. 'Hope it falls down.'

'Don't think so,' replied Mark, 'I was guaranteed that you didn't have any hand whatsoever in building it.' Mark folded up with laughter. 'Took me first shit in me new house as well, Ben,' Mark said after a while.

'Well, that also must have been nice for you, Mark. Just hope you left the john in the nice state you found it in, unlike you do here.' Benny was trying to get his own back. Mark was already laughing before he spoke.

'Well at least the place was still standing when I left it.' Danny laughed out loud.

'That were no fault of mine,' retorted Benny quickly.

'Did you here about that, Phil?' asked Mark. I shook my head.

'He went to the shitter one day; you know that cabin thing over there?' Mark pointed to the hut that contained the toilet, 'and the whole thing collapsed while he was in there!' Even Benny found it funny.

'It was a bad construction,' said Benny in his own defence.

'It was a bad smell,' said Mark, now crying with laughter.

Poor old Benny was regularly teased when Mark had nothing better to do and even when Mark did; but he seemed to take it well and laughed along with him most of the time.

Animal House

Following my confrontation with a snake I was now only too aware of the care that had to be taken around the site as far as wild animals were concerned. So when Danny told me to shift some planks later that had piled up in an overgrown area of the site, I took my time. In fact when Danny returned an hour later I had only moved ten planks.

'What ya been doin', Phil? Benny could have done better than you.'

'I'm just being cautious. These planks have been here quite a while and I thought that there was a good chance another snake or perhaps a Black Widow might be lurking somewhere, or...'

'Yeh, good point,' Danny agreed. 'Let's see what we've got under here then.' He started to turn over the planks with his heavy working boots. Some small spiders and lice crawled away from under each plank but there were no snakes. Danny continued turning over the planks. He was soon shifting them with his ungloved hands and chucking them to me, to be stacked. Rather you than me, I thought. Suddenly Danny leapt away from the pile of planks.

'Ahhhhhhhhh....!' he yelled, jumping away. He tripped over a plank and crashed to the ground. I was already half way across the building site. Danny got up, brushed himself off and then looked up to see me watching from some distance. He laughed.

'Hey, Phil, it ain't another snake.' I screwed up my face and smiled. A couple of the brickies were already calling out 'Snake charmer'. Danny turned back and cautiously approached the pile of wooded planks and I returned to see what he had found. Danny seemed to be studying something.

'Wow, you were right, Phil, take a look at this.' I approached slowly. In between two of the most rotten planks were four Black Widow spiders.

'I know every creature on God's earth has a right to live, Phil, but these little buggers can kill a man; they gotta' go.' With that Danny picked up a spade and started to whack the planks with all his might. Fearing one might be thrown out I stood well clear as Danny was bringing the spade down on the planks like a man possessed. All the Black Widows were soon squashed beyond all recognition and any others lurking must have been well and truly frightened off. Benny came over to see what we were doing and started laughing.

'You two ain't frightened of a few little spiders are ya?'

'Benny, I can tell ya if you was turning these planks, you'd have shit yourself!' answered Danny.

'Well I tell ya what, next scary job that comes along I'll do it on my own. What with Phil and snakes and you and spiders. I bet all the reptiles will be more scared of me than I am of them.' Danny stood up.

'Benny, I don't care what you say, these are scary little buggers.'

'Perhaps we'll get Mark on the job next time,' chuckled Benny. Benny would have loved to see Mark attacked by a whole family of Black Widows.

That day I returned late again to find no Paul and no Mark. Richard didn't know where they were either and so we went ahead and ordered pizza at the local Dominos. Paul and Mark eventually turned up at ten o'clock having been on the golf course for most of the evening with their bosses Steve and Brian. I was being attacked by snakes and Black Widows and they were playing golf.

'How come you end up with your job then, Phil'? asked Richard after we had heard about Mark and Paul's golf.

'Favouritism,' I replied sarcastically.

The next few days seemed to gel together. We all worked during the hot days and swam in the evenings. Our eating habits were again rapidly going downhill and we were all putting on weight. Having been careful about what we ate upon our return from Myrtle 'Toilet', we were now so hungry in the evenings we ate almost anything. Drinking beer didn't help much but we felt we had to do our American bit with the Budweisers. I put on over two stone while we were in the States.

Over those few days Paul began to get increasingly wound up by Brian. It seems he had been working closely with Brian and had received a severe earbashing about 'The Good Book' and the God Squad.

'I mean it's OK if somebody wants to spend their life devoted to the Church and praying during breaks and the like; you know each to his own. But it gets too much when they push it onto you all the time.' Paul's northern accent always came to the fore when he was annoyed.

'Is it that bad?' I asked.

'Is it that bad? It's worse.' Paul was laughing as he spoke. 'Go on, Mark, you tell him: Brian's always on about going to Bible classes and things, isn't he?' Mark nodded.

'Why don't you just tell him that you respect his right to do whatever he wants and that he should respect your right to do what you want as well?' I asked.

'I have. I've told him on a number of occasions. The trouble is I think he needs other people to join him, to justify what he's doing. He claims he "saw the light" after doing a stint in a drug rehab' centre. Well, I mean that shows you how unstable he is and how much he needs to cling to something.

'And now,' Paul continued, 'he's convinced that Mark and I are going to turn up to church this Sunday.' I started laughing.

'Are you going then?' I asked.

'I don't see how we can get out of it now.'

'Ah well, Paul, when in Highpoint...'

Benny was now in the habit of giving me a lift back from work as Danny had his son staying with him for a while. Benny's car was a small Chevrolet; too small a car for such a big bloke. It was predictably an absolute tip inside, with odd bits of crisps and sweets, pieces of paper and tools everywhere. I owed Benny some money (he had leant me some for lunch) and I gave it to him one evening. While he was putting the money away I couldn't help but notice his wallet glisten in the sun, almost as though it were made of silver.

'That's an impressive wallet, Benny'

'Ah, thanks, Phil. Made it myself ya know.'

'You made it yourself?'

'I've been makin' wallets now for over ten years and this one is the best I ever made. I make 'em for friends and anybody else that wants one. This one, if you brought it in a shop, would cost you close to four hundred dollars.'

'Four hundred dollars!'

'Yep, pretty stupid really because I never have that much in it,' he laughed. 'But its expensive 'cause its made out of different types of snake skin. Ya see all the different colours.' He passed it to me. It was extremely flash, and each different skin shone as it caught the bright sunlight.

'Could you make one for me, Benny?'

'Yeh, of course. You just have to pay for the skin of the animal you want, and then I'll sort out a pattern and fix you one up.'

'That would be cool, Ben, thanks.' But although I kept on at him over the weeks the lazy git never did make me a wallet.

The Friday of that week reached record temperatures. The weather channel on the telly didn't have a dark enough red to indicate how hot it would be. Consequently I felt pretty whacked and while I was sitting on a wall waiting for Benny to finish locking up, I looked at my hands. They were rock hard from all the digging and loading I had been doing over the weeks and covered in cuts and marks. My jeans were thick with mud and my upper body dirty and dark brown from having worked in the sun all day every day. It was a world away from my industrial placement work in the City of London. In fact I was in such a terrible state I would probably have been thrown out of a labourers' pub in London.

That Friday evening we all played 'Crazy Golf' with Steve, Mark and Paul's boss; we also met his wife. She was large and short, just like Steve. She was also pregnant and found even the small crazy golf course a bit of a strain. She was quite pretty and, like Steve, a funny, likable person. We would meet her again.

The week had been tough and we spent all Saturday afternoon by the pool. The weekends were the only time the pool even became remotely full, even then it was only with a few kids, but it was a great opportunity to relax. I couldn't participate in the serious action stunts that the other two were up to because of my ear. Any swimming I did was slow and deliberate, making sure my ear was kept dry; I wasn't even supposed to be swimming, but I would be doing a lot worse before our time in the States was over.

Tired of resting, we decided to do our Born Free bit and took an exhausting trip to the zoo on the Sunday. It was really more of a safari park than a zoo with walkways and paths leading from one area to another from where you could look out over large open spaces inhabited by a variety of different animals. Although there was no guarantee of a close look at a specific animal it seemed a much better way to keep animals, if it needs to be done at all, than to have them in cages. This philosophy managed to include Paul, who soon roamed off somewhere. One of the main paths through the zoo split into two, Richard, Mark and myself took one path and Paul took another, trying to catch up after taking photos of the zebra. We didn't really care where he was, he knew where the car was, and we continued our trip through the zoo. It was great to see the animals in open surroundings and a photograph from any angle would have anyone believing that it had ben taken in the bush in Kenya. The trip finished with us all reuniting back at the car at about the same time. It turned out that Paul had unwitingly been following only a few minutes behind us but had never quite caught up.

Radio Days

Benny had arranged to pick me up on the Monday morning to take me to work. He had to give the car to his wife during the day for the whole of the week and for some reason would be driving past Richard's apartment. Benny was usually at work early and thus picked me up at seven am. His wife was in the car with him and I was introduced to her for the first time. Benny's wife was huge; she must have been all of six foot three and looked as though she weighed about twenty stone. Benny's small car was hardly the perfect form of transport for the two of them; here was someone who really could have done with a gigantic pick-up. It fact the both of them were so large that sitting in the back of the small three door Mazda I could hardly see the windscreen. It was difficult not to smile at the comic situation that might easily have been a clip from a Steve Martin movie. Benny and his wife were an extremely happy couple though and laughed and joked with each other all the way to the site. The pair of them filled the front of the car so completely that I didn't dare watch when Benny started to grope for the handbrake.

When we arrived at work, Danny and Mark were already there discussing the day ahead. They had both been in early as there was much to do. I walked over to them, having thanked Benny and his wife for the lift and left Benny then to say goodbye. Mark and Danny were both grinning.

'She is one big woman ain't she, Phil?' Mark commented.

I looked back.

'She sure is!' Mark laughed.

'How on earth can Benny kiss her like that, Phil?'

'Well, maybe they love each other,' I said.

'You know I think I'd rather put my mouth around that waste disposal pipe over there,' said Mark, motioning to a pipe under a bungalow. The comment made the three of us laugh but it was cruel and it was a clue to the sort of day that poor Benny could expect.

'Hey, Benny, let's get on with things eh?' Mark called out. Benny watched his wife squeeze back into the car and gave her a little wave as she left.

'Jesus Christ, Benny, you'll see her this evening.' Benny walked over.

'Sort of cuts me up saying goodbye every day to her, ya know,' he said.

'Listen, Benny, if anyone needs cutting up it's her!' said Mark laughing. 'Now let's get to work.' Benny swore under his breath and Mark looked at me and winked, pleased he had wounded Benny so early in the day.

Later that morning I walked out into the bright sun from one of the bungalows to see Mark and Danny walking towards me.

'Come on, Phil, stop standing around in there and come with us, we've got some stuff to collect,' shouted Mark. 'Where's Benny?'

'He's in the toilet,' I answered with a smile and instantly regretted it: this was curtains for Benny. Mark grinned broadly and started to run toward the upright plastic cabin that housed the toilet. Danny and I walked on behind. Danny was shaking his head.

'God, those two are such kids; at each other all day, every day.' he said.

'You in there, Benny?' shouted Mark as he reached the cabin.

'Yeh, I ain't gonna be long,' came a muffled answer from inside.

'You watch what you're doin' in there now, Ben,' Mark called. 'We want the place to be standin' when you're finished.' Mark started to shake the plastic portaloo.

'Hey, what ya doin'? I swear, Mark, when I get out you're in real trouble.' The brickies and plasterers now looked over to see what the noise was and there was laughing from all around the site. Mark was now rocking the loo to and fro; it looked like it was about to fall over at any moment. Benny's shouts became ever more desperate.

'I swear if this thing falls over... ah... Mark, you son of a bitch!' We were all laughing quite loudly.

'Heh, Benny boy, you'd better get a move on,' called Mark. Suddenly Benny emerged and there was a cheer from the whole building site as he started chasing Mark. They ran round and round the big plastic toilet, much to the delight of the rest of the site workers who shouted encouragment. Eventually poor Benny ran out of breath and swore that he'd get his own back another time, but he had to suffer taunts for the rest of that day from Mark.

Benny picked me up again the following day. We had to get up even earlier as there was so much to do at work before the deadline. I was up at 5.45 and Benny arrived with his wife in his little car half an hour later. The dawn had not yet broken and it was freezing cold, which made a pleasant change. I had never known it so cold in all the time I had been in the States, but then again I hadn't been up before dawn before now.

We started digging trenches almost immediately we reached the site so that we could warm up and be able to make the most of the cooler weather before the sun rose and it became unbearably hot. As it was, we dug all day. The trenches had to be dug manually as there was not even enough room for the Bobcat to reach between some of the bungalows. It really was a tough day's work and my hands, although already hardened, were bleeding and blistered at the end of it.

During our morning break we had a delivery. Mark, Danny, Benny and I were all leaning against Danny's pick-up at the time. A large lorry drove onto the rough site with some wood and once it had stopped, out jumped the blackest bloke I had ever seen. He was literally as black as midnight. He walked over to us.

'Now, where can I find the foreman of this delightful building site, boys?' he asked.

'Right here,' said Mark and walked up to the guy to sign his delivery note. While he was away sorting out some confusion over the delivery, the lorry driver suddenly turned to me.

'Bet you ain't never seen anyone as black as me before has ya, boy?' he said, flashing his pure white teeth. I was rather taken aback but Benny saved me from talking.

'I have,' he said.

'You can't have, man, I just come back from holiday and I reckon I'm the blackest person in the U S of A.' He laughed.

'Hey man, you white boys wanna here some jokes?' he asked. I was struck dumb by this guys good nature toward everybody's colour.

'They had better be good,' said Danny, laughing.

'OK,' the driver said. 'What's the four worst words a white man can hear?' We were silent awaiting the punchline. 'I is the President!' We all laughed out loud.

'Hey, here's another for you, boys. There's this white guy and he's walking along the beach and he sees this lamp. Thinking it might be magic an' all he picks it up and rubs it, and makes a wish. After he made his wish he stops, looks down into his trousers and says "naah, that ain't no magic lamp" and throws the damn thing away. Anyhows he gets home and as soon as he's inside there's a knock on his front door. So he turns and opens it and there in front of him is this guy wearing a white hood and cloak and behind him are hundreds of other members of the Klu Klux Clan with burning crosses and the rest; an' this guy with the hood says "are you the son of a bitch who wants to be hung like a nigger?"'

I couldn't believe that this guy, undoubtedly the blackest guy I had ever seen, was telling racial jokes. I remember thinking how nice it would be if everybody in the world cared as little about colour as this guy did. We chatted a while longer until Mark eventually returned and informed the driver that he should drive further on into the site where the carpenters would help him unload. Mark was surprised by the cheery goodbye we gave the chap and we all returned to our tough digging work and blistered are hands further.

I thought we would get a rest the next day but the digging continued, only the location changed. We were back at the church school, scene of the near-disaster with the JCB. Larry was already there when we arrived, digging a trench with the Bobcat. (I never did find out why he didn't arrive for Paul that one morning.) Danny and I set to work with spades. Poor Benny was left at the bungalow site with Mark for the day, although I supposed that without an appreciative audience the ridicule might stop.

While we were at the church school Lenny arrived: the 'Big Cheese'. He was one of the joint owners of the company and looked exactly the same as all the other builders except that his checked shirt was new and clean, rather than covered in mud, and his pick-up truck was sparkling, rather than beaten and old.

Lenny had some work to discuss with Danny and they drove off to another site, leaving me to spend the rest of the day there with Larry. Oh no, I thought as they left, Larry 's reputation for working long hours might be true and he was my only way back to Highpoint. We worked hard, but at a steady pace, and managed to rectify the church school drainage problem completely. Larry kept things lively with his hunting stories and again invited me to the mountains for a hunting trip.

At the end of the day we cleared the site and loaded the Bobcat onto the trailer and towed it away with the 'Tonka' truck. This was my first ride in the truck and it was so big that the occupants had to use a ladder to get into the cab. It was essentially a dumper truck, and pulling the trailer with the Bobcat on was no easy task as the rear view was almost non-existent. The enormous truck had sixteen gears and as we left the site Larry had to reach third before the speedometer registered any sort of speed at all; however once we were going the mighty engine took us on quickly. It really was quite an awesome truck.

It was early when we left the church school and I thought I was going to get away with an early evening; but it wasn't to be the case. On the way back we took a road I didn't recognise. I looked at Larry out of the corner of my eye and thought that we were headed for another site to continue work. Oh no, the day's not over I thought. We drove on, taking a few turnings and with each the road became narrower. We finally turned down a small dirt track that had an old steel and wood mesh fence set back from the road on our right, with just a few houses scattered around on our left. Larry stopped in a siding by the fence and pointed.

'See in there, Phil? I've been watching this overgrown area for a while now, there's a whole pile of really decent wood behind the fence left there after they finished building a while ago, and nobody has come back to claim it. It's almost hidden in the undergrowth now. So I reckon I'll have it cause nobody else wants it.' He paused to open the door and then looked back at me. 'It's quite a few hundred dollars worth I reckon.' He jumped out of the high cab. I jumped out of my side and we unhitched the trailer with the Bobcat on and left it in the siding. Larry then got back in the cab and drove off for about twenty yards, leaving me standing by the fence wondering what he was up to. Then the reversing lights came on and the truck reversed straight for me. I literally dived out of the way and into some undergrowth.

'Mind out there, Phil!' Larry called from the cab. Bit late for that I thought. The truck continued back at greater and greater speed, passing the trailer with the Bobcat on, and smashed through the fence, crushing everything in its path. The air brakes came on with a loud hiss and Larry jumped from the cab.

'Shit, that made more noise than I thought it would,' he said. I stood dumbfounded. He had just demolished a strong metal and wood fence, - probably worth a lot more than the wood he was after. And his so called 'overgrown area' looked suspiciously like somebody's garden.

'Come on, Phil, somebody might have heard us.' I ran after Larry and we threw all the wood on the Bobcat trailer. I wasn't too worried about spiders and snakes. I figured I'd rather take my chances with them than with a fat, sweating, merciless, gun wielding cop from the local police station, answering an emergency call about ram-raiders crashing into somebody's garden. I was in no hurry to go to Alcatraz for this pile of wood, and worked hard to get the trailer loaded. The whole escapade only took about five minutes and there was a visible look of relief on Larry's face once we had finished. He jumped back into the cab and drove it back out onto the road. I waited by the trailer, constantly looking around to make sure nobody had come out of their house to find out what all the noise was about. I rapidly hitched up the heavy trailer, cutting my hands on the chains in the process, and ran up to the front of the truck, making a jump for the cab door as Larry began to drive off.

'Wow. That all went pretty smoothly, Phil.'

'Let's just hope we don't have to outrun the cops in this thing.' Larry laughed.

We took the wood to the house that Larry used during the week while working in Highpoint and left it in the back garden with what appeared to be about another ton of good quality timber; Larry had quite a store. By the time all the wood was unloaded, I was completely knackered and the adrenaline that had kept me going had ceased pumping. But the day didn't finish there.

'Thanks for helpin' us with the wood, Phil; I know its seven thirty already but we just have to make one more trip over to see Lenny, you know the guy who went off with Danny earlier, to drop off some keys.'

As befits the owner of a construction company Lenny's place was large. It stood on a smart housing estate; but not the sort of estate where your neighbour was sitting on top of you. Here your neighbour was just about visible on the horizon. It was a massive place. In the States there is so much land that everything is spread out that much more; and town planning seems to be the least of anybody's worries. If there isn't a spare acre for a house to be built on it's simply built further out where there is unlimited room.

Lenny's wife and daughters were outside the front of the house when we arrived, saying goodbye to somebody or other. The family were all very hospitable, too much so, and had me involved in another question and answer session, this time the subject was Princess Di. But I was eager to go after a thirteen hour day, most of which had been spent digging in 100 degree heat. It was a struggle making polite conversation for another thirty minutes and answering extremely open-ended questions such as, 'what is Europe like?' and 'do you think your Royalty are good for your country?'

I eventually got back to Richard's at eight thirty.

'Where have you been?' Mark asked.

'Well I haven't been playing golf,' I answered. 'If I mention the name Larry to you, you might get some sort of clue.'

'Well he does have this reputation for working long hours, Phil,' said Paul with a broad smile; so I jumped on him and started to fight him on the sofa.

'Well, Phil, we were waiting for you to get back 'cause we're off out to the cinema, when you've stopped messing around,' said Richard. I released Paul from my Hulk Hogan Death Grip.

'No, you lot go on.' I said. 'I'm shagged. Besides it will take me a while to get showered and things.'

'OK.' So the others left to see 'Nightmare on Elmstreet' part 3 and I crashed out in front of the T.V.

The last few days had been long and tough, so when I got to work the following day and discovered that Danny and Mark were off working somewhere else for the day, I was relieved, to say the least. Now Benny and I were 'unmanaged' we didn't miss the opportunity for an easier way of life and having spent the morning chatting and drinking Coke in the shade we left for an early lunch at eleven with the 'ZZ Top' plasterers. We returned just in time to do an hour's work in the afternoon. On the way to lunch I was quizzed for a second time since arriving at the site about Benny Hill.

'You have Benny Hill in England, don't ya, Phil?' one of the plasterers asked.

'Yes, he's English.'

'I just think he's the greatest. He's just so popular over here. Only thing is, he's on so late at night you have to stay up to see him. I tell ya, I don't know anybody that doesn't watch it over here, he's just the greatest.'

The easier day meant that I was able to join the others for a swim in the evening. I swam tentatively as my ear was still supposed to be kept dry, but it was such a relief to be able to cool down after another hot day.

Benny and his wife picked me up early again the following morning. The small car still hadn't been cleaned inside, in fact it had got worse. Benny and his wife were laughing and mucking around in the front as usual.

'Hey, Phil, you know what day it is today?' Benny asked.

'No.'

'It's my good lady wife's birthday.'

'Happy birthday!' I said as Benny's wife looked around expecting the greeting.

'Thank you, Phil.' The rest of the journey continued with the two of them lovingly fondling each other; but it was not until we were approaching the last turning before the site that the fun really started. On the radio, we all heard: 'and Benny would like to say a big happy birthday to his dear wife Rachael and say how much he loves her; so happy birthday to you Rachael from Benny and here's a record for you...' Benny's wife couldn't believe she had heard her name on the radio and that they were now playing a song for her, while I couldn't believe that things could get any more lovey dovey than they were already.

They couldn't and Benny's wife was so shocked that all she could do was hit Benny and laugh. With Benny's larger than life wife whacking him viciously for the remainder of the journey and him squealing with laughter, I myself was laughing wildly by the time we arrived at the site, unnoticed by the two lovers in front.

Die Hard

That day saw the return of the Bobcat to the site and I spent most of the day inside it, much to my delight. I became overconfident on several occasions, attempting to manoeuvre the machine and control the bucket all at the same time, often in a confined space. As a result, some of the bungalows at the back had strange looking marks in their brick work about five feet up the exterior walls before the day was over, and some of the steps were chipped.

As well as clearing various areas on the site, I was also moving rubble from one bungalow gully to another. A certain amount of broken brick was needed for drainage and had to be put into the gullies around the base of each bungalow. This task almost caused the extinction of the Bobcat. We had filled a number of these gullies and Danny was supposed to be guiding me as to how close I could get to each of the remaining bungalows in the Bobcat without the weight of the full bucket tipping it forward. We were struggling with a particularly awkward one, at the front of the site, where the approach was steeper than the others had previously been.

'Plenty of room there, Phil, come on,' shouted Danny above the noise of the Bobcat engine. I edged closer.

'What about the slope?' I shouted, pointing down.

'That's OK, just lift the bucket as you approach.'

'I can't any more; that's as far as it goes.'

'Well just keep bringing the Bobcat forward; it'll hold, come on now.' We were filling the gully of the bungalow next to where the brickies and a few plasterers were currently working.

'Danny, this is going to tip!' I shouted. The brickies started to look around to see what was going on.

'No, plenty of time yet,' Danny insisted.

'OK.' I continued to edge further forward with the bucket at about head height - as low as it would go without coming down onto the porch.

'Ahhhhhh!' Danny suddenly leapt for his life as the Bobcat tipped forward. My heart was in my mouth. I was leaning on the joysticks to stop me falling out of the caged cab. The Bobcat's bucket had crashed into one of the porch roof supports and the small roof came away from the main structure. Then the Bobcat, with its engine still revving, fell onto its side and down the slope into the gully. The brickies and plasterers were all staring in disbelief. Was this Bobcat driver intent on destroying the whole site? Danny was on his feet now and rushed to hold the porch roof up with Benny. A couple of plasterers threw down their tools and ran to help and put a couple of planks of wood under the porch to relieve Danny and Benny of the tremendous weight. Meanwhile I was crawling from the cab of the Bobcat, which now lay on its side in the gully, its engine still revving.

'What the fuck ya doin', Phil?' shouted Benny.

'What do you mean, it was me who didn't want to go any further,' I shouted back, defensively.

'My fault, my fault,' admitted Danny before Benny and I had a chance to get into an argument. Benny turned to Danny.

'Well what the fuck are you doin' then?' Benny laughed. Realising that it was only a porch roof that had come away and that nobody was injured, the two plasterers that had supported the roof with planks started laughing.

'God, if Mark were here this would be your job, Danny,' one said. Danny didn't laugh; this was serious damage and it was indeed fortunate that Mark wasn't around to witness the Bobcat's incredible demolition potential, but we had to tell him as a new support for the porch roof was needed. We used the brickies large fork-lift to right the Bobcat and tow it out of the gully. The cage was dented on one side but beyond that it seemed to be unharmed. During all the commotion I hadn't given a thought to my own safety and neither had anyone else, come to that. Getting an arm or a leg caught as the Bobcat turned over would have done some serious damage.

The tipping of the Bobcat made me a star on the site, above and beyond the recognition I gained for my snake charming abilities. As with that incident, guys I had never met before came up and made comments such as, 'Heard you tipped the Bobcat, Phil, have to teach me how to do that some time!' Even Larry, working miles away at another site, got to hear about it and when he next saw me he asked if I knew the price of a new Bobcat.

That afternoon Benny and I set about building a fire. Rotting wood and general rubbish from around the site needed to be burnt and. Our fire raged for the rest of the day with everything we burnt having been in the hot sun and consequently dry as tinder. In fact the fire was so successful I was soon having problems finding things to keep it fed. It had a massive, insatiable appetite. Benny had left long ago to talk to Danny about having some time off. It was left to me to keep the fire going. Benny returned, running.

'Oh shit, Phil, oh shit!' Benny was laughing.

'What's wrong?'

'Well, Danny asked how the fire was goin' an' I said we was havin' trouble keepin' it fed. Then we sort of got talkin' about when we were going to start pouring concrete into the porches. Danny said he hoped next week some time but he had just been to look for the wooden supports he had made for the job and couldn't find 'em.' He paused and laughed a little. 'He didn't link the two conversations. I think we burnt the supports he made, Phil, trying to keep this fire fed!'

'Oh shit?' I said with a smile.

'I think Danny might be on his way over to ask you if you've shifted 'em somewhere. Just say you ain't seen 'em.'

'Yeah, I will. Tipping the Bobcat and burning some carefully constructed handmade supports all in one day isn't very impressive.' Benny and I continued to mess around with the large fire, pretending not to notice Danny as eventually he walked over to us to ask the anticipated question. Benny was standing on the other side of the fire and peered through the flames as Danny approached, as though he were hiding.

'Hey, Phil, you seen those wooden supports I built a couple of days ago?' Danny asked. 'The long ones for the porches.'

'Er...no.'

'You didn't move them at all while we were doin' the gullies earlier?'

'No, I don't think so.' Danny fortunately didn't think that anybody would be as stupid as to mistake his supports for firewood.

'Bet those carpenters took 'em.' He said. 'Got to watch those boys, when they see wood around the site they assume it's theirs; they've probably made them into chairs or something by now.'

'Yeah, probably, Danny.' I said. Danny walked off. Benny smiled at me through the flames. I smiled back; it was him who had brought the supports over to burn; he really was stupid.

We tended the fire for another hour or so and did some more digging late in the afternoon with Mark turning up to supervise. Having dug the pipes up at the church school, he didn't want to have to dig these pipes up again. Mark was around and had an audience he couldn't resist winding Benny up.

'Say Benny, how's that good lady wife of yours?' he asked.

'She's fine, thank you, Mark,' he answered slowly, half expecting a nasty comment.

'I was thinking maybe you and your good wife might want to come over and have dinner with me and my wife.'

'Well that would be...'

'And then I thought again and realised that we couldn't afford the food bill!' Mark added quickly and started laughing. As with all Mark's comments it was witty but nasty.

'What is it with you, you God damn asshole?' Benny shouted. He threw down his shovel and started to walk away across the site.

'Hey, Benny man, only jokin'. Hey, Benny come back,' Mark called. Mark's done it this time, I thought. I couldn't blame Benny for walking off.

Benny turned around with a smile on his face

'I sure scared the God damn shit out of ya there didn't I, Mark?' Mark and I started laughing. Benny had got his own back just for once but he was no match for Mark. Benny returned, but it didn't take long for Mark to get bored and start teasing him again.

Psycho

That weekend Paul, Mark and I were all in high spirits; we only had one week left to work. We swam and played tennis for most of the weekend. On Saturday evening Steve - Mark and Paul's boss - invited us all over to play cards and have a bite to eat. I had met Steve and his pregnant wife previously at the crazy golf course and their jokes and good humour hadn't diminished any. They lived in a neat little house on the edge of a wooded area and were great hosts. Steve told us a bit about the MG we had seen outside and the endless bills he had to pay to simply keep it on the road. He said it would have been cheaper to have started from scratch and built the car himself with new parts, such was the cost. His wife concurred and we could see that it had been a sore point in the past.

We all sat in the lounge and chatted until supper was ready. On our way into the dinning room, annexed to the kitchen, we nearly tripped over the cat and it proceeded to become the topic of conversation. The cat was really quite beautiful, pure white with big blue eyes and very fluffy. Steve told us that it had been kept inside all its life (a cat litter was neatly hidden in the corner). Its claws had been removed and it had been house trained at an early age to make it the perfect indoor pet. Steve then told us of the other pets that he had.

'We've a horse, couple of goldfish, a bird and about fifty other cats.'

'Fifty other cats?' Mark exclaimed. We all looked around in search of this wild number of cats. 'Where are they all then?'

'We keep them in a barn that we own.'

'Do you breed them then?'

'No, not specifically. We just sort of keep them really, and let them do what they want in the barn; they look after themselves.'

'Do you feed them?' Richard asked.

'Yes we do; and it's expensive.' There was a pause, then Steve said, 'but we keep the numbers down so it doesn't get out of hand. We just love cats.'

'How do you keep the numbers down then?' asked Richard, 'Do you sell them or something?'

'No, we shoot them.'

'You shoot them?'

'Yeh. When there's too many I just go out to the barn with a shotgun and shoot a couple and bury them.' We all stared at Steve in disbelief. Was this the same happy fat chap we had got to know, who would have trouble saying 'boo' to a goose? 'They sure know when it's comin' too,' Steve continued. 'They scatter around that barn like crazy.' We couldn't believe the way the conversation was going. Was Steve in fact a crazed psychopath who was as nice as pie during the day but a mass serial killer at night? Had we been invited to supper, or were we the supper? Was this yet another movie set? A horror movie in which we were the unwitting cast. Being on the edge of the wood the film The Shining sprung to mind.

'Isn't it slightly hypocritical to say you're cat lovers and then once in a while blast a few to death with a shotgun?' Richard asked slowly and thoughtfully. We all laughed waiting for Steve's answer.

'I suppose so. But we keep 'em an' feed 'em and most of 'em have a pretty good life. Besides if we didn't keep the population down, there wouldn't be enough food to go around.' We saw his point of view, but it did seem slightly harsh on the poor old cats.

A spread of food like no other was laid before us that evening. There was so much that we initially wondered whether there were any other guests joining us. The meal was immense, they had overestimated our appetite on a grand scale, but we all ate well having spent the day outside swimming and playing tennis. For dessert we were offered large wedges of chocolate cake. We ate a thin slither each, as it was all we could manage. Steve and his wife were concerned that we weren't eating properly.

'What's wrong, don't you like the food?' Steve asked.

'No it's great thanks, Steve, but I think we're all absolutely stuffed.' I said. We all smiled at Steve's wife. But Steve was convinced that we didn't like his home made chocolate cake. He made his way to the freezer.

'Got some other things in the freezer here you can have if you fancy something else. We've got er...'

'No honestly, Steve that was great, I just don't think we can eat any more,' Mark said.

'Even got some budgie here,' he said taking a small plastic bag out of the freezer. He smiled at us.

'What? Some budgie?'

'Yes. We only got that bird you see there quite recently,' he said, pointing to a budgerigar in a cage in the corner of the room. 'We used to have a budgie that we were very fond of and when it died we decided to freeze it and keep him around.'

'Ahhhheeeeee!' exclaimed Mark. We all looked at each other agog.

'It probably seems a pretty strange thing to do, but he's not doin' any harm in there so we'll probably keep him a while yet,' said Steve, still holding the plastic bag aloft. He smiled broadly. 'Just gotta make sure we don't eat him by accident!' We all laughed; we had heard of pet cemeteries, but keeping an animal in the freezer was in a different league.

After a cautiously-sipped cup of coffee we all settled down in the lounge to play cards and then chatted until about two in the morning. We were offered food throughout our card session, but left Steve and his wife to polish off the remaining three quarters of the chocolate cake.

When it came to leaving we all stroked the beautiful cat and were fed some more info on the perfect house pet.

'And to stop the cat causing any damage due to sexual problems, we had it castrated,' said Steve.

'You didn't do it with a shotgun did you?' joked Mark and we all laughed. But Steve joked back,

'No we didn't, but we've kept the cat's balls, they're in the freezer with the budgie!'

On the Sunday we were again entertained. An English lady Sarah, who occasionally catered for exhibitions run by Richard's company, had invited us over for a Bar-B-Q lunch. We would be leaving just after Paul and Mark had come back from church. They had relented to keep 'Bible Brian' happy and they came back with some amazing stories about the church and its wealth. Apparently the whole of the floor of the church was covered in a thick blue luxury carpet and rather than the vicar talking through a small microphone to his congregation, the church was blessed - if that's the right phrase - with a complete sound system, thousands of dollars of top of the range electronic wizardry. I reminded Mark and Paul of the bungalows I was building and how they would still remain the property of the Church, even after they had been sold to elderly couples; but Paul topped all the stories about the immorality of the Church by telling us that apparently the former preacher for the area and the chap whose church they had just been to, had left over ten million dollars in his will, but that not a cent of it had been left to the Church. There appeared to be an unlimited number of worrying stories about the Church, both in our local area and in the country as a whole, some, or perhaps all of which may have been true. But there are two sides to everything and most of the stories we had head had come from those who hadn't attended Church, and didn't look as though they would even make an attempt.

We eventually made it over to the Bar-B-Q at Sarah's that afternoon and had a great time. There were about fifteen people there in all but Mark, Paul and I spent most of the afternoon chatting up Sarah's sixteen-year old daughter. On the way there Richard had informed us that the father had apparently run off with a twenty year old tart while they had been in the States, so we didn't enquire about his absence. Sarah's daughter was English like her mother but now fully settled in the States and was really quite beautiful with long blonde hair and a friendly personality. None of us were very successful in our attempts to charm her as we spent most of the time making her laugh by ripping each other to pieces with witty comments. Within a short space of time each of our characters were in tatters, giving the impression that not a decent word could be said about any of us. When we left we blamed each other for our unsuccessful efforts but finally decided chauvenistically that she must have been a lesbian.

The next day should have been a work day - Monday - but it was in fact a national holiday, Labour Day. The holiday is always in September and marks the end of summer and the school holidays. Anyone who had showed the slightest interest in hiring us in Myrtle Beach had wanted us to work through Labor Day and beyond. All the American college kids would have to think about classes for the new term and would leave holes in the vacational employment market. Here in Highpoint, however, we could spend Labour Day relaxing by the pool and watching the Canadian Open golf on TV. Looking back, we probably should have made more constructive use of our days off; taken trips to local areas of interest etc., but we were just so tired after working on the building sites that we spent all our free time resting.

Benny's wife no longer needed the car during the day and this meant that Benny didn't need to collect me at such an ungodly hour on the Tuesday morning. Work didn't seem the chore it had done over the previous week; probably because these were my last few days on the site and the thought of a few weeks' holidaying did me the power of good. I drove the Bobcat most of the day, always looking for an excuse to use it. I was soon at the stage of simply using it as transportation from one side of the site to the other - it made a change from walking in the heat. As it had been a long weekend, everybody on the site seemed to be lethargic that day; but even Danny, who usually cracked the whip over Benny and I in Mark's absence, took an unusual number of breaks and trips to the local 'Circle K' to buy Coke.

Psycho II

The following morning 'Bible Brian' kindly gave me a lift
to work. Benny was no longer passing by the apartment
on his way to work and Paul and Mark said Brian would
oblige rather than cause Richard any hassle in having to
take me to the site at awkward times. He turned up first
thing in the morning in a green, beaten up old Ford saloon
with literally hundreds of religious stickers plastered all
over it, saying such things as 'Thank God for Jesus', and
'God is the Light of The World'. As the car swung into
the apartment complex, with the radio blaring out hymns,
Paul looked at me.

'Told you,' he said with a broad smile. Brian jumped
out, greeted Mark and Paul and shook my hand
enthusiastically. From the inside, the vast array of religious
stickers covered the rear window, almost completely
blocking out the sun. The radio was turned up as we drove
off, to make sure we felt the full impact of the stirring
hymns. We drove a little way before the hymns suddenly
stopped and the religious station began discussing the finer
points of the gospel of St. Luke. Again the radio was turned
up for fear that this may be our last chance to 'see the
light'. We all remained silent in the car until we stopped at
a petrol station where Brian got out to fill up. Paul turned
down the radio and turned to look at Mark and I sitting in
the back.

'You see what I mean, Phil?' he said shaking his head,
'This guy is a complete and utter fruit.' Mark and I laughed
but Paul was taking it seriously. 'I tell ya if you show him
you're just the slightest bit interested in religion he'll have
you in that church before you can say God Squad.'

Brian got back in the car after filling up and buying some
gum and we drove in silence along the wide roads to my
site. I thanked Brian for the lift and then smiled at Paul; he
was looking toward me and away from Brian and he rolled
his eyes in despair as they drove off causing me to start

laughing. Mark didn't turn around in the back but just made the motion of strangling himself as they drove away. They both had a full day of worshipping to look forward to.

Danny and Benny were already hard at work by the time I arrived. As we were so near completion, we would be spending the next two days clearing up - which meant more Bobcat driving and more fires - and also completely waterproofing the gullies that almost cost the Bobcat and myself our lives. The first I knew about it was the appearance of Danny and Benny from the tool trailer, wearing blue overalls and protective orange gloves. They walked over to me with mine and told me to put them on.

'We'll be using some pretty nasty stuff for this waterproofing lark,' said Danny, 'you'd better stick these on.' I took the blue overalls and orange gloves and then, for the first time noticed what a comic pair Danny and Benny looked standing before me. Benny was, as ever, still wearing his red baseball cap and kept a stony expression as he stood in front of me and watched Danny give me my gear.

'What do you look like, Benny?' I laughed.

'You shut your mouth, Phil, you'll be wearing this shit as well.' he said.

'Yeh, does look sort of stupid with those orange gloves an' all don't he?' exclaimed Danny, looking at Benny with a smile.

'Well you look just as stupid, Danny,' Benny said.

'No I don't.'

'Yes ya do.' There then ensued an argument about who looked worst, which eventually turned into an argument about who was the best looking, and thus into an argument about who could pull the most women, and who had had the most women.

We were waterproofing with a black tar-like substance which stank to high heaven and was as thick as treacle. Danny was mixing and stirring, while Benny was down in one of the gullies preparing the area. Mark had been preparing an area to be treated since first thing that morning, but was now sitting out of the sun - as usual - and watching the rest of us work.

'Don't you get any of that black stuff on your face now Benny,' he called out, 'cause with your beard and baseball cap we won't be able to see who ya are.'

'Well, if I did get this black stuff on my face and you didn't know who I was, then maybe I'd get treated a bit better by ya, than I do at the moment; couldn't get treated much worse,' Benny called up to Mark.

'Ya could, Benny, I might think you were a nigger.'

Mark howled with laughter at his own joke and Danny and I smiled. Benny managed a wry smile but as before, the teasing was starting to get to him. That joke of Mark's was, in fact, the first racist joke I had heard from a white person all the time that I had been in the States. I had forgotten the stories that Charlie had told me about racism in the south, while we were working at the furniture warehouse. He had said that the Klu Klux Klan were still very much in evidence in certain areas and that venturing into certain counties in certain states was asking for trouble. But if there had been racism in North Carolina, or in the area in which we were working, it must have been underground. I suppose not being black it was difficult for me to judge; it might have been around every corner.

During the day we of course managed to cover ourselves in the thick black tar-like substance and Benny somehow managed to get some on his face. While we were working, Mark became bored with teasing Benny and started to ask me questions about where I lived what I did in my spare time etc. Danny and Benny joined in as well. I had been working with all three of them now for almost two months and they probably realised that they didn't really know that much about me. As this was my penultimate day they decided they'd like to know a bit more about Europe and about England before I left. They were intrigued to hear that a lot of people in England travelled to other countries for summer holidays. Like those who worked at the furniture warehouse, they had rarely travelled out of the State. I also told them that I had spent the last year working in a bank, in The City in London, which was the equivalent of their Wall Street.

'Jesus, Phil!' exclaimed Mark; 'six months ago you were working in a bank in London, and now you're in a ditch, waterproofing the side of a bungalow with Benny. You have truly worked at the two extremes of life.' While we were all laughing, Benny flicked some black tar at Mark.

'Hey you stop that, Benny, you God damn maniac.' Mark got up from the porch shade, where he had been sitting and started to run off.

'Hey, look Danny, look Phil, we managed to get him up off his arse at last!' Benny laughed. Poor old Benny though, once again, didn't get the last laugh; in his excitement he stepped back into the narrow gully and lost his balance falling over a large tin of the black tar and managed to spill it all over the sand floor of the gully. He toppled further backwards and ended up sitting in a mess of black 'treacle'. Benny was now hidden from Mark's view but Mark came running back to stand and almost cry with laughter at Benny's escapades. On top of this Danny started hitting Benny over the head with his baseball cap for spilling all the black stuff he had spent time mixing. So there was poor Benny sitting in 'treacle' wearing blue overalls and orange gloves, being hit over the head with a baseball cap by Danny, who was also similarly dressed. It really was Laurel and Hardy or a scene from a John Candy movie. Mark was proud of the fact that he had been responsible for the incident and spent the entire day telling the rest of the site about it. Benny smiled about it all, happy to be the centre of attention.

We had succeeded in getting more tar on ourselves than on any bungalow gullies that morning but left the areas we had actually managed to cover to dry in the afternoon sun. The fire had been going all the while and we continued to feed it with further rubbish from the day's work. Danny and I took our overalls off as soon as Mark had said that we should leave the area to dry; it was hot in the overalls and a relief to get rid of them. However when the word had come from Mark to finish in the gullies Benny had been in the tool trailer and hadn't taken his overalls off. This was to provide even more fun for Mark - and the rest of us on the site - a while later.

We had all been clearing up the site, with the aid of the Bobcat, and we were all standing around the brightly burning fire. Even though it was almost the end of the day, Mark was still charged with energy and in high spirits from the earlier incident and he began playing around with the fire. Benny meanwhile was daydreaming, standing by the fire with the rest of us, but looking away, staring at nothing in particular. While Benny was in this semi-conscious state, Mark pulled out a piece of lighted wood, circled around the fire and approached Benny slowly and silently from behind. Desperately trying to restrain his laughter, he held the burning piece of wood under Benny's black tar-covered backside. It caught light almost instantly. Benny turned quickly and immediately realised what was happening.

'Ahhhhhh! Mark, you fuckin' crazy son of a bitch,' he cried as he jumped up away from the burning wood; but it was too late and he looked down at his backside and saw that it was on fire. He screamed at the top of his voice and raced across the building site, half running, half jumping toward the water hose, with smoke and flames coming from his overalls. Mark collapsed with laughter and Danny, who only ever really smiled at Mark's pranks, now started to laugh as well at the sight of Benny hopping and jumping across the site. I was laughing aloud myself as were most of the brickies and plasterers that had been fortunate to witness the comic capers. It was a comedy classic.

Benny managed to reach the waterhose, turn it on and extinguish his backside, covering it in water. He wasn't hurt at all, as it was only the tar that was burning and not his overalls or anything more. To finish the scene, Benny shook his fist at Mark from across the site, much to the delight of a cheering workmen on the site. He stood by the hose for about five minutes, soaking the back of his overalls and with a look of comic relief on his face and when he returned he explained that his wife would want to know how he had burnt his backside, but worse than that, 'I won't be able to take a shit for three weeks!' He promised a laughing Mark that he would get his own back one day and smiled. Mark laughed for the rest of that day and almost had to be driven home he was in such a state!

Romancing The Stone

During the evening Richard, Paul, Mark and myself all went out to a Japanese restaurant in Greensborough. We were treated to a display of 'food throwing'. We all sat around a large, flat, metal hot plate with about eight others and watched as our orders were individually prepared and cooked at lightening speed by Japanese chefs. Fish, meat and vegetables were all thrown to their separate little areas to cook. While we waited the chef further entertained us with an over the top display of salt and pepper cellar throwing, knife juggling and meat chopping. But not everyone seated around the silver cooking area was interested in the display and two in particular were a couple of men sat at one corner of the hot plate talking in a serious tone about business.

The chef assumed that everybody had come to watch him perform and smiled when gasps of admiration came from around the hot plate. But the two chaps in the corner were not in the least impressed and when it came to serving up the food they simply kept on chatting. The chef was now flipping all the food around and throwing various items onto each plate. While he was doing this he accidentally threw a prawn at one of the two men chatting. The prawn hit him on the chin and fell back on the hot plate. Everybody seated around the hotplate looked toward the chap with a smile, thinking it was all good fun, but the man's expression remained sour and he looked the chef up and down, as if to say 'is all that crap really necessary?'. I thought it was quite funny, but the chef's smiling face gave me the impression that if he wasn't careful one of his chopping knifes would find its way into somewhere painful.

Having enjoyed ourselves at Sarah's barbeque, Richard had arranged that the four of us meet Sarah and a friend of hers for a drink after we had finished at the Japanese restaurant. Richard said that there were various bars we could visit and perhaps we could move on to a night club.

We were all for it and so before we had left to go out that evening we had searched hard to find a pair of jeans that weren't mud covered from site work or ripped beyond repair. We met Sarah and her friend Mel - who we had been intrduced to at the barbeque - at a bar and sank a decent amount of Budweiser; apart from Richard who was driving. We were happy puppies by the time Richard suggested we all venture on to a night club. We hadn't been able to go completely crazy while we had been over in the States and so we were looking forward to dancing until four in the morning and chatting up some American chicks.

We journeyed out to a night club called Trips, which apparently was pretty cool. As we approached the entrance though we noticed two things, firstly that everyone entering was considerably better dressed than any of us and secondly those that didn't posses identification were being turned away. The six of us walked up to the door and smiled at the two gorillas guarding it. A huge hand was put flat against my chest as we attempted to saunter past.

'You got any I.D., son?' There was a pause as I considered a smart response but Sarah and her friend instantly said that none of us had I.D. as we were from England and assured the bouncer that we were over twenty-one, the minimum drinking age in the State.

'Sorry, no I.D., no entrance,' said the gorilla. 'You two ladies can go in but these wise guys can't.'

'Look, we're all together, we won't be any problem and these guys are all over twenty-one,' Sarah's friend pleaded. But they didn't give way.

'Anyway, even if they had I.D. we wouldn't let them in looking like that,' one added. 'They look like a bunch of beach bums.' Richard was tired by now and couldn't be bothered to argue and suggested we all wend our way. Paul, Mark and I were disappointed, but we did look like beach bums, with our deep tans and scraggy shirts. We all made

our way to the cars in the warm night air; Sarah and her
friend Mel had come in a car each and as we approached
the cars in the large open car park Sarah and Mel called
goodbye and went on to their respective cars. Sarah then,
having unlocked her car looked back and said, 'Phil, you
want to come with me?' I suddenly slowed down my
walking pace and came to a stop. I looked at the others;
they gave me the briefest of smiles and continued on to
Richard's Golf. I didn't really need asking a second time.
This sort of thing only happens in the movies, I thought. I
looked at Sarah for a while and for the first time noticed
what she was wearing, noticed her features and her beautiful
smile. She was standing by the open door of her car and
had such a relaxed manner that I instantly felt as though I
had known her for years. I walked over to the car and got
in without a word; she started up the car and we headed
out of the large open car park and onto the road leading
directly out of Highpoint.

It felt great to just drive off and feel as though I was
completely letting go for the evening. Amazingly we talked
quite a lot on the journey, both happy to chat about
anything; and the new surroundings of the car and her
voice made a refreshing change as we drove toward her
house. It was eerily quiet when we arrived and as she closed
the front door of her house behind me she motioned to
keep quiet as her daughter was asleep upstairs. The open
lounge area was illuminated by one table lamp which gave
a warm feeling to the house. The whole character of the
house had changed from the lively atmosphere that I had
witnessed when we all attended the barbeque there. No
longer was it brightly lit by the sun's daytime rays, vibrant
with the sounds of chatter. Now it was like a house in the
country in England, softly lit and homely.

I followed Sarah into the kitchen. She instantly headed
for the fridge and opened it quietly. The light came on and
lit her body and features against the dark. She was wearing
a blue skirt and light silk blouse. She pulled a bottle of

white wine from the fridge and smiled, commenting that she thought it would be a good idea to start drinking it. We moved to the softly lit lounge and sat on the sofa, talking quietly and drinking the cold white wine. I was happy to let her invite me back and take the lead role, it created such an easy atmosphere. I didn't feel as though I needed any carefully constructed conversational lines, or to try and impress her; I didn't feel that I needed to worry about how far I could take things or about any of the usual hurdles that frustrate couples trying to get to know each other. We both knew where we were headed. With the wine only a third finished we quietly went upstairs.

Before I knew it it was morning and I had to be at work for seven. I felt like staying at Sarah's all day but that day was my last on the site and I couldn't just miss it. We were up at five so that I could return to the apartment and get ready, and were in the kitchen when Sarah's daughter came down for breakfast. She was just as pretty as I had remembered, with beautiful long blond hair and bright blue eyes; all of it real natural beauty. But she seemed a lot younger than I had remembered. When we had first met her she I would have put her age at anything between sixteen and twenty-three! But seeing her in her home environment again made me realise how naive and young she was, talking about her school and how much she enjoyed her time there. I had been doing my hardest to charm her a few days previously and when she appeared that morning I was aware of how much mental difference there was between us. I obviously had more in common with her mother now. Just like Dustin Hoffman in The Graduate. The daughter had initially caught all my attention. But it was Sarah, her mother, who had invited me back that night and who I had gotten to know. It was Sarah who had taken the leading role...'Are you trying to seduce me, Mrs Robinson?'

So Mrs Sarah Robinson drove me back to Highpoint that morning with 'Graduate' thoughts filling my mind.

They were briefly interrupted, though, as we entered Highpoint. The large smart brick wall that had 'Highpoint' in large white letters on it, lay in rubble. Someone had obviously driven into it during the night, judging by the long black tyre marks in the road and two parallel tyre tracks on the grass up to the wall. Whether they had been sober or not was not an issue!

When we finally arrived outside Richard's appartment I told Sarah of our planned trips on from North Carolina but said that we would be back in a few weeks before we left and I would see her again. The guys greeted me with a sheepish grin when I returned. Paul and Mark didn't know how to respond and waited for Richard's reaction after my Brief Encouter with a friend and business associate. He sarcastically asked me if I had had a good time and I knew that my actions weren't completely condoned; but the others thought I had done my bit for England and badgered me for the details.

Shadowlands

I was quite sad at the prospect of leaving the guys on the site; Danny and Benny were sad that I would be leaving as well. On this last day we continued waterproofing the bungalows with the black tar and made sure that the roaring fire had consumed all the trash there was around the site. On the Monday they would be thinking about the interiors of the bungalows and the final touches to the outsides; soon they would be finished.

The work was interrupted on that last day by a comment from Danny that he had managed to secure the deal of a lifetime. He had bought about a hundred Playboy magazines from a friend which stretched back over the last eight years or so, for 'almost nothing'.

'God damn man, what a deal,' exclaimed Benny as he stood up, in his overalls, in a bungalow gully.

'Tell your friend that he could have sold 'em to Benny at twice the price,' said Mark with a laugh. 'See old Benny wake up when you mentioned those magazines,' he continued. Benny ignored Mark and asked Danny where they were.

'Got them in the back of the truck right now, but...' Before he had finished, Benny had leapt out of the gully and was running across the dusty site heading for Danny's pick-up. Mark and I started laughing.

'What would your good lady wife say then, Benny, if she knew you were looking at those magazines?' Mark shouted. 'Bet ya don't find a picture of her in there, Benny boy.' Benny looked around at Mark as he ran, pretending to be annoyed at the comment; Benny reached the truck but found it was locked.

'If you'd let me continue,' called Danny, 'I would have told you that it's locked. You can see 'em at lunch time.' So that's precisely how Benny spent his lunch hour, and most of that afternoon. By the time Mark was rushing off to his new house that afternoon, Benny had managed to persuade Danny to let him borrow a few of his favourite months. Mark called from his pick-up as he left, 'I'm on my way to find your wife, Benny, to let her know what you've been doin' most of the day.' He had forgotten that I was leaving that day and the last I saw of Mark was him laughing out of his pick-up window at poor old Benny.

Danny took me back to Richard's apartment at the end of the day after I'd said good-bye to all the carpenters and other guys on the site and they all reminisced with me about the past couple months and the times we had. I extended my farewells to Benny and Danny, thanked them for the work they had given me and all the memories that I would return with. I said that they should look me up if they were ever in England, but I knew I would never see them again and at the time wondered what they would all be doing in five years time.

Some while after returning from the States I learned that the company they all worked for, Golden Triad Construction, had gone bust. Danny would surely have moved on to another building company but Benny probably would have changed jobs completely. The occupations that he had had throughout his life suggested he didn't stay in anything for too long and I thought that he was probably making someone smile somewhere else. Mark would almost certainly still be in construction, having been the only one with qualifications; but who knows.

After that last day was over I took time to think and talk to Paul and Mark. We had arrived in the States in the knowledge that we would have to work; but we couldn't help feeling that perhaps other BUNACer's had probably not been digging ditches with bleeding hands from dawn 'til dusk to earn a buck or two. But we didn't regret it. In between the hard work we had had some good times on the sites and met a lot of great characters; that's probably what made the trip so memorable.

High Plains Drifters

So that was it, we had finished work and from now on there was nothing to do but have a good time. We were leaving for Florida that Saturday and were preparing for the trip all Friday. I paid a visit to the medical centre so that they could check on my ear again. I had finished my antibiotics a while ago and my ear hurt slightly and I was worried it was infected. I called a taxi to take me to the centre. The trip took an hour, when it was usually a twenty minute drive; the driver didn't have a clue where he was going.

'Sorry about this, sir, it's my first day today.'

'Don't worry about it,' I said through clenched teeth as we turned down yet another strange road. The sun was shining and I wanted to get out and enjoy it. My first day out from work and I get to spend most of it in a taxi cab, I thought.

'I'll give you a discount, sir, on the cost of the journey.'

'Thanks. Don't you come from around here then?' I asked.

'Yeh, lived around here all my life. But obviously the medical centre is quite new and so I don't really know where it is.'

'Oh!'

'Tell you what, sir, when we get to the end of a road you can say whether you recognise it or not and we'll see how we get on, OK?'

'Well don't you have a map?'

'Well yeh and we're in the right area, it's just that the place is new and I think there are a few new roads around here as well.'

'Oh!'

We eventually found the clinic and I left the taxi driver having only paid for a twenty minute trip. I walked into the centre to find the place full of construction workers again. They could easily have been the same guys that had been there the last time I came. We hadn't had a serious accident at the site throughout the time I was there - although we had had some close shaves. Nevertheless I couldn't help feeling that there was either a lot of construction work going on in the area or these guys must have spent their time jumping off buildings and lying down under forklift trucks; there were loads of them.

The doctor saw me after a short wait. It was a different chap to the one I had seen previously, he was older and spent most of the time telling me how he loved England and that he had been fourteen times. He took a quick look in my ear and gave me the all clear but told me to keep it dry for another month or so. I walked back down the corridor to the waiting room somewhat relieved that my injury was healing. It had been enough of a nightmare as it was and I didn't relish the thought of being put on some pretty serious antibiotics, unable to swim or even drink beer during our trip to Florida: the only things we intended to do. Perhaps I would have been staggering with one of those large buckets of orange juice that Charlie had told me about. I called for a taxi from the medical centre. Incredibly I was sent the same taxi to pick me up as had taken me.

'Good grief.' I said to myself. My heart sank as the chap welcomed me back into the taxi with a broad grin. He said that he was going to get me back in double quick time to make up for the outward journey, but we immediately took a wrong turning out of the medical centre onto a 'new' road and we were lost again. An hour later we arrived home.

'I tell ya I'll get the hang of that journey yet,' he said with an embarrassed smile.

'You married?' I inquired as we arrived outside Richard's apartment.

'Sure am, only a year.'

'Well if your wife becomes pregnant, when she goes into labour I should practise the route a few times,' I got out and handed him a twenty minute fare through the window.

He turned the car around and waved goodbye. I stood and watched him take the wrong turning out of the apartment complex toward a dead end.

'Amazing!' I said and turned and walked toward the apartment.

We called BUNAC later that afternoon to check on our flight which we were pleased to hear was still leaving at the scheduled time, on the scheduled day.

We had MTV on throughout the day while we prepared for our trip to Florida and popped in and out to play tennis and to visit the pool. On MTV they repeat a number of videos throughout the day. It happened on this day that whenever we returned to the apartment they were always playing the same video. It was a fantastic video by a group called Poison. We didn't mind seeing it more than twenty-six times during the day as it featured an absolutely gorgeous girl and a number of other scantily clad females; it was so politically incorrect it was mind blowing. The song was called 'Fallen Angel'. It was about a girl from a small town in the south, who had left home after arguing with her parents while still young. She travelled to the Big City to try and find fame and fortune, had some pictures taken and became a star. After a while though she was old news and nobody wanted to know her; she was mamma's 'Fallen Angel'. It was a fantastic video and what was even more amazing was that the MTV presenter told the story of how the girl who actually starred in the video had originally come from a small southern town to seek her fame and fortune as a model. She had worked in a shoe shop until she was given the video part. But after the video she was unable to find work anywhere and had been forced to return to the shoe shop and eventually back to her home town. None of us could understand why the girl had been unable to find work; she had a body like a goddess. To see a rock video twenty-six times in one day might be some people's idea of hell, but to see this girl's body was like heaven, absolutely outrageous.

Saturday we were up and away. We left at 8.30 and drove for about ten hours. Richard did all the driving as there was no way Richard was going to let an idiot like me take the wheel of his 16 valve Golf GTI. The time in the car passed quickly and we stopped periodically to buy some fresh fruit from stalls by the side of the roads. Because the States is so massive the roads are rarely crowded and on a long drive there were almost times when it was so 'trafficless', it was eerie; miles of hot deserted road, as far as the eye could see.

We arrived in Florida in good time and found our hotel quickly. We were in the centre of vacation land, opposite the famous 'Wet 'n' Wild', a water theme park, and not far from Disney World. We had saved most of our money for these last two weeks and we were determined to have a good time. We each ate a large steak meal that evening for the price of a starter in England and then took a quick look at the local area before retiring to play cards for the rest of the evening. This was it, the holiday we had wanted and an excursion over the road to 'Wet 'n' Wild' would be our first port of call.

So the following day we eagerly arrived with towels and swimming gear. We each paid one price for the whole day and proceeded to get wet and wild. The first thing we noticed was that the place was crawling with gorgeous female lifeguards in red swimming costumes: Baywatch Babes. They had perfect tans from working outside all day and amazing bodies. We were all very dark brown after our building site work, and having 'eaten earth' and mixed with manual labourers for the best part of two months, would have liked nothing more than to have got to know a few of these female lifeguards.

'Do you think the term Wet 'n' Wild refers to the place or the female lifeguards?' I asked.

'I'd like to find out' said Paul. But we figured that they were probably asked out fifty times a day and anyway we didn't want to waste time getting rejected, we had some serious fun to be getting on with.

The extensive array of water rides ranged from tamer rides, where you travelled along a stream of water, down a winding tube; to a ride where you basically threw yourself off the top of a platform down a vertical shoot. On this, the best ride in the whole place, you didn't actually touch the shoot for most of the time, you just travelled down vertically as though you had jumped off a cliff feet first. Eventually the gradient narrowed and you stopped in a spray of water.

Often you pay your money at a theme park and the rides fail to impress; but this water ride took you so close to terminal velocity and serious injury that it really gave you a thrill. Of course, I had to curtail my fun somewhat due to my ear; the doctor would have been none too impressed with my antics as I wasn't even supposed to allow my ear near water. We left 'Wet 'n' Wild' when the place became overcrowded in the afternoon, having not wasted a second of our time there.

We went out for a Mexican meal that evening. We were all ravenous after our water sports and had to watch we didn't spend all our hard earned money on a single meal. We played cards in the hotel in the evening and drank the local beer.

The next day was Disney World, the centre of the universe as far as the tourist is concerned. Richard, who had been before, suggested we did it in two days; on the first day we would visit the main Disney areas and Fantasy Island and on the second we would visit the Epcot centre.

We were there as the park opened and all the attendants at the gate greeted us with big teethy smiles. The car park is so large that we had to take a tram from our car to get anywhere and apparently Disney World is so big that you can fit the whole of Disney Land - which is the smaller park in California - into its car parks; land is not at a premium in the States. Again a single entrance fee covered all the rides. We walked in through the main gates and took in the spectacle of the main street. It was brightly coloured and decorated with various souvenir shops, with the Stars and Stripes flag displayed from the balcony of each.

So here I was again, on a movie set. I would see the Disney castle soon, the dream castle that used to begin each and every Disney film and was such an emblem of the movies. I was surrounded by the atmosphere of movie making, it felt likes a huge props room or a film factory, heaving with people all wanting to make that movie, or draw that cartoon.

The rides were great, more a spectacle than an out and out thrill, and arriving early we didn't have to queue much. Each ride had its own special attraction, be it educational, emotional or spectacular.

We returned to the main street in time for the parade at 3.00pm, when all the famous Disney characters appear and produce a colourful spectacle. On the way we were fortunate enough to encounter 'Chip 'n' Dale' and 'Goofy'. These creatures were hot property and we wrestled with our cameras to get some snaps in before they disappeared to prepare for the parade. I had my picture taken with Chip and Mark had his taken with Goofy. Everybody was keen to have a picture taken with Goofy, so Mark had quite a job trying to attract his attention. He kept on tapping Goofy on the shoulder after he had finished each snap with another group, but failed to get noticed; the smaller kids were given priority. Mark soon got tired of chasing Goofy and the scene started to look quite funny, Mark chasing a huge colourful, full size Goofy for a quick picture; an event that you had to believe you were dreaming to believe. Mark eventually showed his frustration by pretending to hit Goofy around the chops while Goofy wasn't looking causing a few tourists to shy away and Richard, Paul and I to laugh. No matter how hard Mark tried Goofy wasn't interested and the only way Mark finally managed to grab him was when Goofy was just about to leave the public and sneak in through a doorway. Mark caught Goofy sneaking off though and quickly pulled him out of the doorway through which he was just about to disappear. Goofy's huge smiling facial expression didn't change, but I bet the guy's inside the costume did. A happy Mark finally got his photo taken with Goofy.

The 3.00 o'clock parade brought out all the Disney favourites and was good to see. It progressed along Main Street smoothly and the hundreds of characters and many floats quickly seemed to appear and then turn a corner and disappear. There didn't seem to be any mass gathering of characters before hand and no gatherings afterwards as the back of the parade caught up with the front sections; it was all very slickly done. Actually it was too slickly done. It didn't give the impression that it was a special parade at all, performed especially for those watching, which it should have. It was all without feeling and the smiles were false Hollywood smiles. The parade passed off so quickly and efficiently that you may as well have watched it on telly. But I suppose if you're involved in the parade on almost every day throughout the whole year, it probably does become very much a job of work and very mechanical. Nevertheless a bit of tomfoolery by a few of the characters wouldn't have gone amiss.

Free Willy

We all felt like we had money to burn and that evening we again set off for a luxurious meal out. We returned to our hotel, played cards and then went for a quick swim in the pool just before it closed and had a chat about future attractions.

'Sea World tomorrow boys,' said Richard as we dried ourselves by the pool.

'You've been before haven't you?' Mark asked.

'Yeh, but it was a while ago. It's well worth a visit and besides it gives us a rest from Mickey Mouse for a day.'

'It can really get on top of you, can't it, Disney World?' I commented. 'It's a lot of fun but before you know what your doing you're swearing and cursing at having missed different things and it all becomes a chore.'

'It bloody does, my feet are killing me,' said Paul.

'Ah stop whingeing, you northern woman,' laughed Mark. Paul and Mark began an argument about who was in fact the most manly and would therefore be up at the crack of dawn to swim fifty lengths of the pool. They bet on it but it was made null and void by Mark saying that by his calculations the pool wouldn't be open until well after dawn which was far too late for him!

The next day seemed especially hot. We were travelling around in the loosest of clothing but the attractions Florida had to offer needed time; rushing in the heat would only result in us all getting annoyed. Seaworld was great. There were the usual pools for penguins and sealions and show times displayed everywhere for the killer whales and the dolphins. There were shops and restaurants and little signposts telling you which path to follow for which attraction. We planned our day around the times of the shows and so first set off to see the more exotic fish and sharks. We were shown the usual pool of piranhas that seems to grace every aquarium throughout the world and given the line about how 'this pool of piranhas can strip an elephant down to the bone in under two minutes.' The most interesting feature before the shows was the shark pool. There was a long underwater tunnel which we could walk through, and which - we were assured - was made of toughened glass. The sharks swam all about us and over our heads and there were plenty of them. With the right equipment you would have been able to take some amazing photos; but a Dixons £4.99 disposable Super-Snapper wouldn't really produce the goods.

It was soon time for the first show and we all trouped off to see the killer whale 'Shamu'. Every shop at Seaworld was packed with 'I love Shamu' stickers, cuddly toys and T-shirts, so we were dying to see what Shamu was like. We arrived quite late for the show and had to sit near the back, quite a way away from the action and too far for decent pictures. The large seating area surrounded a huge light blue pool, with two further pools behind that were all interconnected. The show was all about man's friendship with the killer whale and an old totem pole that told the story of how a small Indian boy was saved by such a whale. It was an Indian legend, and the legend - or the whale in it, I'm not quite sure which - was called Shamu. The large pool was thus decorated with totem poles and the speakers told us of this legend while Shamu the killer whale swam around the pool and jumped out of the water at exactly the right time to open the show. My first site of Shamu filled my soul with pity. When the huge beast leapt out of the water, rather than a bright black and white energetic whale, Shamu appeared to be old, with fading colours. The poor thing seemed to be a sad sight to me and I remember instantly thinking that I would have preferred to have seen such a magnificent creature in its natural habitat. The poor animal would have to go through the whole routine twice a day, every day and the strain was showing.

Shamu did perform some great tricks, though. He used his tail to absolutely drench everybody in the first three rows and he managed to leap almost entirely out of the water with a human assistant standing upright on his nose. The show was quite good and it took quite a number of red wet-suited trainers to put it on. Towards the end - as if we hadn't realised already - it was explained to us that Shamu was now getting quite old and that soon his place would be taken by his son 'Baby Shamu'. Upon this announcement the water gates into the main arena opened and in swam Baby Shamu, much to the delight of the crowd and an ocean of flash bulbs lit his entrance. The pool had a transparent perspex side to it and thus the baby and big Shamu could be seen swimming side by side. Baby Shamu seemed somewhat keener than his father to swim around the pool at top speed and perform. In fact he looked like a cheeky little rascal who enjoyed the antics of the pool and the crowd's attentions. He had already tried to ruin the show by making so much noise at the back, in a smaller pool, that the trainers had to frequently apologise and commented that we would be introduced to him later. Baby Shamu had probably never seen the sea, I thought, and I wondered if his eagerness would have been somewhat tainted had he known the life that might have been his in the ocean.

Before the show ended we stopped taking photos as we were too far away from the action - even with a medium-sized zoom lens - and decided that we would return and watch the show again from a closer seat to get some action shots.

After the Shamu performance we headed toward the dolphin arena. This was where the dolphins performed the usual plain vanilla, Windsor Safari Park tricks, like singing and leaping out of the water to great heights. The dolphin show was actually entitled 'New Friends' as it also featured a number of whales who also performed a few plain vanilla tricks and who we were supposed to make friends with. We were introduced to a stream of different dolphins and whales and Mark eventually turned to me and said,

'There'd better not be many more New Friends or I'll run out of film.' I laughed, partly at his joke and partly at how stupid we had been recently: taking photo's of anything that moved. We had gone completely overboard with photography and I started to reduce my picture taking from then on. In fact I took a total of 864 photos during our time in the States and it cost me an absolute fortune to get them developed. Rather than the 'free film' I received for each that I had developed, I should have received a free car for doing the job lot.

We decided to end our trip after seeing Shamu once again, so we made our way to the whale arena early. We sat on the third row this time, where there was a sign warning us that the row on which we were sitting was liable to flooding during the show and that we were likely to get wet. We had seen the show before though and jumped out of the way to save our camera equipment just at the right time. Someone who didn't was a poor little girl of about five years of age. She was right up against the perspex glass as Shamu began his routine. Her parents had their eye on her and had not been too alarmed at the small sprays of water that Shamu had caused in his warming up period. Now the show had begun, it was going to be a different kettle of fish and as Shamu crashed his mighty tail into the water early in the routine, a huge wave came over the side of the pool. It absolutely drenched the little girl, as though someone had just stood above her and emptied a large bucket of water over her head. She was so shocked she didn't know what to do and just turned and looked at her parents. Her parents were howling with laughter along with the first three rows and her father had caught the whole thing on video. Realising she was getting no sympathy at all from her parents the little girl burst into tears and her mother came down to collect her, still laughing. It was quite funny to see.

We drove back to our hotel for a swim after Seaworld and then continued our crash diets with a large steak and chips each.

Just around the corner from the hotel was a crazy golf course. Wherever we travelled in the States, there always seemed to be a crazy golf course nearby. Some had been quite spectacular, especially those that were floodlit and this was such a course. Mixed in with the elaborate scenery of caves, waterfalls and bridges on this course, there were a number of hidden gem stones. We were presented with a card with a number of clues on it from which we had to ascertain the whereabouts of the gems. They weren't real of course, just small glass pieces hidden at specific locations to add spice to your Crazy Golf game. I can't remember what the prize was but it must have been reasonable as after every hole we spent quite a time looking for the gems. We found only one. Having not used our grey matter for about three months it really was a strain just reading the clues; building site orders were about the limit of our reading recently. Were we all in for a shock back at university.

We made sure both our days at Disney World were week days to limit the tourists; tomorrow would be Wednesday having made our first trip there on the Monday. There were also fireworks planned for the Wednesday night and we would try to catch them if we were still there later at night. So off we set on the Wednesday morning for Epcot.

The Epcot Centre is designed to incorporate fun with education and almost all the rides were sponsored by some company or other. The first sight you see when approaching the Epcot Centre from the car park is the large silver globe called Space Mountain. It looks simply like an expensive piece of design upon arrival but inside there is a rollercoaster ride in pitch darkness. Our trip also took us to The Living Seas (about the sea and sealife), a 3-D movie starring Michael Jackson, and a completely enclosed garden area in which plant research was in full swing. All the rides were spectacular, very informative and interesting. To think of Disney World, and especially Epcot Centre, as one long roller-coaster ride is a mistake; it's more an education, in science, geography, photography and tourism!

We were getting tired after our day at Epcot and it was seven o'clock before we knew it. The fireworks were not due to start until nine and we couldn't be bothered to wait around so we left Disney World and headed back to the hotel in the Golf.

On the way back we saw at least three cars, all within the space of a mile, stopped for speeding. The national limit of 55 mph was difficult to stick to on the wide Florida roads and the police seemed to be everywhere that evening. It seemed a bit harsh to have a speeding blitz just outside Disney World, we thought. You really knew you were out of fantasy world once the copper slapped the ticket in your hand; that was it: Game Over.

We swam for quite a while when we got back and I rang my parents (reverse charge) to let them know what time our flight would land at Heathrow airport. We also tuned the TV into the weather channel that evening to catch up on the only thing that was ruining our southern trip - Hurricane Gilbert. September was hurricane season, and each hurricane was given a name. Most die out before they reach the US mainland but Gilbert was already causing destruction toward the south of Florida and was cutting off all access to the famous Florida Keys. Although we realised that there was probably a fair amount of exaggeration in the reports, we didn't want to risk being cut off out on the Keys or in southern Florida.

'We'd better keep an eye on that baby,' I said as we lounged in front of the TV.

'Yeah!' exclaimed Mark, in a sarcastic tone. 'With a quick overnight move it would be upon us and then we would be stuck. We would probably miss our plane, miss the start of the university term, which would mean we would fail our degrees and never, ever, ever get a job and go hungry and die!'

Richard looked at his brother, shaking his head.

'That is the most exaggerated comment I have ever heard in my life,' he said.

'Not as big as the exaggeration he told that girl at Wet and Wild,' I said. Paul and Richard laughed. 'Yes, I did rather underestimate,' retorted Mark.

We woke the next morning to find that Gilbert was still gathering momentum. It was moving slowly but still gaining in strength. We would continue our tourist trip at a smart pace and hope to see all we planned.

2001

We drove on to the Kennedy Space Center the following day, armed, as ever, with our cameras. The Center catered well for tourists and as we entered the grounds we saw the rocket bodies from previous Apollo missions lying horizontally along the ground. They were an awesome sight. Their size left us amazed at how they ever left the ground, let alone reached the moon. The sun glistened off their massive black and white bodies and moving further down each we eventually arrived at the engines, the largest of which, we were told, produced about half a million horsepower. Statistics were posted by each Apollo to tell you about its history and its awesome power. We joined the other tourists in taking pictures of each other by the engines of the largest Apollo and needless to say we were each dwarfed by the huge black cone-shaped engine covers and it made for a spectacular picture.

We moved on to the museum. Inside there was a documented history of various Apollo missions right up to the present space shuttle missions, and some of the return capsules and vehicles used. The technology of the early space capsules looked incredibly dated and nowadays most people would probably have been embarrassed to have it in their kitchens. All the buttons and switches were made of old, hard plastic or bakelite and peering inside a capsule was a real eyeopener.

We were all keen to take a picture of an authentic space suit standing in the corner of one room. I approached the white suit and large helmet slowly, adjusting my camera. I wondered whether the suit was dressed on a mannequin, or perhaps supported on a wire stand, allowing the helmet to be removed and for me to get a picture trying it on. I examined it all closely and then took a close-up shot of the large gold coloured reflective visor. The visor was like a mirror, actually being covered in a thin layer of real gold. (Apparently NASA had found that gold was the best

material to protect the eyes from the sun's glare in space.)
The others were behind me taking pictures of the suit from
a distance. I eventually touched the suit and squeezed the
arm to see whether it was simply supported by a thick wire
frame. The whole suit suddenly moved and made a grab
for me.

'Ahhhhhhhhhh!' I yelled and jumped in instant shock.
Somebody was inside the space suit and had been standing
motionless all the while. I got the shock of my life; made
all the more frightening by the reflective visor which came
close to my face. My sudden surprised yelp was the sort of
yelp that only happens when you are truly shocked. I
couldn't recollect ever having shouted involuntarily with
such fright in all my life. The astronaut suit casually walked
away, around the corner. I looked around at the others
who had of course witnessed the entire escapade. They were
reeling with laughter.

We travelled on through the museum, laughing about
the incident. It wasn't long though before we saw the
astronaut again, in another part of the museum, sitting in
a moon buggy, again absolutely motionless. Other tourists,
specifically a large American man in red checked trousers
and his family, were quite close to the space suit, admiring
the moon buggy and its occupant carefully; were they in
for a shock! But we didn't hang around to see it happen,
instead we moved on through the museum, to wait for a
bus to take us around the outside of the space centre. There
were a number of buses, all silver with a blue and white
stripe down them, ferrying people around the site on a
guided tour. We were taken to see the transporter that
moves the space shuttles out to the launch pad and filled
in on the statistics of the beast. We were told that it
consumed over a hundred gallons of fuel for each foot that
it moved the shuttle. The massive vehicle had a number of
tracks - like tank tracks - in which each individual link
weighed over a ton; it apparently took all day to get the
shuttle out to the launch pad. We were also shown the

building in which the shuttle is constructed and our guide informed us that it was so large that clouds sometimes formed inside it, requiring large extractor fans to be put in the roof to keep the air circulating.

We were then taken out to the launch site itself at The Kennedy Space Center, where the space shuttle Columbia was waiting to take off. We were fortunate to have been able to see it; the launch of Columbia had been delayed for a day due to bad weather. A zoom lens on the old Pentax was a must here as from the viewing point the shuttle was still a speck in the distance; we nevertheless took some decent shots of the thing.

Our day finished with another look at the massive Apollo rockets that were situated by the entrance. It had been well worth the trip and as we drove on I pondered the days sightseeing activities at the Kennedy Space Center, full of bumf, buttons and bastards dressed in astronaut suits!

Beaches

We continued south that day to Coco Beach. We were keeping a constant check on Hurricane Gilbert in case it trapped us in the south for a few days; our schedule was quite tight and reaching the JFK airport in New York to catch the plane was our number one priority. We planned to spend a couple of days simply relaxing on the beach. Coco Beach, as well as being a popular holiday spot, was famous for harbouring Ron Jon's Surf Shop. None of us were really 'into surfing man' but Ron Jon's was supposedly the largest and most famous surf shop in the world; so we had to check it out.

As we cruised into Coco Beach it seemed to look like the other tourist resorts we had visited, full of shops and souvenirs, but not as over the top as Myrtle Beach. It was by now towards the end of September and past peak season, so it was relatively quiet. We booked into a motel and headed for something to eat. The days in Disney World, Sea World, the Epcot Centre and The Kennedy Space Center had been all go and at last we had a chance to unwind before our journey back. After we had enjoyed yet another burger at yet another fast food joint we headed towards the supermarket and bought a case of Budweiser - reminding us of the days when we would come back from a hot day on the building sites and polish off a case of Bud between us. However, we all felt like getting smashed and decided that one case wasn't enough and bought another before headed back to our motel.

The morning brought the sun in through the window of our motel room. We were again all crashed out in a single room, deciding that staying in a motel with a our own bathroom and TV was better than having a room each in a fleapit with no facilities whatsoever. The morning light revealed the depth of our alcoholic binge. Over forty cans littered the floor and tables of the motel room but this mess paled into insignificance when we woke and discovered how scrambled our brains were.

We left everything where it was and stumbled on down to the beach - about a hundred yards away - to sleep further. It was only in the eighties that day and the beach made a comfortable bed; but it was still humid. We didn't want to waste the day, though, and by mid-morning we were recovered enough to try our hand at surfing, figuring that the beach was quiet enough to ensure that only a few hundred people would be able to laugh at our attempts. I suppose not being able to surf in Coco Beach is like not being able to ski in St Moritz. We initially hired two foam beginner's boards from Ron Jon's, at their suggestion. This was a good way of learning, they assured us. But the foam boards turned out to be worse than useless - or was it us?

Mark, Paul and I tried every conceivable means to surf; even paddling the boards out ridiculous distances in an effort to catch the waves.

'These are crap,' said Paul as we all staggered back up on the beach.

'Yeah, like trying to surf on a mattress,' Mark said. 'Let's get some decent boards.' So we ventured off to find the experts at Ron Jon's Surf Shop once again and finally returned with the most up to date, expensive, all singing, all dancing, professional boards the guy had in the shop. These were no better though.

'Cheap rubbish,' Richard said after being thrown up onto the beach by a wave, on his twentieth attempt to ride some surf.

'Yeah, they're useless aren't they?' Mark said with a smile. Mark decided that all the boards were probably faulty and we gave up trying to surf. However, Mark, Paul and myself had now been in the States almost three months and our hair was thick and our bodies black, having been continuously in the sun; we looked like real surfing beach bums. So our final trick was to stick our expensive surf boards upright in the sand in full view and lay back on our towels to give the impression that we were the coolest surfers in Florida. The chicks were mighty impressed!

We left the beach later in the afternoon, cleaned ourselves and the room up and then went to the local shopping mall, where we took in a film. I can't remember what we saw, but like all the other films we had seen, it was much less movie-like than our everyday experiences.

The next day began with a breakfast at Burger King. What a treat that was. Our stomachs were beginning to suffer withdrawal symptoms from the lack of fast food we had eaten in Coco Beach. We were getting 'cold turkey'. The Burger King breakfast really did taste frighteningly good.

'You know, when we return to the UK I think our bodies are going to reject any fresh fruit and vegetables we have,' said Paul as we ate. 'Think my body will probably reject any liquid other than beer as well.'

'I know, it's scary,' I said. 'At university all we do is play squash and keep fit, and out here I've put on almost two stone.' Mark looked at me and laughed.

'Tell you what,' he said, 'bet we've spent thousands of dollars on burgers and beer since we've been out here. We'll end up looking like a McDonald burger if we stay out here much longer.'

While we had been sitting in the Burger King the weather, unseen by us, had been closing in. There was a crash of thunder and rain swept the glass windows. We were all taken aback and looked at each other wide-eyed.

'Gilbert!' we all said as one, referring to the hurricane.

'We're in some pretty serious shit if we hang around here, guys,' Mark said. Everyone else in the joint had the same idea and nervously people started to make for the exits, hiding their anxiety.

'Let's go,' said Richard. We hurried to the door and ran through the rain back to the motel. As we ran Paul called out,

'Suppose the Florida Keys are out of the question then.'

'Fuck the Keys,' Richard called back. 'The only ones I'm interested in are the ones for my car.'

Reaching the motel we scrambled our belongings together, checked out and Richard drove like Steve McQueen in Bullet to get us out of Coco Beach. Although we were probably safe we didn't want to risk it and we headed for home early.

We still had a day or two to kill so we decided that on the way back we would stop in Charlotte in South Carolina. Well, actually Richard decided he didn't really want to drive straight back.

'No, we're not going to drive straight back to Highpoint. If you think that I'm going to spend about eighteen hours behind the wheel while you clowns sleep all the way, only stopping to buy some luxury fruit from the fruit stalls, you're very much mistaken.'

'No, not us, Rich!' said his brother with a cheeky grin.

The only stop we made that day, in fact, was at a Waffle House. These had been scattered occasionally along our long journey on the way down to Florida and we thought we would stop at one for lunch. Richard brought the car to a halt directly outside the Waffle House and we all climbed out and headed in. As we made our entrance about twenty heads turned to look. Each one of them belonged to the roughest looking manual labourer I had ever seen; each guy dressed in the familiar thick checked shirt and dirty jeans. It was worse than walking into a locals' pub in the smallest village in England when all heads turn, look you up and down and then talk about you until long after you've left.

Mark looked at me and I screwed my face up in a frightened expression. We all walked to the nearest table and sat on bench seats at a yellow table. A waitress approached and handed us four laminated menus. We looked at her as she dealt them out and hurriedly left us.

'Was I imagining that or does it really exist?' Paul asked distastefully. Richard was as shellshocked as Paul and replied, 'Yeah I saw it too' he said. 'That woman had a beard.'

'She did,' continued Paul. 'That woman had a beard and moustache; and along with her warts she was probably the ugliest person I have ever seen in my life.'

'Keep the noise down,' Mark said 'All the guys in here are probably sleeping with her.'

'Sleeping with it, don't you mean,' said Paul. 'And if they are, well you might remind them there are better looking dogs in the road than that.' Mark and I burst out laughing, attracting glances from the now hushed bunch of mean-looking labourers. We had to suppress our laughter as she returned to take our order. We stared in disbelief at her features as she wrote our orders on a dirty piece of paper; it was only when she had left that we began to notice the standard of hygiene in the place. The table was literally thick with old grease, all the cutlery was filthy and the plastic menus - that only offered savoury or sweet waffles - were covered in pieces of last week's food.

'This place is disgusting,' Richard said as we all made sure we hadn't sat on a discarded egg or something.

'That waitress sort of fits in quite well here, doesn't she?' Paul remarked.

'God knows what the food's going to be like.'

'Well, if it's in the same tradition, Marky, we haven't much to look forward to.'

Unfortunately it was in the same tradition with all the waffles unbelievably greasy and tasting like rubber; the whole lunch had been a complete nightmare. None of us ate more than a mouthful.

'Let's get out of here,' Richard said. So we asked for the bill, hurriedly paid it and walked for the door. We all wore a look of disbelief at how disgusting the place and staff had been and a comment or two reached the ears of the other guys around. As we scrambled into the car, annoyed faces stared out through the windows.

'Don't spare the horses,' I said to Richard, as we screeched out of the car park.

'Don't think we'll be welcome there for a while,' Paul remarked. 'Anyway, wouldn't want to go back. That is the most disgusting place I have ever encountered in my entire life,' he continued.

'Bloody hell, and you're a northerner as well,' said Mark, 'It must have been bad.'

'Oi, watch it!'

We had heard how beautiful parts of Charlotte were and how it was supposedly the oldest part of America, full of character and old world charm. We entered Charlotte at eight in the evening. We stopped at the first motel we came to - a 'Best Western Motel' - and asked about accommodation and prices. We were quoted a very reasonable price and decided to give them the pleasure of our company that night. Tired from the journey we took a quick walk around the motel vicinity and then headed for bed.

The next day we did the tourist spots in Charlotte and Charleston, venturing down older roads and side streets to find the ornate classic houses we had been told about. They were worth seeing in all their splendour, huge symmetrically-square houses straight out of a film set from Gone With The Wind. These southern American houses all had balconies jutting from the upper floors where we imagined the residents would sit each evening after supper in the hot and humid night to try and catch a cooling breeze. We had passed a number of these impressive houses on our journeys into the southern states and we all envied the present occupants of some of the most majestic residences. I remember taking quite a number of pictures in Charleston, of the beautiful old houses, the streets and some of the great trees that still draped along the roadsides. But I subsequently lost the film, which was ironic, because out of all the rolls of film that I took, that was the one that would have yielded pictures that would look more like pictures from a film set than any other.

Our shortened holiday trip ended in the afternoon when we set out for Highpoint. It was a few more hours drive back to the apartment, but with frequent stops made to buy and then scoff loads of fresh fruit, the trip passed quickly. It would be good to get back to the places we knew, the pool and the tennis.

American Graffiti

Highpoint hadn't changed much and after a hot journey, a cool drink and a swim beckoned. We were short on provisions and had to take a trip to the shopping mall first. We reverted to our old practice of attempting to chat up the checkout girls in the supermarket; feeling more confident now that we were seasoned travellers and that we could die happy having seen that first wonder of the capitalist epoch, Disney World. Our attempts brought smiles from the checkout girls but little else. Nothing had changed in Highpoint.

The return back to Richard's apartment was not the end of an adventure, but the beginning of one. We would be setting off for New York in three days and we had to plan our route, sort out our bus tickets and save our remaining dimes. We were apprehensive about the trip; having travelled by Greyhound bus before. There was a lot to do before we left and we would start the next day with a trip to the furniture warehouse, where we had first been employed some three months previously.

We were all up early that day and travelled into the warehouse together. Mark and I had to pack the golf clubs that we had purchased and Paul had to take a trip to the social security office - which was only a short walk from the warehouse - to pick up his social security number; without it he would have had to pay tax on all he had earnt. We didn't really believe that any of us would be thrown out of the country for not registering with social security, or be barred from ever entering again, but it was better to be safe than sorry. What an embarrassment it would be travelling to the States in years to come with your wife and kids, on a trip to Disney World, only to be arrested as you tried to enter the country and being told that the FBI had been after you for the last ten years, suspecting you of being the mastermind behind an intricate network of tax evasion schemes, just because you hadn't paid up for the 'fistful of dollars' you had earnt one summer when you were a student. Stranger things have happened!

When we entered the warehouse we were thrown all sorts of compliments by the secretaries. They hadn't seen us since we left a few months ago. When we had first arrived from England we were white and drawn and probably looked to them as though we were about to keel over. Now we were deeply tanned and looked like beach bums, displaying the brightly coloured T-shirts we had bought at Ron Jon's surf shop in Florida.

'Don't you both look so well,' exclaimed Anne, the secretary that lived near Richard. 'You know when you first arrived from England we didn't know what to think. You were pale and white and wearing heavy clothes even in the hot weather over here. But now well you look like natives!'

'I'm not sure whether that's a compliment or not, I think it's meant to be,' said Richard with a smile, encouraging the other secretaries to follow suit. Richard headed for his office as it was a normal working day for him. Mark and I walked passed his office and out into the warehouse that we knew so well. Nothing had changed here either. The smell of furniture polish hit us as we turned the corner. There was Cheryl with a leather apron on polishing a table top, and Danny was sanding down a large chair. Cheryl looked up.

'Hey, how ya doin', guys?' he called He stopped his polishing, wiped his hands on his apron and came over to shake our hands.

'Both got a nice tan there.'

'Yeah, we've been working outside a lot since we left here,' I informed him, 'and now we've just come back from Florida.'

'Wow! Bet it's nice down there, wouldn't mind going there myself one time. Good to see ya both.'

'How've things been here?' Mark asked

'Oh nothing ever changes here, ya know. Everybody comes in for a day's work and goes back home to argue with the wife.' We all laughed. It was probably true. 'I think the orders are coming in OK and we're getting a bit of business, so that can't be bad.'

'How's the shooting going?' I asked. We were by the table in which he kept his polished silver gun and as I asked him I opened the drawer.

'Yeh, it's still there,' Cheryl said with a smile. 'Had another M-16 competition couple of weeks back and did real well, so I'm pleased about that. And I got some more exercises coming up with the army soon, so I'll get a chance to shoot there too, which is good. So anyway, when you boys going back to good old England?'

'Two days,' Mark said.

'Really, so this is sort of a last visit to see us then is it?'

Just then Mike - Cheryl's brother - came round the corner. He wasn't expecting to see us and it took him a second to recognise us. He walked over smiling broadly.

'Mark and Phil, ya God damn lazy assholes,' he said 'Why ain't ya working?' We laughed and shook his hand. He was as thin as ever and his blond moustache seemed to have grown a little thicker.

'They've just come back from Florida,' Cheryl said.

'Well, I knew you two couldn't hack the pace of work in here. Had to take a few weeks off in the sun to rest a while, did ya?'

'Ahhh, you never do anything here,' Mark answered 'and you're the most God damn lazy son of a bitch I've ever known.'

'At least I ain't as ugly as you!'

'I heard that all the secretaries voted you the ugliest son of a bitch in the area.' We were all laughing.

The friendly banter continued until it was decided that neither side was going to win. Mike asked us about what we had done since leaving the warehouse; he remembered we had said something about Myrtle Beach. We told him

what had happened, what a disaster it had been and how
we had come back to work on building sites in Highpoint.
We had now come full circle and had come to say goodbye. Mike was just off in the dark green company van to
pick up some piece of furniture and we promised to stay
around until he came back. While we were talking to Mike
and Cheryl, Danny had continued with his work. He had
always been quiet and when we passed him to wrap our
clubs at the back of the warehouse he just said 'Hi', and
gave us a smile. At the back of the warehouse were the rest
of the gang, Roland, Steve and Jack. Charlie, the massive
ex-'Nam solider with the outrageous sense of humour, was
the only one missing, which was a shame; we would have
liked to have said goodbye. Roland asked how much
alcohol we had consumed since we had last seen him and
we continued chatting while we packed our golf clubs.

'We'll be back to collect these later, Jack,' I said. 'We
need to go off and get a bus ticket now, if that's all right?'

'Yeh sure, you can leave 'em here. See you in a while
then?'

'Yeah. Cheers,' Mark and I said in unison.

We had to walk to the Greyhound bus shelter to buy
our tickets for the return journey. Paul was going to meet
us there after his trip to the social security office. Amazingly
he was there when we arrived and we walked in to the
offices together and up to the counter.

'Could you tell us the times of buses to Washington
please?' Mark asked. The lonely chap behind the counter
was as old as he was stupid.

'I could do,' he replied smiling broadly. Oh my God I
thought, it's going to take an hour to buy three tickets
from this guy. We all remained completely silent, totally
unmoved by his feeble attempt at wit. Noticing this, the
guy's expression changed to one of anger and he reached
for a large timetable book stored under the dusty counter,

'Well now, let's see. When do you want to go?'

'Wednesday,' Mark answered.

'And that's to Washington, is it?'

'Well, we want to buy a ticket all the way to New York but we want to stop off in Washington.'

'You can do that on these tickets.' He looked up. 'Three of you then is there?'

'Yes.' He reached under the desk and pulled out three tickets and began to fill them in.

'We can leave at any time then can we?' Mark asked. The chap looked up angrily.

'Hang on there boy, give me a chance, I can only do one thing at a time.' He looked down again and we all smiled at each other.

'That's three tickets to New York leaving Wednesday,' he said handing them to us. He told us the price and that the bus would leave at 9am.

'And these give us the opportunity to stop in Washington for a while do they?' Mark was confirming our route.

'Well, where do you want to go, boy, New York or Washington?' He was now quite angry for no reason whatsoever.

'Well, we said we wanted to stop in Washington for a while.'

'You said you wanted to go to New York, boy. Now which is it?' I took Mark and Paul aside.

'Listen, this guy's as thick as concrete,' I said. 'Let's just confirm that the bus goes through Washington and leave. It's best not to confuse the guy by talking about stopping.' We turned back to the counter.

'So these tickets take us to New York via Washington?'

'Yes. But you said you wanted to go to Washington and not New York!' he answered.

'These are what we want,' said Mark. We paid and left.

'Wow, was that guy stupid or what?' Paul said. We all prayed that our tickets wouldn't land us in New Orleans instead of New York.

Steve - Paul and Mark's building site boss - came around that evening. We played crazy golf at a nearby course and returned to drink coffee and laugh about Steve's frozen budgie. He had brought around a cake that his wife had made for us. She was quite heavily pregnant now and found it difficult going anywhere for the evening, so had sent a cake in her absence.

Mrs Robinson II

The next day was our last and we spent it as we had many others before, swimming, playing tennis and sunbathing. But there had been a phone call for me first thing, just before Richard had left for work. He poked his head around the door

'Sarah's on the phone for you, Phil.'

I looked at Mark and Paul.

'Careful, Phil,' laughed Paul. 'Before you know it you'll be staying here, marrying, having kids.' The others laughed as I walked through to the phone. I chatted for a while about my trip before once again 'Mrs Robinson' took the lead and asked me over for the evening. I didn't take as long as Dustin Hoffman to get used to the idea and she arranged a time to pick me up.

'I'm going to stay with Sarah this evening,' I said nonchalantly as I returned to the front room.

'You'd better rest up today then, Phil, you'll need all your strength this evening,' said Paul; the others laughed.

'Jealousy doesn't become you, Paul,' I answered.

'Well, Phil, you were the only one of us to pull a woman in all the time we have been over here,' Paul continued. 'Pretty miserable performance really.'

'Think she pulled me actually,' I said, sitting back down in an arm chair and Paul laughed.

'Well that's even worse then! Why aren't there women flocking to our feet, we're all good looking guys and now we're all as black as the ace of spades, what's stopping them?'

'Paul, there are two reasons why you lot haven't pulled since you've been here,' commented Richard as he headed for the front door. 'Firstly you lot haven't been working where there was ever likely to be an abundance of women that you could get to know; and secondly by your age most women over here are married. See you guys later.' With that he left for work.

'He's right, I suppose,' said Paul after a brief silence. 'The only girl that we have even met that was worth chatting up was Sarah's daughter and any chance there has been knocked on the head 'cause Phil's sleeping with her mother!'

So after a day's swimming and tennis I was picked up by Sarah in her classically large American saloon. I had done all my packing earlier and so I only needed to worry about Sarah returning me to the apartment in time to catch the Greyhound the following morning. We journeyed to her house along the wide roads and talked and it was again good to feel detached from the routine, albeit a pleasant one, that I had been following with the others. After a while she asked,

'You're at university, aren't you?'

'Yes I am,' I replied. 'Why?'

'Well, you know that friend of mine that you met at my party and then again when we went out?'

'Yes.'

'Well I told her about us and how old you are and that you are at university and she has started calling me Mrs Robinson.' I smiled at her.

'That's just what I've been thinking,' I said.

'Is it?'

'Yeah. This could be straight out of the film.' We didn't say much else during the journey, both of us feeling relaxed and happy in each other's company. Sarah's daughter was staying with a friend for the night but our conversation was just as quiet back at the house as we again drank some wine and chatted. Sarah was more casually dressed than when we last had seen each other, wearing smart fawn trousers and a white shirt. I'm not sure if Mrs Robinson ever wore such clothes, but I'm pleased to say Sarah followed the rest of The Graduate script to the letter.

I was taken back in the morning in plenty of time for my trip back.

'I don't like long goodbyes,' Sarah said as we pulled up outside Richard's apartment.

'Likewise,' I said. We said a brief farewell and I got out and walked around to her window.

'I'll probably never see you again,' she said.

'I know,' I said. 'But what the heck, Mrs Robinson.' She smiled, slotted the car into first gear and pulled off. I walked into the apartment. Paul had his head in the fridge looking for something to eat for breakfast and Mark and Richard were drinking coffee.

'Morning, guys,' I said with a smile. They cheered and made the usual crude jokes, all at my expense.

Being There

We were to be taken to the Greyhound bus depot by Richard to catch the bus at nine but Paul was moving nervously around the flat when the time came to leave.

'Have any of you lot seen my ticket?' he asked.

'Oh no!' Richard exclaimed.' If you've lost your ticket we're all going to beat the living hell out of you.'

'No seriously, guys, I think I've lost it. I had it this morning and put it down somewhere.' We looked at him in disbelief that he could loose such a vital piece of luggage. We all searched intensively. You could have bet your last pound that when the time came to leave Paul would forget or lose something.

'Here it is,' called out Richard from the living room.' It was on top of the TV.' We all sighed with relief and loaded our rucksacks and golf clubs into Richard's car. After all the travelling we had done in 'trains planes and automobiles', this was the beginning of our final journey and it wasn't without a solemn air that we left Highpoint. We looked at each of the places we had gotten to know as we passed them in the car, for the last time. The bars, the fast food joints, the shopping mall, the signs for the golf courses and the roads which led to the building sites on which we had worked. We all remarked that we might return one day, but leaving the area seemed to have a permanent air to it.

We thanked Richard at the bus stop and he too, I think, was sad to see us leave. Although it had been a squash in his apartment, we had had many good times.

Much to our surprise the bus was exactly on time. We boarded and started out for New York. We were to have an eventful trip back which began with everyone being dumped off the bus about an hour's ride outside Highpoint. We weren't really sure where we were. The other passengers seemed relaxed and we assumed the stop was scheduled although it wasn't on our tickets. We were out in the heat once again, sitting on tarmac. It was about ninety degrees and we had our gear stacked up by a wall.

'I hope this is right,' I said. Paul and Mark smiled.

'Well, it would be in keeping with the rest of the trip if we ended up in somewhere like Virginia and missed our plane,' said Paul.

'Well, it certainly hasn't been the holiday I thought it was going to be, I'll grant you that,' Mark said. There was a pause.

'I suppose some BUNAC students must land good jobs in restaurants in California or somewhere and spent a lot more time travelling,' Paul continued.

'Well, possibly. We did cock our trip up, wasting two weeks and a lot of money in Myrtle "Toilet".' I said. 'If we had got those building site jobs straight away we would have been laughing. Hardly any accommodation expenses to pay and food was quite cheap. We would have been able to do the west coast as well; time and money would have been on our side.'

'Well, we've really lived the States and seen it from an angle that the holiday makers don't, that's for sure,' Paul said.

'Yeah. And you can't say it hasn't been eventful.'

'You still keeping your diary up to date, Phil?' Mark asked.

'Yep. I'm going to write a book. A lot's happened, you know.'

The trip to New York took nine hours. We slept most of the way. Well, only two of us slept at any one time while the other kept a wary eye on the other passengers; they were as motley a crew as we had encountered on our first Greyhound bus after originally arriving in New York. The only noticeable absentee was the psychiatric patient.

As we had requested of the Greyhound ticket officer in Highpoint, we stopped in Washington. It was dusk when we arrived and we immediately faced the problem of trying to catch a local bus that would take us past all the tourist spots before nightfall. We also had our luggage in tow. We headed out of the bus terminal and walked toward the nearest main road; outside the terminal was a taxi cab rank.

'Heh, you guys want a taxi?' a fat black chap called from a big beaten-up yellow estate car, with no hub caps. We all shook our heads. There was no way we could afford a taxi for the entire evening and anyway we didn't want to go to any single place. We walked on, constantly looking for directions or bus stops. When we had reached the end of the road the same taxi driver caught up with us. He leant out the window of his massive estate cab.

'You sure you guys don't wan'a taxi, man?' We all looked at each other. I walked up to the cab.

'Can you tell us where the nearest bus stop is? A bus that'll take us around the city?'

'What do ya want one of those for, man?'

'We want to see the sights; and before it gets dark.'

'I can take you to see the sights, man.'

'We haven't got much in the way of cash,' I said. His face turned serious.

'How much you dudes got then?' By now Mark and Paul had walked over to the cab and we all fished in our pockets.

'Well, we've got forty-five dollars between us but we need to keep fifteen to get something to eat.'

'So you got thirty dollars spare?'

'Yes.' He paused to consider the deal.

'OK thirty dollars. I'll take you round the sights. But real quick mind you.'

'Yeah sure, that's great.'

'Chuck your stuff in the back then.' We all smiled and threw our stuff and then ourselves in the back. As it turned out we had gotten ourselves quite a deal.

He took us to the White House, the Kennedy Memorial, the Lincoln Memorial, passed the important government buildings and by the river. We were literally seconds at each sight.

'OK boys, White House,' the cab driver would call out. We would leap out of the beaten up taxi while it was double parked, snap away with our cameras - so we all had a picture of ourselves by each monument - and jump back into the cab. The wheels would screech on the hot road and we would be on our way to the next port of call.

'Lincoln Memorial, boys,' our driver called. We jumped out of the cab and sprinted up the steps. But time had now caught up with us. The sun was sinking fast and we had to hurry to catch the last rays of light. After jumping back in the taxi the driver sighed.

'That's it, boys. I don't think you're gonna get much more in tonight.'

'OK, well, thanks for taking us around,' Mark said. We were all genuinely pleased we had managed to catch so many sights.

'I can't just leave you three here. You want something to eat? I know somewhere, it's cheap and the food's good.'

'Great, thanks; but we've no more money,' Mark said.

'Don't worry about that. I'm on my way there anyways.'

'Thanks.' The taxi driver was a decent guy. Our thirty dollars had gone a long way. He was not only decent, he was by far and away the most intelligent guy we had come across in the States. He started to ask us about our political opinions.

'Now, the Labour Party in England is chiefly funded by trade union contributions, right?'

'Right,' I said and laughed.

'What's wrong?'

'Well, it's just that most people we've come across don't even know where England is, let alone know anything about its political structure.'

'You just ain't been talking to the right people,' he said with a laugh. 'Anyway the system you have out there seems pretty good. The problem with the system over here is that you have to have money to get into politics in the first place. It costs a lot to run for any political post, so the poor people don't really get heard. OK, so some guy may say he's workin' for the poor or the blacks in the community, but the guy has to get funds from somewhere and business or the Mob are the only two ways to get it; so it's a bad system over here, really.'

'Well, our system isn't perfect,' I answered. He continued to talk politics and had even heard of the Liberal Democrats. After politics we moved onto the subject of 'Who Rules Britain.' Our cab driver had the answer to some of the major questions in this field of study and explained his answers with reference to the British class system. He really was a complete genius, this cabby! (Unless he had a Ph.D. in social sciences which he hadn't told us about.) We next moved on to the subject of 'Who Rules America'

'Well I tell ya, there is no doubt in my mind who rules this ole country of ours, and that's the Mob, the Mafia. You can't do anything nowadays in any major city without the Mafia getting in on it. They've got their finger in every pie from the building sites to the kids on the streets. You know nothing is built in New York without at least one or two fictitious characters appearing on the payroll; and their money goes to the Mob as sort of protection money.'

'Surely the authorities must know this goes on?' asked Paul.

'They sure do, man, but they can't prove anything. It takes an age to collect information on the top guys in the "families" as they're called. And once you get these guys to court you can't have a proper trial; all the jury are threatened and they can afford to hire the best defence lawyers in the business.' He paused before sidestepping onto the subjects of banks.

'An' another thing that I reckon', man, all this drugs war that's supposed to be going on; the government spending millions to fight drugs on the street and the barons in South America. Well, you know what, if they wanted to, they could stop most of the drug problem overnight; but they don't. They just put up a front to show the media and the public that they're doing something about it. And you know why they don't really want to stop it over night? 'Cause they can't, it would mean the end of the American economy. You see, so many banks have leant money to South America that if the countries had no income from drugs there wouldn't be any money comin' in to pay off their bank debts and the banks here couldn't afford that. They'd go bust, man, and the top guys over here know it too.'

We continued our conversation until we reached the restaurant that he had recommended.

'All the taxi drivers come here, it's real cheap and the food's good.' We didn't believe a word. Everywhere we had eaten in the States had been either burgers or steak. We parked up, collected our stuff out of the back of the cab, thanked the driver once again and walked in a small entrance and down some steps. The place was quite full and to our surprise was not just serving burgers. It was decorated in the style of a 'Little Chef' restaurant and had a self service system. Our driver left us to talk to fellow cabbies and we each selected a hot meal of lasagne. Washington was growing on us. Although it supposedly had the highest murder rate in the States, the places we had seen were reasonably clean and the streets seemed more British than anywhere else we had visited.

We sat for quite a while in the restaurant; we had time to kill before our next bus and we coincidentally left at the same time as our cabby friend. I'm sure he didn't think it a coincidence though, the three of us standing out in the street with all our luggage looking tired and forlorn. With a sigh he walked over to us and asked where we were headed. Stupid question really as we were completely lost and so tired that given the chance would have slept on our rucksacks in the middle of the road. He didn't give us that chance though and offered to whisk us off to a part of the city where bars and a few shops were still open, for free. Our thirty dollars had been well spent.

The Remains of the Day

Having thanked the driver yet again, we parted company and walked along a street that contained expensive bars and boutiques. We didn't know where we were and didn't really care. We looked in a few shops and I managed to rustle up some money to buy a bag. I needed a smaller bag for the plane; I only had my rucksack and loads of trash to take back that I didn't want to chance in the hold. We walked a while and eventually came to a major road junction. We wanted more than anything to just sit and rest. We were all still in good spirits and as with our outward journey our nervous energy was keeping us going.

'Excuse me, could you tell us if there's a bar nearby where we could get a drink?' I asked a girl as she passed us. She looked us up and down and then smiled.

'Sure, follow me.' I'm not sure whether her smile was one of friendship or in fact she was smiling at the fact that we looked like beach bums who had lived on a beach all their lives and never travelled to a big city. We followed her.

'You from the university here?' she asked as we walked, 'or just visiting it or something?'

'Well...' I started and was going to explain who we were, etc. but I really didn't have the energy, '...something like that,' I smiled.

She lead us down some steps after about a hundred yards, and into a basement area. Inside it was full of university students sitting around dark wooden tables. It was a great little bar and we felt right at home.

'Thanks,' I said out of the blue. The girl turned.

'That's OK,' she said and walked on to join her friends. We sat down on the nearest bench and stacked our stuff behind it.

'I thought our luck was in then,' exclaimed Paul. 'Thought she might introduce us to her friends and we might all end up back at the University.'

'Dream on,' said Mark. 'The way we look at present no girl would even let us in their room even if we just offered to clean it!' He was right, we were all very well tanned but a complete mess. Who cared.

'Usual then, boys?'

'Please, Phil,' Mark and Paul said in unison, and I went to stock up with Budweiser.

We sat in the bar for quite a while. Our Greyhound bus left at 4.30am and we decided that spending our last money on beer and getting steadily drunk was the best idea in the world. We were chucked out at closing time.

Once again we were on the streets of Washington, lost and with time to kill. We walked.

'Hey, what's that? An angel is appearing before us on the streets of Washington,' said Mark. He was more drunk than I thought. I squinted. Surely it wasn't an angel we could see illuminated against a night sky, way off in the distance. Had we in fact all been mown down by a mad gunman in the bar and were now on our way to heaven? I racked my brain but couldn't remember any such happenings. We continued walking.

'I recognise it, though,' Paul said.

'I know,' said Mark. 'It's the Lincoln memorial, lit up.' Sure enough it was. Was he ever an angel, then, I wondered, my drunken mind working over time to try and link all pieces of the conversation together. The memorial shows Lincoln carved in marble sitting in a large chair, enclosed in a temple-like structure, but only Lincoln himself is lit, giving a spectacular, yet spooky tourist attraction at night. We walked up to the memorial, staggered up the steps and collapsed at the great man's feet, ready to sleep for ever and a day. There was silence for quite a while and we might well have dozed off with our rucksacks on our backs were it not for a group of students who came to join us. We noticed in fact quite a few tourists and general spectators around the memorial on this hot Thursday at midnight. Paul was messing around with his camera.

'What the hell are you doing?'

'This, Phil, is probably one of the most spectacular photo opportunities we've come across in all our time in the States.' he exclaimed. I turned to look at Lincoln. There he was towering twenty or more feet above me, beautifully silhouetted against the dark wall at the back.

'Yes, you're right.' The walk to the memorial had sobered us up a bit. We spent the next hour taking dramatic shots of the Lincoln memorial, and discovered that in the distance was the Kennedy memorial, just as beautifully lit and offering as impressive a sight.

By the time our photo escapade was over, the other students were the only people left. We watched as they played dice on the steps of the memorial and we were soon invited to join them in a game. We were introduced to Rick, Kathy, Charlie, Sara and Neil. So here we were; it was approaching 2am and we were playing poker dice on the steps of the Lincoln Memorial in Washington with five strangers. Mark turned to Paul.

'You know, Paul, if somebody had said three years ago, before we started university, that in three years time we would be doing this at this time, I wouldn't have believed them.'

'Oh shut the fuck up, Mark,' Paul said, laughing.

We even outlasted the students that night. We, who had been mostly awake for twenty-four hours and had little prospect of sleep in the next twenty-four, were left on the steps when the others decided it was time to go and get some kip. There was nothing else for it, we would have to make our way to the Greyhound bus shelter and wait. A cab took us to the bus terminal for a set fee; our leftover dinner money. Once at the bus terminal we parked ourselves and our luggage on the floor. We were still half drunk.

'Hey!' came a shout. I woke with a start. A broom was being jabbed into my ribs by a black cleaner wearing blue overalls and a nasty expression. We had all fallen asleep on our rucksacks.

'Ya can't sleep there. Get up.' I was too tired to resist and besides his broom was a lethal weapon. The others were also woken as he cleaned around their motionless bodies. We got up and stood around aimlessly, three-quarters asleep, barely able to keep our eyes open. He watched us as he moved along with his brush. We all returned his looks, waiting until he was out of sight before we sat back down. He poked his head back around the corner, but stayed away. Two girls had sat down next to us; they too were travelling around the States they told us and were both nurses. Unfortunately they were heading off in the opposite direction from the bus terminal, such had been our luck with the fairer sex.

We talked until the time came to board the Greyhound. We hadn't noticed but the bus terminal had been gradually filling up with people and there was now quite a throng around the leaving gate. We joined the queue and said farewell to the two girls. As the bus was leaving so early in the morning it was still pitch black outside. We were checked on board by a young black guy in a tracksuit.

'He's one laid-back puppy,' I said as we chucked our stuff in the massive luggage stores beneath the silver bus.

'Who is?' asked Paul.

'That guy in the track suit. If he's our driver he should be wearing a uniform shouldn't he?'

'Yeah. Perhaps he isn't.' None of us really cared. We clambered aboard the bus and fell into some seats. Our real driver stepped aboard, an old white guy with a small potbelly. He tipped his cap at a lady sitting in one of the front seats, put down a small bag by his seat and sat in behind the wheel.

'Oh no, I knew it was too good to be true,' said Mark. Paul and I looked at him inquisitively. 'Take a look at the bus driver, guys,' he continued. Paul and I hadn't noticed, but our driver's face was as red as a cherry. We all looked at each other.

'Maybe it's just the bus' night lights that make his face look like that,' I said.

'Let's hope it's that or a severe case of sunburn.' Mark said. 'If not, then there's a real chance that this driver is going to keel over at the wheel.' Paul and I smiled. We were too tired to care about this either. Almost everybody on the coach was asleep immediately after we left.

The final stage of the trip to New York would take another five hours. Once again we took turns to sleep; one always keeping an eye on our hand luggage and making sure that our rucksacks weren't unloaded from the coach before New York. While I was on 'watch' I was entertained by a tremendously fat bearded chap wearing a Stetson and an old woman who was perhaps his mother, reading verses from the Bible out loud. They were not seated next to each other but either side of the aisle. He would read a passage in a quiet tone and she would reply,

'Alleluia, and praise the Lord!' She did deviate slightly by saying 'Praise be to God,' and 'Lord have mercy,' now and again. Here were another two Americans completely fruits about religion. But 'Bible Brian' who we had previously encountered was not a patch on these two. The man continually read from the Bible and when he came across a really important or profound piece of the Lord's Book he would lean right over to the old lady and almost whisper the extract, emphasising every word. Her reply would be louder than any of her others: 'Praise the Lord!' This would cause a few sleeping passengers to stir from their sleep and groan at the noise, but she was oblivious to thinly disguised complaints. The pair of them were seated about five rows in front of where we were and after a while I found myself straining forward to listen to the passages being read. I was almost up out of my seat when the important pieces were whispered. Before long I was on edge, and hanging on every word the guy said. Mark and

Paul were still sleeping soundly. I leant as far forward as I dared to listen to another quiet passage. But when the chap had finished this particular extract there was no 'Praise the Lord' or 'The Lord have mercy' from the old woman. Instead, both of them slowly and deliberately turned and looked at me, as though they had a sixth sense and had felt my gaze. They stared at me. In an instant I thought about the strange situation in which I now found myself. I was on a Greyhound bus on my way to New York, before dawn, staring into the eyes of two religious nuts, with nobody else on the bus awake. They seemed to be staring at me for an eternity.

'Would you like to join us in celebrating the good news the Lord has to bring, my child?' asked the old lady.

'No. Thank you,' I answered, embarrassed. Their faces turned sour and their eyes opened wider. The only noise was the constant hum of the coach tyres on the tarmaced road; inside there was complete silence, with nobody awake to help me if they had suddenly forced me to eat the Bible or something! I hadn't been taking the mickey out of their devotion, but that is how it now looked. As far as they were concerned I was now a devil worshipper. I slowly sat back into my seat. They turned back slowly and continued with their readings. I sat motionless for a few seconds, then I quickly woke up Mark so that he could keep 'watch'. I wanted a little time to myself, to pray for God's forgiveness, before He struck the bus with lightening, gave the driver a heart attack, or worse still unloaded our luggage at the wrong stop.

We were all awake but dazed as the bus entered New York. We arrived just in time for the morning rush-hour and were stuck in traffic for about an hour. We finished the journey where our first Greyhound bus had begun, at the Port Authority bus terminal. We were different individuals from those that had left three months previously. When Mark and I had left New York we were pale, ill-looking and apprehensive. Now we were a sort of deep mahogany colour, looking well (fed), and pretty laid back.

We had planned to spend this final day in the 'Land of Opportunity' seeing Manhattan Island by boat. A three hour trip around the island was apparently the best way to capture all the tourist sights without having to negotiate traffic, people and strength-sapping pavements. We dumped our rucksacks in some lockers at the Port Authority and headed toward the BUNAC offices on the ground floor of the YMCA. We knew the way and wandered through the streets talking of the events of the last three months. The YMCA looked the same, with its canopied entrance and massive frontage. It was all as classic as we had left it. Steam rose from a drain in front of the YMCA, and a police 'black and white' cruised passed. We were back on the best film set in the world. Although other places had had that movie atmosphere about them throughout the States, New York was the place where you most expected a director to jump out at any moment and shout 'Cut!'

We collected our Airport bus tickets from the YMCA and set off to the department store 'Macy's'.

'Here it is!' I exclaimed. We had stumbled across it. No large signs, no rows of flash window displays, nothing; just a large building which needed renovation and a luminous sign far above our heads. We all went in. It was similar to Debenhams. We soon left!

The boat trip was next and we made our way down to a pier and instantly picked out the long boat on which we would travel. It was quite old, with the lower deck covered by a blue tarpaulin. In the middle there was the bridge and what we were later to discover was a small, extremely overpriced shop. We paid thirty dollars each for the boat trip and it was another thirty dollar bargain. We saw some of the classic shots of Manhattan Island, the sort you see in opening sequences at the movies with the tall skyscrapers surrounded by water picked out as the film crew in a helicopter swoops down. We also saw the Statue of Liberty, massive and majestic. The Statue was, of course, a present from France. America and France must have been very friendly at one stage. Today, if such a statue were presented there would be cries of: 'What a waste of public money' and 'Great, you get a beautiful statue, we get EuroDisney.'

We glimpsed Wall Street, were told about each bridge as we passed beneath it, were shown the Greenwich Village and Brooklyn areas of New York and told about each skyscraper as it came into view and the date upon which it lost its status as the tallest building in the world. The trip lasted for over two hours during which time we constantly snapped away with our cameras.

The trip had been well worth the money and it filled a substantial period of the time we had before our flight. We now headed back to the Port Authority to pick up our luggage and walked back to the YMCA where a bus would take us to JFK Airport. We had plenty of time and ambled through the streets of New York for the last time. We were still surviving on nervous energy and how I made it the few blocks from the Port Authority to the YMCA, with my massively heavy rucksack, my hand luggage in my newly bought bag and my weighty camera around my neck, in the New York heat of late summer, with precious little sleep in the last two days, is still beyond me. I do remember bumping into Paul though as he stopped abruptly in front of me to avoid a car. We both shouted at the car; there had been no indication from the driver as to his intentions, he just swung into the road we were crossing at high speed. Our shouts brought few looks from the rest of those on the 'film set'; it was in the script, the sort of thing you would expect from native New Yorkers.

The bus that turned up outside the YMCA was just as awesome as the one that had brought us there from the airport - even in the light of day. The massive shining steel sides and the crash bar at the front glistened in the sun. The windows were slightly tinted and the tyres and wheels as tall as a man.

'This bus JFK Airport,' the female BUNAC rep was calling. We waited in a short queue and gave our names. A horrible thought flashed across my mind. What if we've got the wrong day, what if we are a week early or a week late? We've only a few dollars now between us. But we were right on cue.

On the bus we chatted about all we had seen and all we had done; all the roles we had played and all the action we had seen. There was no doubting that we had had some good times; but we had also had some bad times. We had had a memorable time, an eventful time and certainly had worked hard for all we earned. Without a doubt though, we had seen the States from a viewpoint that no tourist ever would; we had had a front row seat all the way. We would leave with many memories to reflect upon; images that would be with us always. The States had been a film set, and we had been in the script.

The airport was packed and the queue for our check-in desk looked a mile long. It was snaked around the whole of the airport. There are two airports that service New York: JFK and Newark.

'If Newark Airport is as small as JFK is, then they need another airport,' I said to Mark.

'Yeah, this is a bit silly. About twenty buses arrived at once.' Mark said. There was a BUNAC rep moving up and down the queue to collect different cards and to check our passports and tickets. Judging by the length of the queue, it would have probably been a safe bet that the aircraft would have been over-booked; it was.

'Right, can I have your attention please?' called a stewardess over a microphone to the packed departure lounge; and then came the customary airport bribery.

'I'm afraid the plane is over-booked,' she said. There was a groan from the whole of the departure lounge. 'So if there is anyone who would be willing to wait for the next flight,' she continued 'would they come forward please. There will of course be a compensation of some sixty pounds paid to those who are willing to wait for the next flight.' We didn't join the stampede.

We slept on the homeward flight and the combination of jet lag and lack of sleep would mean we would be completely spaced out by the time we reached London. We were fortunately not in the company of some wise guy who liked the sound of his own voice, and who would later recommend we visit Myrtle Beach.

We landed at Heathrow and there was a cheer from a group of BUNACers across the aisle from us.

'They obviously had to work even harder than we did,' Mark said.

'Chance would be a fine thing,' said Paul, rolling his eyes. Mark and I laughed.

'You know what, guys?' I said. 'Next time I go to the States, I'm going to take a video camera, and make some movies.'

'Talking of cameras,' said a searching Paul, 'has anyone seen mine?'

'You've lost your camera now, have you?' Mark said.

'Yes, I have,' Paul replied, still searching. I laughed.

'Well quite frankly, Paul, I don't give a damn.'